Chinese Gold: From Following to Surpassing

Liu Shan'en

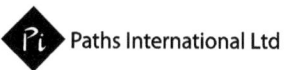

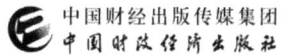

CONTENT

Preface 1 ·· 1
Preface 2 ·· 1
Foreword ·· 1

1	Gold Control Arising from Resource Shortage ············	1
2	Surging Undercurrent under Firm Ice ····················	23
3	Breakthrough of Gold Market from Scratch ···············	39
4	Top-level Design of China's Gold Market ················	53
5	A Latecomer's Pursuit and Surpassing ···················	89
6	An Encounter on the Road to Internationalization ···	123
7	A Diversified Market System ····························	143
8	Innovative Gold Consumption Demands ·············	177
9	A Gold Investment Market Derived from Development	199
10	A Gold Market with Diversified Means of Transaction ···	225
11	A Gold Market under Progressive Internationalization ···	237
12	Prospect: Thoughts on Future Development ··········	247
13	Gold Market: The Third Segmentation ················	265

Afterword ··· 284
References ·· 287

Preface 1

Over past 20 years, the global gold market has undergone significant changes. The institutional investors was continuing to increase their holdings of gold, and the retail investors also became increasingly interested in gold. With the improved popularity of electronic products, the demand on gold in the technology industry has increased. More importantly, the central banks have transformed from net sellers to important buyers. In 2018, we witnessed the highest demands from central banks on gold since the collapse of Bretton Woods System.

In the last decade, the gold market in China has developed at an astonishing speed, and has completed the transformation of role from follower to surpasser. Today, China is the largest gold consumer and producer in the world, accounting for 23% of global total demand and 13% of global total supply respectively.

Against the background that the world are now full of political and economic uncertainty, we particularly need to ensure the security and stability of financial market. As the leading body of the global gold industry, the World Gold Council is committed to making gold a mainstream financial asset. We will strengthen the cooperation with institutional investors and enhance their understanding on the role of gold in their investment portfolio.

It is very important to build trust and confidence in global gold market, so that the World Gold Council supports an effective regional regulatory framework. People are willing to choose credible and reliable gold products and solutions when investing in physical or financial products, and China flies its own characteristics in this aspect.

Chinese Gold: From Following to Surpassing

The establishment of Shanghai Gold Exchange as well as the implementation of a series of forward-looking policies and measures have created the necessary conditions for China to become the largest gold market in the world. Other markets may use China's model for reference, so as to create an open, transparent and effective trading and investment environment.

In consideration of the fact that more and more attention is being paid to the environmental, social and corporate governance (ESG) principles in the gold industry, in 2019, after extensively soliciting opinions from the public, we issued the *Responsible Gold Mining Principles*, bringing forth the clear expectations for all stakeholders about what responsible gold mining is. These principles will bring confidence to refiners, trading markets, investors and consumers, so as to further make gold a mainstream investment asset.

The recently-released results of our survey on global consumers indicate that the gold is considered as a mainstream investment choice and one of the most stable investment options, only next to savings and insurance. Although there is still a lack of trust in gold, people are still confident and loyal to gold. In the future, we need to consider whether the gold can arouse more profound resonance among young consumers and whether we can open up a road to new audiences through technical innovation. I believe that China may be able to take the lead in such reform again.

We should agree that China and its gold industry are embracing and getting integrated into the wider world, whether from the viewpoint of ESG principles, consumer survey report or market transparency. We firmly believe and expect that China will be ready to play a more leading role in the global gold market. In this process, China will face both opportunities and responsibilities.

The World Gold Council attaches great importance to the leading position of China, and is also fully convinced that China will make more contributions in the future.

David Tait
CEO of World Gold Council

Preface 2

Thinking on Road to Millennium Change of China's Gold Industry
Written for the Publication of *Chinese Gold: From Following to Surpassing*

Gold, as a kind of metal with dual attributes of currency and commodity, is an important component of foreign exchange reserves of various countries. Since its establishment, the People's Republic of China has always been in the dilemma of severe shortage of foreign exchange, so that it has been a priority for the country to increase gold production, an important link in settlement of such dilemma. However, in the early days of the People's Republic of China, the gold productivity was very low. The gold production was only 4.07 tons in 1949, and it was not until 1977 that the gold production reached 16 tons, exceeding the historical record created in 1911.

In order to improve the production capacity of gold, we have made unremitting efforts. In the new century, great changes have taken place in China's gold industry, and China has realized the transformation from a follower to a leader: In 2007, with the gold production of 270.49 tons, China surpassed South Africa which had been ranked No. 1 in the aspect of gold production for one hundred years. After the human beings made great breakthrough in gold productivity in the middle of 19th Century and following Russia, USA, Australia and South Africa, China became the fifth country

Chinese Gold: From Following to Surpassing

which achieved the highest gold production in the world. By 2018, China has occupied the first place in gold production in the world for 12 years. Since 2007, the gold production of China has successively exceeded 300 tons and 400 tons. While the gold production of China steadily occupies the first place in the world, the import volume of raw material of gold has also increased greatly. In 2018, China imported 112.78 tons of raw gold, and the gold supply capacity reached 513.90 tons, more than 100 times the gold supply capacity in 1949.

The growth of gold supply capacity in China has driven the growth of gold demand in China. In 2013, the total consumption of gold in China exceeded that of India for the first time, ranked No. 1 in the world, and the industrial consumption of gold in China exceeded that of USA, ranked No. 2 in the world, only next to Japan. In 2018, the total consumption of gold in China reached 1,151.43 tons, ranked No. 1 in the world for 6 consecutive years. Therefore, in the new century, the gold product market with diversified products and the largest scale in the world appeared in China. In turn, the development of gold product market has made China the largest gold wealth gathering place and the largest gold importing country in the world.

The continuous enrichment of gold products in China has driven the activity of gold transaction and the expansion of scale. After 2002 when it completed the "final kick" for its growth out of nothing, the China's gold market has got the trading volume increased to 59,000 tons (single side) in only 17 years, becoming the third largest gold market in the world. Shanghai Gold Exchange has become the largest spot gold market in the world, and Shanghai Futures Exchange has become the second largest gold futures market in the world.

In China, the industrial chain of gold is so complete and the scale of gold market is so large that they are rare in the whole world. It can be said that, the gold industry in China has changed from a latecomer and follower in the international gold industry to a surpasser and leader. In the new century, the change of gold

Preface 2

industry in China is great. If being placed on the time coordinates of the 5,000-year history of China, this change is not only a change in a century, but also a millennium change and a milestone of gold civilization in the 5,000-year history of China. Gold has experienced the infiltration of human culture for thousands of years and has become the absolute wealth of human beings. Therefore, this millennium change is also one of the important symbols for the fact that the wealth creation power of Chinese nation is ranked top among all nations in the world. In addition, this millennium change happened at the key moment of the revival of the Chinese nation, so that its value surmounts the meaning for gold industry and has more profound historical significance.

The millennium change of gold is the theme of the book *Chinese Gold: From Following to Surpassing*. However, the author does not stop at the superficial statement of millennium change, but takes this millennium change of Chinese gold industry as a case of contemporary economic development of China, so that it rises to the deeply think about the selection of economic development road of China, and the theoretical exploration and upgrading for the selection of development road of socialist market economy. This is also a self-surpassing of the author. The Author is in his seventies, but keeps on working. Over recent 10 years, he has got a new book published almost every year. In this new book, the author extends the development problem of Chinese gold industry to the rational understanding of development road of socialist market economy of China, which is the result of his long-term academic accumulation. The author has published the monograph *Breaking Cocoon: Deciphering the Course of Chinese Gold Marketization Reform* which describes the course of gold marketization reform in China and the monograph *Aspiring to the Throne: Reviewing the Development of Chinese Gold Industry* which describes the course of development of Chinese gold industry. These two monographs provide us with the development track of thoughts in this Book.

The millennium change of Chinese gold industry didn't happen instantaneously, but experienced a long and continuous process of exploration, and the selection of development road for China's gold market is also completed in such continuous process of exploration. Though the gold production has become a key undertaking developed and supported by the State since the 1970s, the development of gold industry is not smooth, but involves continuous innovation upon development road. In the early days of the People's Republic of China, the development road of planned economy was selected, and the State invested a lot of manpower and material resources in order to produce more gold. However, the backward production mode of pure manpower mining made the new China's gold production stay at a low level in a quarter of century after its birth. From 1975 to 1993, the gold production of China entered a continuous growth period of nearly 20 years, and the development achieved in this period was mainly attributable to China's selection of reform and opening-up road in 1978. With the improvement of China's equipment manufacturing capacity, the productivity level of gold industry has also been liberated. The Chinese gold industry began the third adjustment of development road in 1994, and the opening-up of gold market marked the comprehensive marketization reform of gold industry, and this process was fully completed by 2002. The selection of development road of socialist market economy is the sublimation of the reform & opening-up road, and now the Chinese gold industry has gone through the 17 years' practice after taking the market economic road.

  From 1949 to 2018, China produced 7,831.22 tons gold, while from 1949 to 1974, namely the traditional planned economic development period, the gold production was only 192.11 tons, accounting for 2.45% of total gold production of China; the period 1975-1993 is the 18 years when China's gold industry embarked on the road of reform and opening up, with the gold production reaching 783.83 tons and accounting for 10.01% in total gold production of China; the period 1994-2018 is the 24 years when China embarked on the development of socialist market economy, with the gold production reaching 6,855.28 tons and accounting for 87.54% in total gold production of China. In other words, the social market economic

Preface 2

road period during which China produced nearly 90% of gold is the historical period which witnessed the greatest achievement made by China in development of gold production.

In different development periods, the achievements made in development of Chinese gold industry are very different. Through comparison, we understand that the reason why the Chinese gold industry has changed from following to leading is because we selected the social market economic development road.

The development history of Chinese gold industry over in past decades has proved the correctness of the selection of socialist market economic development road, thus strengthening our confidence in selection of this road. This is also the greatest significance of the publication of the book *Chinese Gold: From Following to Surpassing*.

Song Xin
CPC Committee Secretary and President of China Gold Association

Foreword

China is the only country which has the uninterrupted culture among the four great ancient civilizations in the world. However, in the five-thousand-year development history of China, except for a few dynasties or a few historical periods of a certain dynasty during which there was the light of gold, the gold production of China was very low and could be calculated in *liang* only. This situation has not changed fundamentally until the establishment of the People's Republic of China. Therefore, we failed to be the protagonist for a long time in the historical dramas on the stage of civilization history of human beings. China's lack of leading role in creation of gold civilization was an important sign for lack of social wealth and delayed development of commodity economy in China.

With the beginning of the 21st Century, a new page has been opened in human history, and many historical events occurring in the first 10 years of 21st Century have become the key to a turning point. China, as the marginal existence in international gold industry, has begun to shine the light of gold and become the leader in global gold industry and market.

In the autumn of 2002, after being waited for more than half a century, the China's gold market emerged from the cocoon. Though 17 years' development, it inadvertently achieved the transformation from follower to surpasser, becoming the leader for future development of international gold market.

In 2007, with the gold production of 270.49 tons, we unexpectedly surpassed South Africa which has been the champion for one hundred years and won the first place, completing the transformation from a gold-poor country to a gold-rich country. For us, the 21st Century wrote the story about Chinese gold which achieved a

Chinese Gold: From Following to Surpassing

millennium change, and also interpreted the rise of the Chinese nation.

In the first decade of 21st Century, why could China get its gold industry developed greatly, achieve the comprehensive historical surpassing in all links in upper, middle and lower reaches of gold productivity, and form a complete world-leading gold industrial chain through? Is it the favor of fate, or there is any other fundamental reason? We have to explore and think deeply. Because of the writing of this book, I began to seek the answer. The journey to explore the source of light of gold started from the bewilderment, and finally I came to the conclusion that the source is China's unique system. Though this conclusion is obtained after understanding the development of gold industry in China from outside to inside, but I was still very worried, so that I had to build a theoretical support for the conclusion. For this sake, I expanded my vision to the theoretical dimension of human economics, and looked for the true reason for great development of China's gold industry in first decade of 21st Century in the development process of human economics.

First, I should find out what "system" is. The answer is that, the "system" is culture, and is the behavioral rules and regulations formed under a certain cultural condition. The "system" of human beings is diversified, but there are two kinds of behavioral rules for achieving the goal of economic development, one is the rules of "invisible hand", namely market competition, and the other is the rules formulated by "visible hand", namely government. For the relationship of these two "systems", we also experienced a process from discovery to understanding.

After a long "barbaric" development period, the human beings finally found a new development road, namely market economy (commodity economy) development road. The opening of this road made the human civilization reach a new level, and thus the human beings produced the market omnipotence theory based on market worship. However, in 1929, more than 200 years after the birth of classical liberalist economics, the global economic depression caused by the economic crisis in USA revealed that the self-healing

Foreword

capacity is a short board of market, and the human beings began to look for ways to improve the economic repair capacity after the breakage of balance of market. The Hoover administration which did nothing in face of the crisis went out, and then a series of "new economic policies" implemented by the President Roosevelt who came to power became the bright spot in the crisis at that time, providing a direction of thinking for answer-seeking people. This thinking led to the birth of neoclassical economics. Government, as a powerful force to repair economic imbalance, was named as "visible hand", while market was named as "invisible hand". From then on, "visible hand" and "invisible hand" have become two special terms used in contemporary human economics.

The two "systems", namely "visible hand" and "invisible hand", have differences in implementation and regulation and are regarded as hot and hot by many people, but the human beings have increasingly understood that both these two different "systems" are needed by economic development, just like the left hand and right hand of human beings. However, there is still one question which must be answered. How can the coordinated and effective interaction be realized between "visible hand" and "invisible hand"? This often falls into the situation that "each says he is right", but the final answer should be obtained by taking the actual result as the only judgment standard.

After World War II, a lot of things needed to be done, which provided opportunities for "visible hand" to play a role. Nowadays, intervening in economy has become the normal status and responsibility of "visible hand". However, the query and opposition to intervention in economy by "visible hand" have not disappeared. This is mainly due to the worry about the wrong intervention and chaos interference in economy by "visible hand", and the worry is not a nuisance, because such a thing is not impossible, but has already happened. Therefore, how to avoid the intervention by "visible hand" or reduce the error made by "visible hand" also becomes a difficult problem for human beings to solve.

As a latecomer, the China's gold market achieved the advancement

Chinese Gold: From Following to Surpassing

from follower to surpasser in the 17 years' development, which has drawn attention from all over the world. However, the largest significance of development process of the China's gold market which has grown in an environment with a strong and powerful government is to provide a successful case for intervening in economy with "visible hand". Under the guidance of free market theory and through the long-term survival of the fittest, the international gold market grew up with competition as the basic element. However, the China's gold market takes a development road based on the top-level design from "visible hand" and the orderly competition, and this is the basic characteristic of development road of China's gold market.

The China's gold market was borne from the transformation from gold control "system" under "visible hand" to gold marketization "system", the "visible hand" is the director in this process, and the development of the China's gold market is the product of top-level design by "visible hand". The China's gold market developing on this road has made the eye-catching achievement, so that the reasonableness of this road selection is proved.

We say that the selection of road for China's gold market is reasonable. First of all, this is based on the progress of reality, and this judgment is also based on the comparison of a larger international background.

Firstly, the international gold markets, which grew up in a development environment in which the regulation was ignored and self-discipline was emphasized, the risk control was ignored and the leverage was emphasized, and the management was ignored and the competition was emphasized and troubled by price manipulation scandal, so that they sought for reform and strengthening the regulation became the trend of reform. What the international gold markets need to do now is what we have done in the past, so that the development road of China's gold market has a reference value for future development of international gold markets. In this sense, the China's gold market has changed from follower to leader.

Secondly, a larger comparison background is the outbreak of USA

Foreword

financial crisis in 2008, which led to the global economic crisis. This crisis exposed the fragility and unfairness of international monetary system with USD as the central currency. As a result of people's reflection on this crisis, many countries built up the financial gate, put the financial security in the first place, and began to rebuild the financial monitoring system and strengthen the information transparency. In the process of this reform, we find that a powerful government is necessary. Therefore, the development road of China's gold market which involves the top-level design has been increasingly understood and recognized. This is the greater value of the development road of China's gold market.

As for the necessity of narration and interpretation of the story about Chinese gold, we still lack the understanding of the role change with respect to the understanding on development road of China's gold market, so that we are also unimpressed with the speech that the China's gold market has become a leader as given by the former CEO of World Gold Council. Therefore, in order to properly tell the story about Chinese gold, China Gold Association specially organized a small-scale "Symposium on Road of Gold Market in China" in Beijing Reclining Buddha Temple Hotel on May 17, 2019, so as to carry out discussion over the conclusion of this Book. More than ten representatives from World Gold Council, China Gold Association, Shanghai Futures Exchange, Minsheng Bank and Jingyi Gold participated in the symposium. As a result, the consensus was reached to a considerable extent, the understanding on Chinese "system" was intensified, and the theme of this Book was further enriched. I would like to extend my deep gratitude to Ju Chengxin of Shanghai Futures Exchange, Dong Hong of Minsheng Bank and Luo Jiang of Shanghai Gold Exchange for their special contributions to the writing of this Book.

1
Gold Control Arising from Resource Shortage

From 1949 to 2002, China has implemented the control over gold for 53 years. The birth of this "system" was based on the long-term shortage of foreign exchange in China. Before the reform and opening up, the foreign exchange reserves of China, a country with a population of more than 1 billion, were only a few hundred million US dollars or several billion US dollars each year. In 1982, the foreign exchange reserves exceeded USD 10 billion, reaching USD 11.573 billion. At that time, against the background that it was very difficult to obtain foreign exchange, the great hope was placed on gold production for changing the situation about shortage of foreign exchange. However, at that time, the level of gold productivity was very low, so that the founders of new China determined the increase of gold production as the undertaking directly led by the State Council, and made all efforts to mobilize all social resources available to increase the gold production. However, the formation of "system" which ensures the gold production will not be achieved overnight, but is a process of continuous exploration and development. At that time, the gold was a hard currency and was monopolized by the government, and the priority was given to gold production as the main channel for increase of foreign exchange, so that the allocation of gold resources was a typical model of planned economy. With the gradual resolution of the shortage of foreign exchange, the gold control began to be loosened and finally ended, and the marketized management was achieved on gold. Therefore, whether China implements the gold control "system" or the gold marketization "system", the supply of foreign exchange is the basic

Chinese Gold: From Following to Surpassing

basis. This is the starting point for us to observe and understand the development of Chinese gold from control to marketization.

1.1 Han Dynasty: A Gold-rich Dynasty

Gold, which exists in the natural world, is extremely special to human beings. It is not the basic demand for survival of human beings, but it is closely linked with the social development of human beings. Its special function in human society even wins the worship from human beings. Therefore, every nation is closely related to gold in the process of civilization. Though the gold culture of Chinese nation is not the most brilliant among the four ancient civilizations, its history associated with gold is very long.

The creator of natural world is unfair, the opportunities granted by it to various nations are not equal, but it is not so stingy for the Chinese nation. The archaeology shows that, the Chinese nation, if not the earliest, was the earlier people who understood and used gold. There is a long gold history in the 5,000-year development history of China. This can be traced back to the Xia Dynasty which existed 4,000 years ago, and the gold ornaments were already available at that time. There are written records in China about the use of gold as currency in Xia Dynasty. In China's ancient book *Royal Document • Yugong*, there is a description of "Tribute, only three metals". What are "three metals "? It is stated in the *Historical Records • On Price Balance* written by Sima Qian, the famous historian of the Han dynasty, that: "The currencies of Xia Dynasty have three colors, namely yellow, white or red." "Three metals" mean that there were three kinds of metal currencies used in the Xia Dynasty, namely gold coin, silver coin and copper coin. During the Warring States period, the gold currency became more diversified, including gold cake, gold collar, gold plate, gold horseshoe and gold toe, which showed that the gold currency had been widely used in China at that time. The Qin Dynasty unified the national currency, namely the copper coin with inner square and outer circle. However, this was the currency used by the masses, and as a superior currency,

1 Gold Control Arising from Resource Shortage

the gold coin widely existed in the upper class. As a result, in the historical books of the Han Dynasty following the Qin Dynasty, there are still records about the use of a lot of gold by emperors, and the usage became more diversified: for bribery, or for reward, or for consumption, or for making currency, or for burial. The gold in the tomb of Liu He, the Haihun Marquis of the Western Han Dynasty, unearthed in Nanchang, Jiangxi Province in 2015, shows us how amazing the number of gold owned by emperors is. We can only use the word "shock". There are 96 gold cakes, 33 gold horseshoes, 15 gold toes and 20 gold plates between the inner and outer coffins of Haihun Marquis Liu He. This reveals that, though the Qin Dynasty had taken copper coins as the unified currency, the gold coins still extensively existed in upper society in the subsequent Han Dynasty, and they were not simply used as an intermediary for exchange, but were used for maintenance of relationship between powerful persons: for tribute, or for gifts, or for commendation. Many of the gold coins and gold articles unearthed from the tomb of Liu He came from gift or reward from the imperial court. For example, in order to defeat his opponent, Liu Bang, the founder of the Han Dynasty, once spent 400,000 *liang* of gold to buy off the subordinates of Xiang Yu. A total of 437 gold relics of which the weigh exceeds 200kg were unearthed from the tomb of Liu He. The gold buried in the tomb of Liu He shows us a gold-rich world of the Han Dynasty, and some experts believe that, the Han Dynasty owned more than 500 tons of gold. Before the middle of the 19th Century, only more than 10,000 tons of gold had been produced all over the world, and the annual average gold production of the whole world was only about 2 tons, so the Han Dynasty with more than 500 tons of gold was really a rare gold-rich country. However, after the Han Dynasty, the gold gradually faded away from the historical records of China. We also did not see the records about extravagant use of gold just like what the emperors of Han Dynasty did. The use of gold in monetary field of China also became rare case. From then on, China ended the gold-rich age and began the gold-poor age which lasted for one thousand years. Thereafter, the annual gold production of each dynasty could only be calculated by *liang* (0.5kg is equal to 16 *liang*, which is the Chinese measurement unit for precious metal), so that "where did the gold in Han Dynasty come from and where had it gone" has become an unsolved mystery.

1.2 Uncover the mystery of gold shortage in China

Where had the gold in Han Dynasty gone? There is a viewpoint that the luxurious funerary was popular in Han Dynasty so that a large number of gold in Han Dynasty were buried underground, and a lot of gold unearthed from the tomb of Liu He of Han Dynasty proves this viewpoint. In today's view, the consumption of gold for luxurious funerary in Han Dynasty may be an important reason, but it is not the main reason for shortage of gold after the Han Dynasty. The main problem should be at the level of gold productivity, and the long-term low level of gold productivity caused the shortage of gold supply. Then, what is the reason for low gold productivity in China after the Han Dynasty? The productivity is often linked with demand.

1.2.1 The gold was noble but not important to people's livelihood in farming society

The Qin Dynasty established a centralized feudal society. Since then, China became one of the countries in which the feudal society existed for the longest time, so that China was a self-sufficient farming society for long term. In the farming society, the self-sufficient natural economy is dominant, and the land and population are the most important social resources, because the land and population determine the development of productivity of social agricultural products, and meet the people's demand on food and clothing determines the stability and sustainability of society at that time. Therefore, the order of social populations was officials, farmers, workers, businessmen and slaves. In order to highlight the great importance attached to farming, the emperors of

1 Gold Control Arising from Resource Shortage

the final dynasty of China, namely the Qing Dynasty, built special courtyards to reflect farming and sericulture in the palaces where they lived, such as Yuanmingyuan and Summer Palace. Because of the sacrificial activities carried out every year, they built large buildings such as Xiannongtan and Ditan. The behaviors of Chinese emperors for highlighting the importance of farming were even imitated by European emperors. In the spring of 1768, the French crown prince, who was only 14 years old, imitated the emperor of China, and held a ceremony for personally and symbolically tilling the land with plough accompanied by his ministers. Therefore, at that time, although the gold was valuable, it was not a key and decisive social resource, so that the development of gold production was not highly valued, and the advancement of gold production technique was very slow. When the gold resources which were easy to be mined in the surface layer were exhausted, the society at that time did not make great efforts to find the gold resources that could be exploited continuously in the deep layer. Without the geological resources, the gold productivity would shrink rapidly even if there was a peak of development. In fact, the situation that China was lack of gold for one thousand years is firstly caused by insufficient discovery of geological resources rather than insufficient reserve of geological resources. Before the Han Dynasty, the abundant supply of gold in China resulted from a large number of gold resources in surface layer, but after these surface resources were used up, there was no new supply of geological resources. Because of this, the gold production in most dynasties after the Han Dynasty could only be counted in *liang*, and the annual output of gold was only tens of thousands of *liang*. Owing to such a small amount of gold supply, the use of gold was limited to the narrow imperial court, and gold was exclusively owned by emperors and became the symbol of royal power. Although the gold always has a high position in the history of China, it was difficult for gold to play a role at the broader social, economic and living level. The suffering borne by China owing to the shortage of geological resources and the depression of gold production lasted to the contemporary era. Since 1949, China has organized the battles again and again to increase the gold production. The first problem encountered was about resources. The reason why the expected results could not be achieved in gold production is that no breakthrough was made in supply of geological resources. In order to achieve the breakthrough of proven reserves of geological resources, China established a rare non-combat professional force engaged in gold geology exploration, namely the Gold Command of Chinese Armed Police Force, in March 1979, and also set up a special gold geology exploration fund in 1986 so as to ensure the supply of fund for gold geology exploration. Based on the need to increase the gold production, China devoted itself to the discovery of new gold geological resources. After the 1970s, although the proved reserves increased, they could only maintain the production, but could not achieve expansion of reproduction. The resources had always been the primary factor affecting the development of gold production. The long-existing problem about shortage of geological resources was not alleviated until 2005 after the proven reserves continued to grow, exceeded 10,000 tons and reached 13,000 tons. The situation that the supply of gold-related geological resources was insufficient and thus the gold productivity shrunk seriously is the main reason for change of gold production in China from high level to low level after Han Dynasty, and is also the explanation given by us for the gold-poor age of more than one thousand years entered by China after the Han Dynasty.

1.2.2 The result of backward development of commodity economy

The supply and demand are two sides of a coin. The shortage of gold supply will limit the demand, while the low level of gold demand will affect the gold supply and then affect the production development, which will make the gold supply insufficient. This is a vicious circle. The shortage of gold supply in China affected the implementation and expansion of social functions of gold, so that the gold could only be monopolized by the upper class of society

1 Gold Control Arising from Resource Shortage

for a long time and existed in a narrow social space. In the early period of modern times, the gold was also monopolized by the State and only existed in the treasury, and people were forbidden to own it. The insufficient gold demand was the result of long-term artificial inhibition, and the insufficient demand also affected the supply. The vicious circle of gold resulted from the backward development of commodity economy in self-sufficient agricultural society. Therefore, although China has a long currency history, the function of currency only stays at the stage of acting as an exchange tool. Due to the backwardness of commodity economy, China's currency did not develop into the capital which could appreciate, so that people's desire to hold gold currency wealth was relatively low. The situation in Europe was greatly different from that in China. Europe also had the problem about gold shortage, but owing to the development of its commodity economy, the currency capitalization was achieved. Gold was not only currency, but also a capital that could appreciate, so that the social power and charm of gold were greatly increased. Therefore, in order to settle the shortage problem, Europe tried every means to increase the supply of gold, and even took getting gold as its top priority. In 1511, in order to obtain gold, the King Perdinand of Spain commanded his army in America to "get the gold at all costs". As a result, the European countries fought hard for increase of gold, and fought for the origin of gold. The European gold wars broke out one after another, and even a war could last for a hundred years. After the gold resources in Europe were exhausted, all countries turned to external colonization and plunder. In the history, the European conquest of Egypt, the eastward aggressions of Crusades in the Middle Ages and the exploration of new continent initiated in the 15th Century were all aimed at solving the problem of gold shortage faced by Europe. The European's fanatical and persistent pursuit of gold is unimaginable for us. Finally, relying on the plunder of America's gold and silver, the European colonists achieved the dream of owning a large number of gold, and also established the gold standard with the plundered gold. The establishment of the gold standard further inspired the European

Chinese Gold: From Following to Surpassing

people's crazy pursuit of gold. In Europe's classic masterpiece *Homeric Hymns* and Shakespeare's *Timon of Athens*, there are descriptions and records of Europeans' obsession and madness about gold. In the eyes of European, the gold is a devil that can turn black and white and change everything. Columbus, the pioneer of European people's voyage adventure in search of new continent, said: "Gold is the most precious thing. Wealth is composed up of gold. With gold, you can do whatever you want in the world. Gold can even make your soul go to heaven." The European people's obsession with gold stands vividly revealed on the paper. Compared with European people, the Chinese people are much more indifferent to gold, and the use of gold as currency is even inferior to silver. This is because Chinese people select a development road which is different from that of Europe.

1.2.3 The road taken by China is different from Europe

The road taken by Chinese nation is different from that taken by Europe. The Qin Dynasty unified the currency and used the base metal copper instead of gold. In case of shortage of copper metal, our solution was paper currency, so that China became the inventor and first user of paper currency. The earliest paper currency of human beings was born in the Song Dynasty of China. However, after going through the Yuan and Jin Dynasties, the accumulation of inflation made it difficult for the paper currency to continue, so that though Zhu Yuanzhang, the founding emperor of the Ming Dynasty, prohibited the use of metal currency, the Ming Dynasty still returned to the copper currency standard in 1435 and changed from base metal currency to precious metal currency in 1525. At that time, the silver coins rather than the gold coins were adopted, and the silver coins were adopted till the period of the Republic of China, so that China is the country which has ever maintained the silver standard for the longest time in the world. The Ming Dynasty turned to silver standard, but there was no developed silver mining industry, and the production of silver was low. Therefore, the silver of Ming Dynasty

1 Gold Control Arising from Resource Shortage

was not self-made but imported, and was exchanged with silk, tea and porcelain during trade with western countries.

At that time, America was the main producer of gold and silver in the world, and the gold and silver of America were occupied by European colonists and became the first pot of gold for Europe to promote the industrialization and develop the commodity economy. However, not all gold and silver possessed by Europe flowed into Europe. It is estimated that about 1/3 to 2/3 of silver plundered by western colonists from America in the 16th Century finally flowed into China through trade. In addition, the price ratio between gold and silver was 1:7.0-1:5.5 in China and 1:14-1:12.5 in Europe, and relatively speaking, the silver was cheap in Europe and was expensive in China. Therefore, a large number of silver of Europe was smuggled to China, and even if it was strictly forbidden, the smuggling did not stop until there was a few of silver left in Europe in the middle of 18th Century. The loss of silver from Europe in a large number led to the shortage of silver, and became an important reason for Europe to end the gold & silver standard and establish the gold standard. Owing to the flowing of a large number of silver into China, the silver became abundant in China for a while, and thus the silver standard was implemented and maintained to the 1920s. Therefore, China has never really implemented the gold standard. China saved gold due to the implementation of silver standard, and thus the shortage of gold was maintained. The gold demand at low level was in equilibrium with the supply at low level, so that the shortage of gold in China was the result of interaction between supply and demand. In the face of gold shortage, our approach was to reduce the use of gold, while the approach of Europe was to increase the supply of gold by all means. The difference between our approach and the approach of Europe is the difference between natural economy and commodity economy. Europe had the demand of appreciation of currency by the 18th Century due to the development of commodity economy, and the supply was relatively abundant due to the inflow of American gold. Therefore, in 1717, UK changed the gold & silver standard to gold standard. Of course, this change was also attributable to the price ratio between gold and silver. In the 19th Century, the gold standard was expanded to the whole world, becoming the internationally dominant currency system and continued to the 1970s. However, China had no demand for currency appreciation due to natural economy, and thus the silver standard could continue. Therefore, the participation degree of gold in China's real economy was very low, the gold currency culture in China lacked depth and breadth.

In the final analysis, the reason for disfavor for gold standard in China is that the demand of currency appreciation was relatively delayed owing to the low level of commodity economy and thus China had not strong desire to turn to the gold standard. The insufficient demand is one of the reasons for the low gold productivity in China. Affected by material shortage, China developed the economy first so as to guarantee supply, and put production before demand. After the materials were abundant, the demand became the primary consideration of economic development, and became the driving force of economic development. This adjustment in thinking is realistic and important for understanding the development of China's gold market, and increasing the demand has been the basis for development of China's gold market.

1.3 The development road is not smooth

The Opium War in 1840 is a sign that China's national fortune changed from strong to weak. After that, China gradually became a semi-colonial and semi-feudal society divided by western powers, which was the suffering period of the Chinese nation. In the social turmoil, our predecessors understood the value of gold in troubled times, but the turbulent social environment made the development of gold production in China enter a low tide period.

1.3.1 The gold industry starting at low level

After China entered the gold-poor age, there was also a short

1 Gold Control Arising from Resource Shortage

development period for gold, namely the 30-year high-tide period for gold production in China from the end of 19th Century to the beginning of 20th Century. In this period, the gold production was increased from the level which takes *liang* as measurement unit to the level which takes ton as measurement unit. In 1911 when the Qing Dynasty withdrew from the historical stage, China's gold production reached 15 tons, creating a historical record of China's gold production. However, it was only a meteor passing by, and did not form a continuous development force, because thereafter a turmoil was coming, and the gold productivity shrank quickly. In 1949 when the People's Republic of China was founded, the gold production was only 4 tons, less than 30% of the historical record (namely 15 tons) created in 1911. This record was kept for 66 years and became the historical peak which could not be surpassed by China after several attempts after 1949, and was not rewritten until 1977. Therefore, the low level of gold productivity in China is embodied not only in the fact that China was short of gold in ancient times and modern times, but also in the fact that China has also suffered from gold shortage for many years in contemporary ear.

After that, in the 1960s, China had a temporary economic difficulty, and the grain production was reduced, so it was necessary to import wheat from abroad and pay with foreign exchange. Therefore, the urgency of foreign exchange demand was increased. Under such a background, the importance of gold as a hard currency at that time was highlighted. In order to settle the difficulty in payment with foreign exchange, the policies about gold production started to change. As early as 1957, the State Council (Government Administration Council) issued the *Circular on Mobilizing the Masses to Increase Gold Production* (here after referred to as "*Circular*"), requiring the leaders at all levels to put gold production on the work agenda and mobilize the masses to increase gold production. However, it was just a directive to act, and there was a long way from reaching the goal. This process is a process for exploration into "system", so that the innovation and abandonment of "system" existed in the whole process of development of Chinese gold industry. Even in the 53-year gold control period, the system was continuously adjusted rather than unchanged.

The *Circular* is the first national-level guiding document for development of gold production, acting as the policy for encouraging the masses to mine the gold. This policy lasted for 31 years, and was not ended until the middle and late of 1980s. From the perspective of Epistemology, the issuance of the policy for increasing the gold production by encouraging the masses to mine the gold was based on the understanding that human is the first element of productivity and increasing the human resources is an effective way to improve the gold productivity and increase the gold production. At that time, in addition to the gold production, the practice to develop production through on mass movement was also manifested in all aspects of industrial production. The policy of mobilizing the masses to increase gold production continued for 31 years. From the perspective of reality, the issuance of this policy was related to the national situation that at that time, China's industrialization was just started, the capital and technology were insufficient, and the labor force was relatively sufficient. However, this also led to the long-term existence of low-level manual gold production mode in China, and the backward production mode is one of the reasons why the gold production in China did not grow rapidly and sustainably. Therefore, in 1958 after the *Circular* was issued, the gold production was increased by 24.26% as compared with that in 1957, reaching 6.89 tons; from then on, the gold production declined continuously, and was only 3.653 tons in 1962, 10.25% lower than 1949.

1.3.2 Reform of "system" and gold century of China

The issuance of the Document No. 63 of the State Council in 1993 marked the start of gold marketization reform in China, but the reform was not completed in one step. Under the situation that the gold control was not released at that time, the marketization of gold price formation mechanism was promoted firstly, so as to initiate the transformation of gold management system from planned economic

1 Gold Control Arising from Resource Shortage

system to market economic system even if no sufficient preparation was made. This is because that, in 1993, while the synchronization between international gold price and domestic gold price was achieved, China cancelled the gold production development fund, so that the fund supply for management institution was cut off, and the reform became necessary. The impact on gold production enterprises is that, while the synchronization of gold price was achieved, all gold-related preferential policies were cancelled, the "visible hand" withdrew its direct intervention in gold production, and the driving force for development of gold enterprises was changed from externally-given type to internally-generated type. This adjustment of gold management "system" seemed to be passive, but it was actually in line with the trend, because the 14th National Congress of the Communist Party of China held in October 1992 established the reform goal of socialist market economy, so that the establishment of gold marketization direction has become inevitable. However, the transformation of management system needed a running in period, and the shift of development momentum also needed a growth period, so that in 1994, as affected by the transformation of new and old management "systems", the continuous growth of gold production was interrupted, and the negative growth of 4.6% occurred. During the 7-year system transformation period from 1994 to 2001, the annual gold production changed from continuous growth to fluctuating growth, and the production declined in 3 years and grew in 4 years. In 1997, due to the transformation between new and old "systems", there was a time lag of adjustment of gold price, so that the domestic gold price was higher than the international gold price. As a result, the gold purchase volume of central bank increased by 50.58% for the first time since 1949.

  During this period, the production fluctuated, but the joint force for industrial development was formed due to the establishment of independent production command and leadership work system, so that the capacity of gold industry to get adapted to change was improved, and the cultivation of built-in power also began to play a role. As a result, during this system adjustment period, the gold

Chinese Gold: From Following to Surpassing

production was still growing, and in 1995, the gold production of China exceeded 100 tons and reached 108.5 tons. China became one of the main gold producing countries in the world.

After the 7-year transitional period for reform, the opening of Shanghai Gold Exchange in 2002 marked the achievement of gold marketization in China, and thus the management "system" for gold industry in China entered the comprehensive market economy period. Such day was also the end of the bear market of more than 20 years in international gold market, and the international gold market began to enter the unprecedented bullish market for gold. From 2002 to 2012, the international USD gold price increased by 5.16 times, while the domestic RMB gold price increased by 3.73 times. The rise of gold price also increased the profit of gold production enterprises, and during this period, the total profits of gold industry increased by 22 times, from RMB 1.528 billion in 2002 to RMB 35.141 billion in 2012. Driven by the bullish gold market, the internal development force of gold enterprises was strong. China also had a continuous growth period for gold production from 2000 to 2014. This continuous growth period was 14 years, shorter than the previous continuous growth period (1975-1993) which was 18 years, but in this continuous growth period, the total gold production reached 4,100.034 tons, namely 5.23 times that in previous gold production growth period and 52.36% of total gold production since 1949, and the annual average gold production was 6.63 times that in previous gold production growth period. More than half of total gold production achieved during the 70 years after establishment of the People's Republic of China was achieved in these 14 years. This is a significant impact of the change of gold development "system" on gold production, and the actual results of development prove the advantages of socialist market economic "system".

Starting from 1949, it took 46 years for the gold production of the People's Republic of China to go up the first hundred-ton step. In the 10 years after 2002 when the gold industry entered the social market economic system, the gold production of China went up 3 hundred-ton steps continuously: it spent 8 years from 1995 to 2003 in going

1 Gold Control Arising from Resource Shortage

up the second hundred-ton step and reached 200.6 tons in 2003; it spent 5 years from 2004 to 2009 in going up the third hundred-ton step and reached 313.98 tons in 2009; it only spent half the time, namely 2 years from 2010 to 2012, in going up the fourth hundred-ton step and reached 403.05 tons, as indicated in Figure 1-1. In 2014, the gold production reached 451.799 tons, which was the highest record in this growth period. As a result, China became the only country with the gold production exceeding 400 tons in the world. The historic breakthrough of gold productivity gave the best endorsement for the advantages of Chinese social market economic "system".

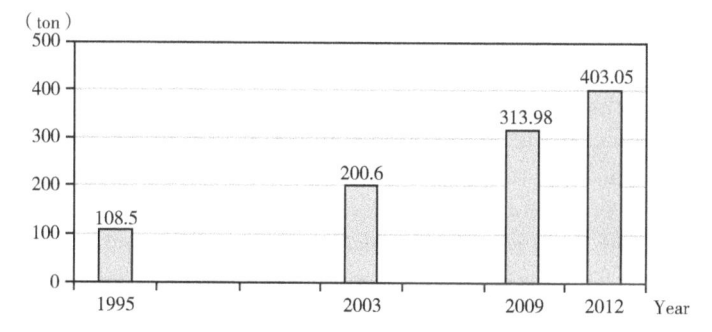

Figure 1-1 Hundred-ton Steps for Gold Production of China
Source: *China Gold Yearbook 2013*.

1.3.3 China won the global crown in the new century

In 2007, with the gold production of 270.49 tons, China surpassed the centennial champion South Africa and became the new champion. As a centurial change, it was announced by international professional institution rather than us. It was somewhat beyond our expectation that China could become the world champion in 2007 our gold production in 2006 was only 240.18 tons, lower than 247.1 tons in Australia, 251.8 tons in USA and 291.8 tons in South Africa, and ranked fourth in the world. For 2007, our expectation is that we could surpass Australia and be ranked third in the world, or surpass USA and be ranked second in the world. Since there was the gap of

Chinese Gold: From Following to Surpassing

more than 50 tons between us and South Africa, we believed that South Africa would still be the world champion. Therefore, when the international professional institution declared that our gold production was ranked No. 1, we even expressed doubts. On the basis of the expectation that the gold production of South Africa would be decreased by about 8%, the China Gold Association declared that our gold production was ranked second in the world. In fact, the decline in gold production in the other three countries was far beyond our expectation. In 2007, the gold production in Australia, the United States, and South Africa fell by 20.57%, 37.56% and 45.68%, respectively, while that in China increased by 12.67%. In such a context, China finally surpassed South Africa by one ton in terms of gold production and became the new champion of gold production around the globe. This is somewhat surprising, but it is an inevitable result of the continuous growth of China's gold production and the stagnation or decline of gold production in major gold-producing countries in the new century.

The bullish gold market has also made the development of gold resources in China a hot spot for geological exploration and triggered an investment climax. Therefore, China is growing continuously in terms of gold productivity and gold output, the proven gold reserves have also achieved a breakthrough. Insufficient gold reserves have been a long-standing problem that has plagued the development of China's gold industry. However, the proven gold reserves from 2005 to 2017 had achieved continuous growth for 12 consecutive years. As of 2017, the proven gold reserves had reached 13,000 tons, ranking second in the world after South Africa. The growth and growth rate of proven gold reserves in China are shown in Figure 1-2. Based on the amount of resources consumed in current gold production, China has been able to meet the static demand for gold production for about 20 years. Therefore, the shortage of gold geological resources has been considerably alleviated or basically resolved. This change has laid a solid resource foundation for the faster development of gold production in China, and it is also a symbol of China's gold wealth developing from insufficiency to prosperity and an important part of

1 Gold Control Arising from Resource Shortage

China's "Golden Light" strategy in the new century. After unremitting efforts, we have finally climbed to a historical peak that our predecessors have never reached. In this process, we are also constantly exploring the market system and keep innovating and sublating in exploration. After the 14th National Congress of the Communist Party of China established the reform goal of the socialist market economic system in 1992, China initiated a comprehensive economic system transformation, which not only brought the gold industry out of a downturn, but also established China's leading position in gold production throughout the world. No matter for the gold resources that have been acquired on the ground or those that have been discovered underground, China has made significant breakthrough in the new century, but our exploration and practice of the socialist market economy system have never stopped and are continuing to intensify.

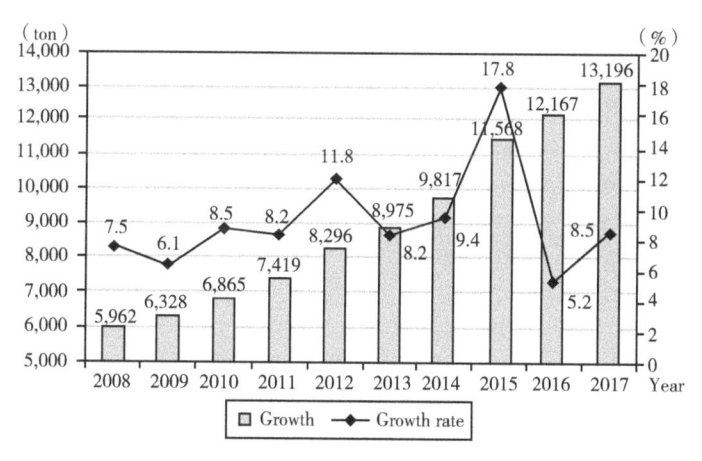

Figure 1-2 Growth and Growth Rate of Proven Gold Reserve of China from 2008 to 2017

Source: *China Gold Yearbook (2009-2018)*.

1.4 Two sides of "invisible hand"

The bullish gold market that began in 2002 has brought a rare

Chinese Gold: From Following to Surpassing

opportunity for the development of China's gold industry, and the "system" transformation guarantees that we can seize this opportunity. However, the market has both opportunities and risks. The gold price began to fall in 2013. In such year, the international dollar gold price fell by 15.4%, and the domestic RMB gold price fell by 18.01%. The profit of China's gold industry fell by nearly 60% (59.44%), and the quantity of loss-making enterprises increased 19.4 times, accounted for 20.49% of all enterprises covered by statistics in such year. The continuous growth of gold production lasted till 2014. In 2015, the production declined by 0.39%, and then the decline was not stopped but aggregated. As a result, the production in 2018 was decreased by 11.22% as compared with that in 2014. The gold market has a development cycle. If it only relies on the market mechanism to repair itself and enters the next bullish market, that will be a long and uncertain process, and the loss will be unbearable. However, China's socialist market economy is not a free market economy, but a market dominated by market mechanism with regulation, so that when there is resistance in the operation of market mechanism, the "visible hand" should play a role, so as to get the gold production out of the downturn period as soon as possible.

Promoting the technical advancement is the first factor for overcoming the bottleneck of market, but the achievement of technical advancement often requires cooperation, which needs the "visible hand", namely government, to play a leading role. In the 1990s, although the gold resources proved by China grew continuously, the low-grade refractory gold ore accounted for more than 50% of proven geological resources at that time, and such gold resources remained in the mine because of the poor refining technology. Therefore, China carried out a pilot project of "exchanging technology with resources" in the 1990s, but the effect was very little. Finally, the problem was solved through technical innovation organized by the competent authority. The breakthrough in low-grade refractory gold ore dressing and refining technology is one of the key factors for the sustainable growth of China's gold production in the new century. Without the breakthrough in low-

1 Gold Control Arising from Resource Shortage

grade refractory gold ore dressing and refining technology, there will be no highlight of Chinese gold in the new century.

In 2015, the gold production showed a negative growth rate of 0.39%. Although it rebounded in 2016, it continued to decline from 2017 to 2018. The reason is that China pays more and more attention to environmental protection, which improves the discharge standard of cyanide containing materials in gold mines, and some mines stop production due to substandard discharge. In addition, the environmental protection also requires that the gold mines in nature reserves to be moved out or shut down. With the challenge of green production to traditional gold production, the innovation of gold production technology becomes an urgent task in reality, and the development of gold green technology is also an opportunity to improve the technical content of industry. Therefore, the China Gold Association takes the lead in promoting the discharge standard for cyanide-bearing materials in gold mines and the innovation of utilization technology, thus pushing the greening of gold production in China to a new level. The breakthrough of this technology will surely be a great driving force for the development of gold production in China.

In addition, with the intensification of opening up of China and the innovation of refining technology, more and more imported resources are utilized, and the utilization of imported resources has become an important way for China to improve the gold supply capacity. This is ensured by "system", while ensuring and promoting the international cooperation is an important responsibility of "visible hand". The international cooperation has become the important factor for maintaining the light of gold in China. Though there was a decline cycle of gold production after 2015, the gold supply of China still remained at a high level, which is attributable to the fact that the intensified international cooperation buffered the reduction of domestic mineral gold production. In 2017, the production of gold materials decreased by 6.03%, and the gold production was 426.14 tons. However, due to the gold production based on imported raw materials increased by 11.46%, reaching 91.35 tons, the total

Chinese Gold: From Following to Surpassing

gold supply of China exceeded 500 tons and reached 517.49 tons. In 2018, the production of gold minerals in China decreased by 5.87%, and the gold production was 401.12 tons, while the supply still remained at the level above 500 tons. This is because the gold production based on imported raw materials exceeded 100 tons. The gold supply capacity of China is 130 times wore than that in 1949. Because of the international cooperation, the gold production of China has the advantage of international competition, while the gold supply capacity of Australia which immediately follows China is only about 300 tons.

The first 10 years of the new century are the decade during which great change happened. During this period, both the mineral gold production and the discovered underground reserves of China were ranked among the top in the world. Therefore, China has achieved a millennium change from a gold-poor country to a gold-rich country. This millennium change also coincided with the key period of revitalization of the Chinese nation, so that the influence of this millennium change is extremely profound and diverse. The process of this millennium change is also a process of continuous adjustment and exploration of gold "system" in China.

The gold control was born in the 1950s, was initially loosened in the 1980s, was further relaxed in the 1990s when the gold marketization trend was turbulent, and was finally ended at the beginning of the new century. Now, the Chinese gold industry has been developing in the market economic "system" for 17 years. The Chinese gold industry has greatly deepened the understanding of this "system" and more rationally understood the "visible hand" and "invisible hand" as well as the laws of their relationship. The socialist market economy is no longer a theory in a study, but becomes the running principles of socialist economic development. Through 17 years' marketization practice, the China's gold market has blazed a development road with Chinese characteristics.

2

Surging Undercurrent under Firm Ice

What we mean by "gold marketization reform" is that the unified gold collection and distribution by central bank was changed to free market trading. With respect to its cause, I have given the political interpretations in my book *Breaking Cocoon: Deciphering the Course of Chinese Gold Marketization Reform*. However, the occurrence of any economic phenomenon must have an internal cause in economy, and the political factor may only be a surface phenomenon or trigger point. The inherent economic factor is the development of gold productivity of China, which changed the supply condition of gold and thus directly affected the gold control "system". Though the lifting of gold control was indicated by the establishment of Shanghai Gold Exchange, it happened in 2002. Before that, with the implementation of reform and opening up in China, more and more foreign exchange was earned, the contradiction of gold supply was eased, and the supply of foreign exchange was continuously improved. Therefore, though the gold control was still imposed in the 1990s, its foundation had become loosened.

2.1 The supply pattern began to change

The gold control policy was an emergency measure taken against the background shortage of foreign exchange. It was legalized by the promulgation of the *Regulations for Administration of Gold and Silver* in 1982. Before the opening of Shanghai Gold Exchange, however, the supply-demand relationship of gold in China had begun to change from official deposit to private deposit, and the legal foundation of gold control had been shaken. This is the fundamental cause of gold marketization in China.

2.1.1 The foreign exchange reserves became increasing abundant owing to opening–up

To a great extent, the shortage of foreign exchange in China resulted from the planned economy. In 1978, China implemented the reform and opening-up, embarking on the road of integration with world economy. As a result, the source of foreign exchange became diversified. In the 1980s, the foreign exchange reserves exceeded USD10 billion; in 1994, China initiated the reform for foreign exchange management system, and got the foreign exchange reserves increased by 1 time; in 1995, the foreign exchange reserves reached USD 75.3 billion, and with the annual gold production exceeding 100 tons, China became one of the main gold producing countries in the world. Due to the joint effect of several improvements in supply of foreign exchange, the necessity and urgency of gold control in China began to decrease.

After 1995, China embarked on the road of rapid growth of foreign exchange reserves, and the growth rate could even be described as extraordinary. In 2000, the foreign exchange reserves exceeded USD100 billion, reaching USD168 billion, and in 2002, the foreign exchange reserves reached USD 403.251 billion. The annual average growth of foreign exchange reserves exceeded USD 100 billion. At that time, what China was facing was not the problem about shortage of foreign exchange, but the question whether there were too many foreign exchange reserves. Therefore, in 2002 when Shanghai Gold Exchange was opened, the problem about shortage of foreign exchange was settled, and it was a well-established move to abolish the gold control and promote the gold marketization. Looking back on the private gold buying tide in 1993, China took consolidating the gold control as the main theme of the Document No. 63 of the State Council in fear of shortage of foreign exchange reserves, thus delaying the gold marketization by 10 years. If we knew that the foreign exchange reserves would increase sharply in the next year, namely 1994, then the countermeasure taken would be different.

2.1.2 The gold demand was mainly changed to private demand

Owing to the increase of foreign exchange reserves, the importance of gold for foreign-exchange payment began to weaken, so that the quantity of gold in foreign exchange reserves decreased rather than increased. In the 1990s, the gold reserves of China were even lower than those in the 1970s. The gold reserves of China were 398 tons in the 1970s, decreased to 395 tons in the 1980s, and then remained unchanged till the end of 1990s. Therefore, for so many years, the gold has not been reserved by the state, but has been converted to the demand of the people. The proportion of gold in foreign exchange reserves has begun to decline significantly: The proportion of gold in foreign exchange reserves of China was 65.79% in the 1970s, declined to 28.11% in 1980s and was only 1.75% in 2000. As a result, the gold reserves have been marginalized in foreign exchange reserves. Though the central bank has increased its holdings of gold reserves since 2009 and the gold reserves have increased to 1,885.5 tons now, they only account for 2.2% in foreign exchange reserves, so that the marginal status of gold in foreign exchange reserves has not changed. This shows that the state is no longer the main demander of gold and thus is no longer the main undertaker of responsibility of gold production, and the gold holders begin to change from government to common people. This change fundamentally shook the survival foundation of the unified gold collection and distribution system, though the unified gold collection and distribution system was still maintained for 10 years till the beginning of the new century, namely 2002.

From storing gold in treasury to storing it among people, the achievement of this change was based on the gold purchasing capacity of people. From the perspective of national reserves, this change was attributable to the fact that the increased foreign exchange was received by China and more gold supply could be turned to meeting the needs of the people; from the perspective of private possession, the central bank was no longer the main holder of gold, but how much could people absorb the gold? In fact, at that time, the relevant department was suspicious, and on the eve of the lifting of gold control, there was a discussion about "how to deal with the draggy sales of gold". However, this worry did not become reality, and this should be attributable to the reform and opening-up of China. Owing to the reform and opening-up, China has become increasingly prosperous and strong. In this process, the common people also got huge economic benefits. Since 1996, although the central bank has reduced the interest rates for deposit several times, the growth of people's deposits has exceeded RMB1 trillion every year. Because the income of individuals and families has increased by dozens times, the middle class composed of nearly 400 million people has emerged. The Chinese people have got the growing purchase power, and the people's demand has become an important driving force for economic development of China, so that the people have the ability to take over the gold after the central bank is no longer a main gold demander.

2.1.3 The consumption upgrading of people drives the gold demand

The growth of purchasing power of the increasingly affluent people is firstly reflected in consumption upgrading. The daily durable consumer goods of residents have been upgraded four times over the past 40 years: In the 1970s, after the minimum life demand was satisfied, the durable consumer goods pursued by common people were old three pieces - sewing machine, radio and bicycle; in the 1980s, the old three pieces were replaced by new three pieces - refrigerator, TV set, washing machine; in the 1990s, the target became car; in the new century, there comes the housing

2 Surging Undercurrent under Firm Ice

upgrading for the purpose of improving the living conditions. As a result, the consumption of residents has experienced the upgrading to RMB 100 level, RMB 1,000 level, RMB 10,000 level and RMB 1 million level. In this process, not only the demand on durable consumer goods, but also the demand on configuration of family assets has been upgraded. According to the *Survey Report on Family Wealth in China (2018)* issued by Chinese Economy Trend Research Institute under the Economic Daily, the growth of family income has promoted the consumption, but the growth of people's income was always higher than that of consumption, and only till 2016, the growth of consumption expenditure became slightly higher than that of disposable income. The difference between income growth and consumption growth is the growth of wealth held by individuals and families. The newspaper pointed out that, the per capita wealth reached RMB 194,300 in 2017, there was the trend in China that the wealth held by common people became diversified and high-grade. With the increase of family wealth, the focus of people began to change from short-term income of wealth to long-term value preservation and inheritance of wealth.

In the tide of Chinese people's pursuit of preservation and inheritance of family wealth, the increased holding of gold as the absolute wealth of human beings is very natural. At the beginning of opening of gold market, the gold consumption of people mainly involved the demand to show off, which was the result of inheritance of gold-related historical culture. Now, the increased holdings of gold by people are based on the demand for value preservation and inheritance of wealth, so that the scale of gold demand is upgraded. This indicates that the economic capacity required for increase of gold demand is obtained, and thus it is feasible for the gold demand to be transferred from government to common people. As driven by the continuous change in supply-demand relationship of gold, the gold control was relaxed and then abandoned. This is the truth hidden behind the surface phenomenon, and the gold marketization is driven by inherent economic factor rather than external political factor.

Under the conditions of market economy, the change of gold demand is the leading force which drives the change of market supply & demand pattern, and the supply side should change accordingly in light of the change of demand so as to achieve a new balance of supply and demand. Therefore, every change in gold demand will cause a change in the new balance point of supply and demand, and this change will determine the scale and direction of development of gold market. In essence, the development of gold market is to continuously pursue the improvement of new balance point between supply and demand of gold, so that creating and forming the new demand for gold is the key for development of gold market.

2.2 The control was loosened under the impact of undercurrent

Although the China's gold market was born in the new century, it was conceived in the 1990s during which the gold control was still imposed. During this period, the change in supply-demand structure of gold in China led to the loosening of gold control. Finally, on the birth date of gold market in the new century, the gold control was abandoned. Rome was not built in a day. The gold marketization did not happen suddenly, but was a gradual process from quantity accumulation to qualitative mutation as the supply of foreign exchange in China changed from shortage to abundance.

2.2.1 The gold supply began to take into account both inside and outside

Since 1975, the gold production of China has entered a sustained growth period, and the extreme shortage of gold supply in China has been somewhat alleviated. In 1995, the gold production of China exceeded 100 tons, reaching 108.5 tons, so that China became an important gold producing country in the world. In 2000, the gold production of China grew by 63.19%, reaching 176.91 tons, so

2 Surging Undercurrent under Firm Ice

that China changed from an important gold producing country to a main gold producing country in the world. At that time, the gold production of China was ranked No. 4 in the world. The gradual improvement of gold supply made it possible for the national gold reserves to be used for livelihood of domestic people. Therefore, although the gold was still under control, the use of gold began to shift from meeting the payment need for foreign trade to meeting the domestic demand. As a result, the gold ban for people began to get relaxed, and this change directly affected the subsequent selection of circulation mode and circulation path for gold marketization in China.

In more than half a century since the founding of the People's Republic of China, the social function of gold was determined as an important national foreign exchange reserve. Before the 1970s, the gold accounted for more than 40% of national foreign exchange reserves, and in some years, such as 1970, the proportion reached 90%. The gold was mainly used for payment for import trade, which is also the reason for the implementation of gold control. Therefore, China strictly controlled the domestic civil use of gold and comprehensively restrained the civil use of gold, so as to concentrate on payment for foreign trade. However, with the improvement of supply conditions of foreign exchange, the gold reserves have new usages.

Firstly, in 1979, China issued the panda gold coin. It was mainly issued overseas at the beginning, and then began to be issued domestically in the middle of 1980s, so that the domestic demand on gold coin was expanded. In the new century, China has developed a variety of gold coin on the basis of panda gold coin. In addition to panda gold coin, it also issues commemorative gold and silver coins with various themes every year. In terms of gold consumption, the gold consumption for gold coin in China has been ranked among the top three in the world. In 2017, the gold consumption for gold coin was 26 tons, 37.1 times that in 1991. The birth of panda gold coin in 1979 shows that, at that time, in addition to the foreign-exchange payment function, the gold reserves also obtained the commodity value-added function, so that people could buy and sell gold in the

Chinese Gold: From Following to Surpassing

form of gold coin. In 1982, the China's gold market took a bigger step, resuming the market supply of gold jewelry which consumes the most gold. The change in number of gold coin issued and growth rate from 2008 to 2017 is as indexed in Figure 2-1.

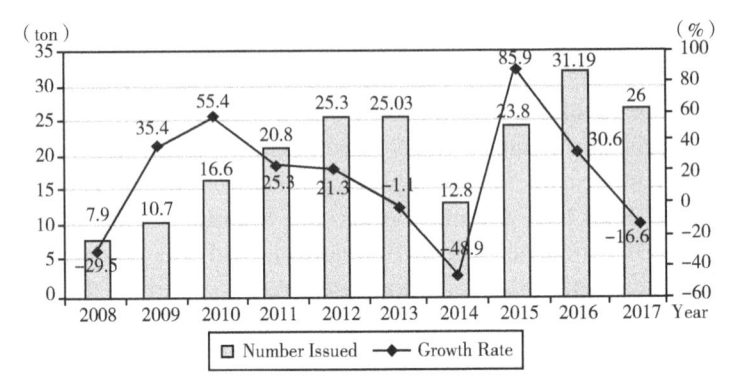

Figure 2-1 Change in Number of Gold Coin Issued and Growth Rate from 2008 to 2017
Source: *China Gold Yearbook (2009-2018)*.

Secondly, in the 1960s, in order to restrain the civil use of gold, China stopped the market supply of jewelry gold. 20 years later, in 1982, China resumed the supply. In 1985, China even used 100 tons of gold reserves to produce jewelry, which was 2.56 times the gold production (39 tons) in that year, and was almost the total gold production in 3 years. For the first time, the gold reserves were widely used for domestic economic development. This is because that, there was serious inflation at that time, and the inflation rate was as high as 18%. At the published price, the 100 tons of gold could recover the currency in amount of RMB 5.44 billion, and could generate a value-added premium of RMB 1.14 billion in the sales link, with the total value-added rate being 71%. It not only could greatly recover the currency and was conducive to suppression of inflation, but also was a profitable business. This shows that, in addition to the foreign-exchange payment function, the gold has also undertaken the function of stabilizing domestic currency. Therefore, after being able to own gold coin, people can also buy and sell gold in the form of jewelry.

2 Surging Undercurrent under Firm Ice

2.2.2 The change in reserves shook the foundation of control

Owing to the implementation of reform and opening-up, the scale of foreign investment in China has expanded continuously. With the development of export-oriented economy, the foreign exchange reserves of China have gradually grown. In 1982, the foreign exchange reserves exceeded USD 10 billion, which was a landmark event. After that, the growth of foreign exchange reserves not only continued, but also was accelerated. By 2000, foreign exchange reserves exceeded USD 100 billion, reaching USD 168 billion. Though this figure is still very small as compared with the subsequently-achieved scale of near USD 4,000 billion, it is more than 200 times the average value (USD 608 million) in the 1960s, is more than 100 times the average value (USD 1.167 billion) in the 1970s, and is more than 10 times the average value in1980s. Therefore, the foreign exchange reserves of China have undergone a qualitative change from lack to abundance, and this change has gradually reduced the dependence of China on gold. The conditions for lifting of gold control began to become mature in the 1990s, and at that time, the people's demand on gold was so developed that it began to challenge the monopoly of gold. The emergence of Ganwang private gold market in Haicheng, Liaoning Province is a typical event, which indicates that the challenge became open.

Till the beginning of the 1990s, owing to the shortage of foreign exchange, China always concentrated its efforts on solving the problem about gold shortage, so that the gold production was the central issue highly concerned by the state. The gold producers were the main player in increase of gold production, so that they had a greater say in the reform of gold circulation system, and were also the leading force which affected the gold marketing at that time. However, at the end of 1990s, the supply condition of foreign exchange was improved, and the main force of gold circulation reform became consumers, so the social attention to gold production was greatly reduced. Whether at the national level or at the level of common people, the reform of unified gold collection and

Chinese Gold: From Following to Surpassing

distribution system has become more revolutionary.

When the supply of gold jewelry was restored in 1982, there were only 38 jewelry processing enterprises in China, the annual output value was less than RMB 80 million, and 60% thereof came from processing for foreign trade. Only a few tons of gold were processed every year, far from meeting the needs of the increasingly wealthy people, so that in the 1990s, many people took advantage of Shenzhen's special status of opening to the outside world, and flocked to Shenzhen and Zhongying Street in Shatoujiao, adjacent to Hong Kong, to buy gold jewelry. This was also a scene of Shenzhen's opening up at that time. At the end of 1990s, the gold jewelry industry, one of the top-ten industries in Hong Kong, began to move to Shenzhen, where the gold jewelry processing enterprises gathered. As a result, the demand for raw gold began to emerge in China. The contradiction between the development of this industry and the gold control was increasingly aggravated, because the control led to insufficient supply of raw gold, impeded the logistics, restricted its development, and made some behaviors getting around the gold control system appear. This also became one of the direct factors which drove the reform of gold management system.

Gold is a kind of special metal, and is the traditional object of trading in the financial market. Owning gold was once the desire of Chinese people which had been suppressed for long term. In the 1990s, with the increase of income, the Chinese people's desire to own gold became a strong behavior impulse, and the underground gold transaction reached a considerable scale and did not stop despite long-term prohibition. At that time, the competent departments of the government also increased the number of anti gold smuggling personnel. Even so, the people's demand on gold investment did not disappear, but existed in a semi-open form, becoming another important driving force for lifting of gold control.

Although the gold marketization reform was completed at the beginning of the new century, it was put on the agenda under the action of dual demands from people on gold consumption and gold investment in the 1990s. The demand on consumption of gold commodity brought forward the requirement on diversification of social functions of gold, while the demand on gold investment brought forward the requirement on breaking of monopolistic management system relating to gold. Therefore, in the 1990s, with the undercurrent surging, the gold control system was already in danger. In 2002, the China's gold market achieved the breakthrough from zero to one and completed the "final kick" of gold marketization, and the whole process was natural and smooth. Since this "final kick" is a natural result, what special value does it have?

2.3 A "final kick" with international significance

The gold marketization is a gradual process. The goal of this reform was determined as early as 1992, and the gold control was relaxed as early as 1982. However, these changes were quantitative changes, and only the completion of "final kick" was qualitative change which led to the fundamental change. The first fundamental change was that the central bank achieved the transformation of role from direct operator of gold to manager of market, so that the leading power for flow of gold wealth in China was transferred from government to the public, and the potential of gold demand from people which had been suppressed for long time was turned into the actual consumption capacity. As driven by the continuous growth of consumption, China became the largest gold demanding country in the world and the largest gold producing country in the world, and changed the pattern of international gold logistics. China changed from a gold exporting country to a gold importing country, and the imported gold changed from the supplementary supply source to the largest supply source, far more than the mineral gold and recovered gold in China. In 2013, China became the largest gold importing in the world. Therefore, the significance of the birth of the China's gold market has surmounted itself, reshaped the international circulation pattern of gold wealth, and further promoted the contemporary international gold logic trend of " flow of gold from the West to

Chinese Gold: From Following to Surpassing

the East", thus making the international influence of the China's gold market reach a new height. This is another international significance of completion of "final kick". The change in quantity of gold imported by China during 2008-2017 is as indicated in Figure 2-2.

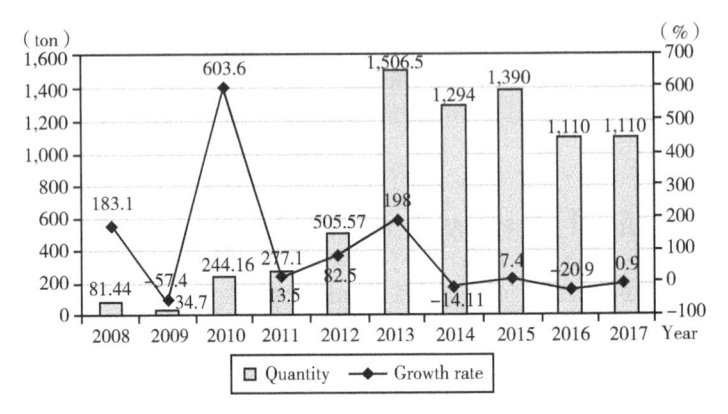

Figure 2-2 Change in Quantity of Gold Imported by China from 2008 to 2017
Source: *China Gold Yearbook (2009-2018)*.

China completed the "final kick" of gold marketization, so that the systematic fetters on Chinese people's gold demand was released, and the potential of gold demand was quickly tapped out. In 2013, China not only surpassed India and became the largest gold consuming country in the world, but also became the only country in the world with the gold consumption exceed one thousand tons. In 2017, China's gold consumption was 1,089 tons, accounting for 76.17% of China's total demand in such year; in 2018, China's gold consumption was 1,151 tons, accounting for 65.41% of China's total demand in such year. The first major area of gold consumption is gold jewelry. Though China resumed the supply of gold jewelry in 1982, during the 10 years before the opening up of the gold market, the average annual consumption of gold in China was less than 200 tons (192.55 tons). However, from 2002 when Shanghai Gold Exchange was established to 2017, the average annual consumption of gold in

2 Surging Undercurrent under Firm Ice

China reached 642.53 tons, growing by 233.7%. Especially from 2013 to 2018, the average annual consumption of gold exceeded one thousand tons, reaching 1,051.57 tons.

The figure above indicates the change of gold consumption demand in China, and the gold investment demand has increased quickly owing to the opening of gold market. In 2004, China opened the gold investment market for common people. The branded small gold bars were firstly launched by the four major state-owned banks, which awakened people's historical memory of "little yellow fish". Now, the gold investment products available in the market have been diversified, and the gold investment has been popular among all walks of life, from ordinary housewives to intellectuals. Many people have participated in gold investment, so that the gold investment market has been multi-layered, so as to meet the diversified needs of different investment groups. The strong gold investment demand has made Shanghai Gold Exchange the largest spot gold floor-trading market in the world only after 5 years' operation. In 2017, the investment demand on physical gold (gold bar + gold coin) in China was 302.39 tons, 4.69% higher than that in 2016. For the perspective of international comparison, this figure is undoubtedly impressive. Except for China, the top-three countries in 2017 in the aspect of physical gold investment were India, Germany and Thailand. The physical gold investment demand of these three countries was 164.2 tons, 106.5 tons and 64 tons respectively, accounting for 54.3%, 35.22% and 21.16% of Chinese market demand respectively. The physical gold investment demand of China was almost the sum of physical gold investment demand of such three countries.

A fundamental change brought about by the opening of China's gold market is that, the demand became the main driving force of the market, the supply met the demand, and the diversified demand brought in the supply side reform. The supply side reform not only affected the production of mineral gold and opened up the market space for the development of gold mining industry, but also drove the development of Chinese gold processing industry and then promoted

Chinese Gold: From Following to Surpassing

the development of Chinese gold circulation & sales industry. Therefore, a basic feature of the China's gold market is that, the gold marketization enabled the leader in holding of physical gold wealth to be adjusted from government to common people. This adjustment drove the growth of gold demand and also drove the diversification of demand on gold products. As a result, the development of gold industry chain in China was promoted, and China obtained a complete industry chain from exploration to processing and then to terminal market. The gold industry chain is complete and every link has the world-class scale, which is unique in the world. Therefore, the China's gold market enjoys strong industrial support and can develop stably. Nowadays, most of the international gold markets are not supported by gold industry, most of them are dominated by circulation and trading, most of them are not located in the gathering place of gold wealth and gold processing industry, and most of them enjoy no complete industrial chain structure. China is supported by gold industry chain, so that the gold market not only undertakes the gold trading function, but also undertakes the function to gather gold wealth. At the key moment of national rejuvenation, this wealth-gathering function of China's gold market is of great significance. For China, the largest significance of the establishment of gold market is that the development of gold economy has changed from the mode directed by "visible hand" to the mode directed by "invisible hand", while the regulation work system of "visible hand" has made the Chinese gold economy develop more quickly. Therefore, the gold market not only provides the gold trading platform, but also serves as the basic market for trading of derivatives of financial market, and fills in the gap of Chinese circulation market. It is the indicator for allocation of gold resources in China and the aggregator of gold wealth, and undertakes multiple social functions for the development of Chinese gold industry, so that it plays an important role in the stabilization of social economy.

3
Breakthrough of Gold Market from Scratch

Because of the development of gold productivity, the supply side and demand side of gold in China were changing from quantitative accumulation to qualitative breakthrough. Almost all the changes before the 1990s belong to the quantitative accumulation. There was a consensus on the necessity of gold control, both at the top level of government and at the general level of common people. Therefore, the unified gold collection and distribution management system was highly authoritative at that time. This management system was maintained consistently from top to bottom without any challengers. During the "Eighth Five-year Plan" period of China from 1986 to 1990, under the support of "visible hand", the average annual growth rate of gold production reached 11.23%, and the annual average gold production reached 52.9 tons, 69.52% higher than that (31.206 tons) during the "Seventh Five-year Plan" period. Therefore, the relevant leaders were satisfied with the gold production work during the Eighth Five-year Plan Period, and believed that China had found the right way for development of gold production. As a result, it was decided that, the stability would be the main focus, no new gold management policy would be issued during the "Ninth Five-year Plan" period, and the current work system for production management and industrial management would not be changed greatly. However, this work arrangement was disrupted due to the sudden appearance of Ganwang private gold market in Haicheng, Liaoning Province. In 1993, the gold marketization reform was initiated under the situation that no sufficient preparation had been made.

Chinese Gold: From Following to Surpassing

3.1 A tinder which ignited the gold marketization in China

The work arrangement of the State Council for the development of gold industry during the "Ninth Five-year Plan" period was disrupted by the appearance of private gold market in Ganwang in 1993. It became the tinder of gold marketization reform. 1993 was also called as the first year of gold marketization reform in China.

Ganwang Town is a remote town located 18km away from Haicheng in Liaoning Province. It is not well known. It neither produces gold nor processes gold jewelry, and is also not a distribution center of gold products. However, it became widely known owing to the fact that a gold marketization reform was initiated from the establishment of Ganwang gold market.

The Ganwang gold market is a private gold market. The so-called private gold market is a market which has completed the registration for enterprise with the industrial and commercial administration department, but of which the gold business has not been approved by the central bank. It traded gold jewelry on the counter and also traded gold under the counter sometimes. More incredibly, this market publicly announced that its gold price was in line with the international London USD gold price and would change as the international gold price changed. This obviously went against the *Regulations for Administration on Gold and Silver*. It is specified in the *Regulations for Administration on Gold and Silver* that, the gold shall be subject to the pricing as well as the unified collection and distribution management by the central bank. Therefore, the Ganwang gold market has violated the relevant provisions of the *Regulations for Administration on Gold and Silver,* and was a reform carried out beyond authority. A town-level leader has no power to promote the reform which is not within the scope of his powers and responsibilities, so that some people believed that Ganwang gold market was illegal and should be closed, but the central bank's opinions on Ganwang private gold market were that the market could exist after making correction. Therefore, the actual situation was that, before the opening of Shanghai Gold Exchange, the Ganwang gold market was always a market with the characteristics of integrating with international market. In 2002 when Shanghai Gold Exchange was opened, the Ganwang gold market was closed owing to disappearance of this special function. In fact, after 1993, a binary gold trading structure appeared in China, that is, the central bank's unified gold collection and distribution market and the Ganwang gold free trading market coexisted. However, the Ganwang gold market was strongly inhibited, and became a market which could exist only but could not develop, so that the existence of Ganwang gold market did not have a significant impact on the central bank's unified gold collection and distribution system, and the gold control lasted for 10 years.

3.2 Interpretation of the Document No. 63 of the State Council

The emergence of Ganwang gold market imposed a certain impact on the unified gold collection and distribution system, because this event was tinder and could lead to a wildland fire which would end the gold control. Would the gold marketization be promoted by making use of this event, or would the market be checked and the gold control system be further adhered to? Therefore, the State Council was urgently required to make clear the processing principles for the new problem occurring. This was the background against which the Document No. 63 of the State Council was issued. At that time, the public generally believed that the Document No. 63 of the State Council was the symbol of gold marketization in China. This may be a kind of misunderstanding, because the Document No. 63 did not start the gold marketization reform, but reiterated and maintained the unified gold collection and distribution system, and the gold marketization was only confirmed as a future direction. We can say that 1993 is the first year of gold marketization, and that's all. Even the gold price synchronization reform which has the

Chinese Gold: From Following to Surpassing

most significance of marketization reform was for the purpose of consolidating the unified gold collection and distribution system, but not for the purpose of promoting the gold marketization reform. Of course, the situation that later the gold price synchronization triggered the gold marketization reform was not intentionally arranged, but occurred unexpectedly.

The reason why the Document No. 63 of the State Council, which consolidated the unified gold collection and distribution system in general, was interpreted by the public as marketization is mainly because that the 14th National Congress of the Communist Parly of China was just ended and everyone was full of yearning for the marketization reform. The basic starting point of the issuance of the Document No. 63 is that the government was worried about the prospect of foreign exchange reserves and insisted on the work system of gold control. The subsequent situation was that, since 1994 when the reform for management on foreign exchange reserves was initiated, China entered a rapid growth period of foreign exchange reserves, and in less than 10 years thereafter, the situation that the foreign exchange reserve was insufficient was changed to the situation that the relevant departments were concerned about the excessive foreign exchange reserves. If in 1993 when issuing the Document No. 63, the State Council could forecast this development prospect, maybe the gold marketization would not be delayed by 10 years to the beginning of the new century. However, the future is uncertain, and the Document No. 63 of the State Council could only take the gold marketization as a prospect of future development on the basis of the reality at that time.

The Document No. 63 of the State Council was issued in August 1993. In fact, 3 months ago, a Circular No. 7 about gold policies was issued, and it was the reply given for the request for instruction about gold policies from five departments. The Circular No. 7 involved the price increase of gold and gold products, and decided that the gold price would be increased by 6.67% (RMB 100), the central bank would increase the sales price by 15%, and the sales price of industrial gold would be increased by 26.58%; no rigid regulation

3 Breakthrough of Gold Market from Scratch

was given on price increase for gold jewelry. In addition, the State Council required the central bank to propose the amendments to the *Regulations for Administration on Gold and Silver* in accordance with the requirements of the *Regulations on Change of Operation Mechanism of State-owned Industrial Enterprises*, and required the State Gold Administration to propose the implementation measures for pilot projects of developing low-grade and refractory gold ore resources by foreign funded enterprises. The Circular No. 7 of the State Council basically continued the consistent work idea of raising prices in small steps and stabilizing gold control, but gave no word on promotion of gold marketization, so that the Circular No. 7 did not achieve the expected effect and the problem was not solved. Therefore, after the Circular No. 7 was issued, the State Council also issued the Document No. 63 to strengthen the solution to the existing problems, and to strengthen the guidance on marketization reform under the condition that the unified gold collection and distribution system would remain unchanged.

If we give a general interpretation of the theme of the Document No. 63, the center is to properly manage the gold products and relax the gold price. At that time, though China's foreign exchange revenue had increased greatly and its foreign exchange reserves were increased continuously after reaching USD 10 billion in the 1980s, the shortage of foreign exchange was just alleviated, but not completely reversed (It was completely reversed at the beginning of the new century). In light of this situation, China could not immediately release the gold control, so that it has to control the products. In order to eliminate the impact from appeal for marketization reform on gold control, the countermeasure was to achieve the synchronization of gold price. Though the Document No. 63 did not clearly specified the initiation of gold marketization reform, it gave response to the appeal for gold marketization, namely linking the RMB gold price with the international USD gold price and letting the RMB gold price increase greatly, so as to meet the demand of gold producers for interests and thus alleviate the impact on unified gold collection and distribution system. At that time, the main appeal of government was to maintain the gold monopoly rather than the profit-making right. The main purpose of the Document No. 63 issued by the State Council was to stabilize the unified gold collection and distribution system. This was the overall situation at that time, while the marketization reform was a relatively minor issue, so that China did not immediately start the construction of gold market, but provided a transitional period.

Properly managing the products means maintaining the unified gold collection and distribution system unchanged, but the state also determined that the achievement of gold marketization would be the final goal and required that great efforts would be made to achieve the balance between short-term goal and long-term reform goal. Though the gold marketization is not the short-term goal, the Document No. 63 defines three tasks for promoting the gold marketization: The first is that, the Legislative Affairs Bureau of the State Council should, in conjunction with relevant departments, propose the amendments to the *Regulations for Administration on Gold and Silver* in accordance with the requirements of the *Regulations on Change of Operation Mechanism of State-owned Industrial Enterprises*; the second is that, the central bank should carry out the preliminary research on construction of gold market; the third is to promote the gold price mechanism reform, achieve the synchronization between domestic RMB gold price and international USD gold price, and make the domestic gold price change as the international USD gold price changes.

The price synchronization is the most valuable reform for eliminating the impact of Ganwang market on gold control work system: firstly, it meets the interest demand of gold producers, stabilizes the work order of unified gold collection and distribution, and plays a preventive role; secondly, though the traditional unified gold revenue and distribution system is maintained, after the synchronization of gold price, China will implement the gold price floating system whereby the RMB gold price changes together with the international gold price, and thus the market mechanism factor will be introduced into the unified gold collection and distribution

3 Breakthrough of Gold Market from Scratch

system, so as to change or improve the operation mechanism of unified gold collection and distribution and become an actual step for promoting the gold marketization; finally, the synchronization between RMB gold price and international USD gold price will really become the catalyst for collapse of gold control. At that time, however, the society has not yet understood this point profoundly.

While determining the price synchronization, the Document No. 63 of the State Council also cancelled the original preferential policies for gold production. However, the policies were not be adjusted in one step, and there was a transitional period. Therefore, another important content of the Document No. 63 was to determine the transitional policy arrangement for gold industry during the transitional period. This arrangement declared the end of the mode whereby the development of gold industry is directed by government as well as the beginning of transformation of the development power for gold industry. If we say that the profound impact of gold price synchronization on gold production enterprise would be revealed 6 years later, then the gold industry institution reform and management system reform were launched immediately. Because the gold price synchronization led to the cut-off of industry management funds, the management institution reform was in urgent need. Therefore, during the Ninth Five-year Plan Period, the gold industry entered a transformation & reform period.

The synchronization between RMB gold price and international gold price actually demolished the firewall for gold producers, and thus the risk of international gold market could be directly transferred to domestic market and finally undertaken by gold producers. This is the direct reason for the gold industry to embark on the transformation and reform. However, at that time, the synchronization between RMB gold price and international gold price got a lot of applause from the gold industry, because the synchronization raised the domestic RMB gold price by more than 90%, and the gold producers thus became the winner of the biggest interest in this price reform. In fact, the Document No. 63 cancelled the preferential policies for gold production, so that the Chinese gold producers were not only the winner of short-term interest, but also the undertaker of long-term risks. In the 6 years after the synchronization of gold price, because the change in international gold price conformed to the interests of producers, or the change was within the allowable range, the market was basically calm, the gold control could also remain the same, and the gold marketization reform was stagnant. The continuous decline of international gold price was the event that broke the peace. The interest pattern temporarily formed by synchronization of gold price was broken, and owing to the intensified contradiction, the costs and risks of gold control were increased sharply. This drove the central bank to launch the gold marketization reform in 1999 by means of small-step trial.

3.3 The reform was re-started after 6 years' silence

Owing to the synchronization of gold price, the domestic gold price was adjusted from RMB 48.2 per gram to RMB 75.85 per gram and then to RMB 94.46 per gram, increased by nearly 1 time (96%). As a result the gold producers were satisfied with the interest obtained, and were satisfied with the reform results that the products were controlled and the price was released. For the People's Bank as the implementer of the policies about unified gold collection and distribution, stabilizing the order of collection and distribution of gold was its largest appeal, and was satisfied with the fact that the management system of unified collection and distribution was maintained. Therefore, the reform initiated in 1993 led to a new interest pattern, and there came a 6-year silence period for gold marketization reform. In such six years, the reform determined by the Document No. 63 of the State Council was not further advanced, and the gold control remained unchanged. The maintenance of this interest pattern was related to the extraordinary stability of international market gold price. The annual average price of gold was USD 384 per ounce (about 28g) in 1994, USD 384.17 in 1995 and USD 387.77 in 1996. In these 3 years, the price fluctuation was

3 Breakthrough of Gold Market from Scratch

only about 1%, so that the domestic RMB gold price was adjusted only four times. Although it was decreased, the decrease rate was less than 1% (0.98%). Therefore, for gold producers, this brought them a very high level of comfort, and thus they had neither desire for change nor motivation for reform. This pattern was not broken by market situation until 1997: The gold price changed from stability to continuous decline, and by 2001, the RMB price of gold fell at nearly 25% or 24.85% every year in average. As a result, the domestic gold price dropped from RMB 95.48 per gram in 1996 to RMB 71.75 per gram in 2001. For the gold producers, the decrease of gold price indicated the decrease of income and profit. At that time, however, the gold control was not finally lifted at that time and the central bank still implemented the unified collection and distribution of gold, so that the gold producers faced with market risk did not called for gold marketization reform again, but requested the central bank to protect the price, and the central bank also responded. If the international gold price was less than RMB 80 per gram, the central bank would purchase the gold at a price which was 3% higher than the international gold price.

This change was a disaster for the central bank. Owing to the unified collection and distribution of gold, the central bank in the gold control system had become the main undertaker of market risks, the operating risks involved in the operation mode of selling at high price and buying at low price were increased, and even all the possible operating losses would be borne by the central bank. In order to avoid the loss from gold operation, achieve the synchronization between domestic gold price and international gold price, the central bank continuously increased the frequency of price adjustment. The frequency was increased from once a year to once a month and finally to once a week, but the synchronization still could not be achieved. This situation not only greatly increased the workload, but also provided opportunities for speculators to carry out cross-market arbitrage, and huge economic loss even occurred in gold operation. In order to solve this problem, the only way was to promote the gold marketization reform and hand over the risk to

Chinese Gold: From Following to Surpassing

the market. In such a situation, the central bank changed from the maintainer of gold control to the promoter for releasing of control. As a result, in 1999, the gold marketization reform was initiated again.

The central bank was extremely cautious about the restart of gold marketing reform, so that it did not directly promote the establishment of gold market, but only planned to carry out some minor improvement for the unified collection and distribution system for gold and carry out some exploration in gold marketization. Finally, however, in order to support the marketization reform, some major reform actions were also be implemented.

In 1999, the year before the millennium, the central bank approved China Gold Coin Incorporation to issue the millennium gold bars. Though the panda gold coin was issued in 1979, this is the first time since the establishment of the People's Republic of China that the gold bar entered the market and could be bought by common people freely. Though the gold bar was named as "commemoratory", it undoubtedly awakened people's memory of "little yellow fish" in 1930s and 1940s, and announced that the gold control was coming to an end.

In 2000, the central bank approved Shenzhen to sell the imported gold in its foreign exchange to the jewelry processing enterprises in need of raw gold. This is difference from planned distribution of gold, but the sales according to demand. This reform provided another gold trading mode in addition to the unified collection and distribution, and was undoubtedly favorable for the development of gold processing jewelry enterprises which had been troubled by shortage of raw materials for a long time. Since Shenzhen seized the opportunity of reform and formed the development advantage, not only the jewelry processing enterprises in Hong Kong, but also the jewelry processing enterprises in Mainland China moved to Shenzhen, so that the gold jewelry processing industry of Shenzhen entered a new development stage. Now, the gold jewelry industry of Shenzhen has become an industry composed of more than 1,000 processing enterprises and more than 10,000 sales enterprises with

3 Breakthrough of Gold Market from Scratch

the characteristics of Shenzhen.

The silver market is a pathfinder of gold market. In 1999, the central bank firstly lifted the silver control and established Shanghai White Platinum & Silver Exchange. The silver market was officially launched in January 2000, but the effect was not satisfactory and the trading was light. So far, Shanghai White Platinum & Silver Exchange also has no developed into the central silver trading market of China. However, the unsuccessful silver market provided a warning for the establishment of gold market, so that the positive significance of the failure of silver market is to provide a practical case for the construction of gold market that can be directly used for reference and reflection, and play an important role in the successful establishment of the gold market.

Although the central bank was cautious about the restart of gold marketization, it had a clear goal of reform, which made the local governments see a rare opportunity and respond positively. After the news of the restart of gold marketization came out, the five cities including Beijing, Shanghai, Shenzhen, Tianjin and Wuhan put forward their wishes to launch the gold market in different forms to the State Council, and finally Shanghai became the winner. This selection was a part of China's strategy to forge Shanghai into an international financial city, and finally improved the missing link in financial market system of Shanghai. At that time, in addition to external driving force, the internal pressure of central bank was also increased. An executive of Shanghai Gold Exchange once wrote that: "For the central bank, by 2000, the monetary policy management and the financial regulation have been intensified, so that by cancelling the unified gold collection and distribution policies and opening up the gold market, we can focus on strengthening the functions such as macro-control, monetary policy management and the financial regulation, which also conforms to the international and domestic market situation as well as the industrial development trend. In addition, the situation about foreign exchange has obviously improved, and the urgency of exchanging foreign exchange with gold has weakened, so that there is the opportunity

Chinese Gold: From Following to Surpassing

for opening up the gold market." Therefore, the gold marketization reform started prudently in 1999 became the clear work target of the central bank, and the establishment of China's gold market entered the action stage in 2020.

In 2000, the preparation of China's gold market started. At that time, many people believed that this meant that the Chinese gold industry abandoned the gold regulation system directed by "visible hand" (namely government) and turned to the management system directed by "invisible hand" (namely market). However, there were two different ideas about the process of this abandonment. The first was that the "visible hand" withdrew completely, and the "invisible hand" assumed all the rights and responsibilities after the withdrawal of "visible hand". The silver market, which took the lead in lifting the control, took this road, but was not successful. The so-called free market theory is more a subjective wish, and is far from reality. The unsuccessful silver market provides reference for the organizers of gold market, so that how the "visible hand" would play a role in making up for the market defects became the key question for another selection. What is gratifying is that, we finally selected the second road, and thus the China's gold market embarked on the development road with top-level design and achieved success.

4
Top-level Design of China's Gold Market

Since 2000, the China's gold market has entered the specific stage of preparation and construction. Based on the lessons learned from silver market, the central bank thought more and decided to take a road which is different from that for silver market. This was not determined at the beginning. There were many programs at the beginning of preparation of gold market, and the preparation program was changed for many times. Finally, the central bank decided to directly intervene and set up Shanghai Gold Exchange on the platform of Shanghai Foreign Exchange Trading Center. In other worlds, the "visible hand" would establish a gold market to be regulated by central bank through strengthening the top-level design of the market. This road is different from that of UK, USA and other important international gold markets. They are gradually improved on the basis of market competition, while Shanghai Gold Exchange is the product of top-level design carried out by central bank. The evaluation on this difference involves the cognition on human economics, so that we should carry out some theoretical expansion for human economics. Of course, this is not a storm in a molehill, but a real issue which contains a great truth and must be explored in depth.

4.1 The cognition of market has not been completed

The development is the common pursuit of human beings. With respect to the selection of development road, the human being finally found the road of market economy after going through a long process, that is, the development and wealth could be achieved through market exchange. Therefore, the human being abandoned plunder and violence and selected commodity production. This is the development road of human civilization. The commodity production began to become the dominant production mode of human beings, and the commodity exchange began to become the dominant life style of human beings. The market is the operational platform of commodity economy and becomes the core of commodity economic system, so that this change in development mode of human beings naturally raises the position of market in human society, and the market has gradually become the center of production and life of human beings. However, the sublimation and summary of market behavior of human beings lags behind the market practices of human being, and is a continuous process of in-depth evolution.

4.1.1 Classical Economic school and *The Wealth of Nations*

After a long time of continuous trial and error, the human beings accepted the market economy, which has gradually become the dominant production and survival way of contemporary human beings. The form and connotation of market economy are all in continuous change, so that the human beings' understanding on market economy is still under exploration, far from over. Therefore, at present, there is no perfect market economic mode that can be universally applied, because the exploration is surely the selection of multiple paths.

The human beings' first systematic summarization and theorization of market economy was completed by the Classical Economic school born in the 18th Century and represented by Adam Smith. The academic foundation work of this school is his immortal work *The Wealth of Nations*, written three hundred years ago.

Adam Smith was a Scotsman who lived in 1723-1790. He was a representative of Classical Economics in the 18th Century, and his most important work, *The Wealth of Nations*, laid the theoretical foundation for economics of human beings. From then on, the economics became an independent discipline of human beings. This is a book which, through the elaboration of industrial development history and commercial development history in Europe, reveals to human beings the role of market as an "invisible hand" on economic development and its operation law, and points out the civilized development road in which work creates value and exchanges achieve value. He put forward the economic liberalism, advocated the free operation, free competition and free trade and opposed excessive intervention of government in economy. It is the epistemological conception arising from this economic liberalism that changed the traditional cognition of human beings on social development. In more than 200 years after the birth of Classical Economics, the Classical Economics was regarded as the classic of Human Economics and the principles of state governance. In the era when the economic liberalism of Adam Smith was popular, the politicians also always regarded the traditional gold standard as a code of conduct, taking the maintenance of free casting, free payment and free import/export of gold coin as their own responsibilities. This is the cultural conditions for existence of gold standard. Without the impact and shock arising from the great economic depression in 1929, people would still be immersed in the faith of perfect "invisible hand".

More than two hundred years after the birth of Classical Economics, in face of the reality that the economic crisis occurred in the 1930s and the market could not get out of the predicament, the human beings found that the market as "invisible hand" was not totally perfect and could not quickly repair the development imbalance, so that they began to seek ways to make up for the defects in market. As a result, the neoclassical economics came on the stage. The birth of neoclassical economics is not a negation of classic economics, but the deepened understanding of human beings on market, and naming it as neoclassical economics aims to indicate that it and classical economics are derived from the same origin.

Chinese Gold: From Following to Surpassing

4.1.2 The Neoclassical Economics were born in danger and disaster

Just after the fire of World War I was extinguished, the world was trapped in the quagmire of economic crisis and could not come out for a long time. The history often has amazing similarities. Just like the crisis in 2007, the economic crisis occurring after the war was also caused by financial crisis, which originated from USA and then spread to the whole world. In 1929, the speculation in USA stock market was out of control. On September 26, Bank of England announced that the interest rate was raised to 6.5% in order to stop the outflow of gold and protect the position of the pound in the international exchange system, and then a large amount of international hot money flowed out of USA and entered UK. On September 30, UK also announced the withdrawal of hundreds of millions of USD from the New York stock market. The rapid contraction of USA funds made the USA stock market lose blood, which led to a sharp drop in the USA stock market. On October 24, it finally collapsed, and people fell into extreme panic. On that day, 11 experienced speculators committed suicide. However, this was not the worst time. By the middle of November, the share price fell by more than 40%, and all hard-earned money of many people was turned into nothing. The economic crisis in USA lasted to 1931, and the general industrial index fell by 53.8%; the profits of private companies fell by nearly 60% (59.5%) from USD 8.4 billion in 1929 to USD 3.4 billion in 1932; Under the situation that the rural population of 11 million is not included, 28% of the country's total population, about 34 million adult men and women, were unable to make ends meet; during the Great Depression, there were 109,371 enterprises in USA going bankrupt. The Great Depression made the world economy suffer a lot and people fell into misery. Influenced by this, the fascist thoughts appeared in politics. Germany, Japan and Italy established the fascist regimes, which laid a powder keg for World War II. In face of this crisis, the Hoover Administration, which

4 Top-level Design of China's Gold Market

believed in free market economic theory, was at a loss what to do, so that it stepped down in March 1933 and the President Roosevelt came to power. Thereafter, the President Roosevelt actively intervened in economy and implemented the so-called "new policy", showing the responsibility of government as "visible hand" for development of economy. The actions of the President Roosevelt's indicate that the government as "visible hand" can do something for development of economy, and also should do something. From then on, "invisible hand" and "visible hand" have become the special terms in economics. However, it was only because of the outbreak of another world war that USA could completely get out of the shadow of the Great Depression. The World War II is the catastrophe of human beings, but it provided USA with a great opportunity for development.

The gunpowder keg buried by the Great Depression exploded in 1938, the World War II broke out, and the human beings were trapped in greater sufferings. However, USA exclusively gained the benefits of war because of being far away from the battlefield, and the vigorous development of military industry enabled USA to make a lot of money. When other countries were generally ravaged by war, USA accumulated strength and then replaced UK as the world's number one.

With respect to the global economic depression in the 1930s originating from USA, its impact on human society is reflected not only in economy and politics, but also in culture, and the important culture achievement generated is Neoclassical Economics, whose representative is Keynes of UK.

Keynes not only summarized the experiences and lessons of USA in dealing with the Great Depression in 1930s, but also summarized the experiences and lessons of UK in dealing with the Great Depression. At that time, UK and USA were the main economic countries, and their gains and losses in dealing with the crisis could serve as the reference for the whole world. Therefore, on the basis of summing up the experience and lessons of UK and USA in dealing with the Great Depression, Keynes put forward a new thinking with global significance for dealing with the economic depression, and established the macro economics, which, together with Einstein's theory of relativity and Freud's psychoanalysis, are called the three revolutions in intellectual circle of human beings in the 20th century. Keynes's neoclassical economics has become the leading ideology of capitalist world economy after World War II, and Keynes is known as "Father of Postwar Prosperity". Keynes mainly studied the relationship among currency, interest and employment. He believed that the "effective demand" is the traction force of economic development, so that creating the effective demand is extremely important for economic development. Therefore, the government should directly intervene in national economy with financial policies and monetary policies, so as to solve the problem of insufficient effective demand. This is the "visible hand" theory in neoclassical economics, which establishes the necessity of governmental intervention in economy. The neoclassical economics overturned the market omnipotence theory, and established the new code of conducts for postwar politicians. Keynes believed that the gold standard affected the degree of freedom of "visible hand" monetary policies, but held a negative attitude towards the gold standard. The Neoclassical Economics changed the form and path of post-war economic development, and made it a responsibility of politicians to intervene in economy with "visible hand". The intervention in market, especially the gold market, has become a common reality, because the intervention in gold market is based on the needs of adjustment of monetary policies, and is one of the means by which the "visible hand" intervenes in economy.

4.2 The intervention from "visible hand" has become the norm

Whether in the gold standard period in the 19th Century or the gold demonetization period in the 20th Century, during the history of more than two hundred years, the gold market has always been a financial market closely relating to the currency market, and the issuance

4 Top-level Design of China's Gold Market

and management of currency has always been the power of "visible hand". In the gold standard period, the issuance and circulation of gold coins were managed by the ministry of finance; in the gold exchange standard period, the gold reserve was the asset managed by the ministry of finance, and its liquidity was controlled by the state. In 1954, London gold market resumed its operation, and its function was to maintain and achieve the stability of international monetary system centering around USD. Even after the gold is no longer currency, the currency of central banks in various countries has not been completely separated from gold. More than 30,000 tons of gold reserve is maintained by various countries as the final insurance for currency, and the liquidity of gold reserve is achieved through the gold market, so the central banks of various countries do not leave the gold market, but maintain the contact with the gold market and its influence on the gold market. Therefore, the gold market is regulated by financial authority of every country. Since the gold market is different from ordinary commodity market and is a financial market which has close relationship with currency, the ministry of finance of every country always participates in or supervises over the trading in gold market by some means or in some forms for the purpose of the balance of receipts and expenditures and the issuance and control of currency by central bank, and this practice has become the norm. Taking UK as an example, its official participation in London gold market involves the following aspects.

The first is that, as the custodian of global physical gold, Bank of England provides the central banks of other countries with the gold custody service, and on this basis provides such central banks with the specific account services and provides such central banks and their customers with the gold trading services.

The second is that, as the agent of the gold reserve held by ministries of finance, Bank of England provides liquidity for gold reserve of various countries, and borrows and lends the gold through the gold market. The gold borrowing & lending behaviors carried out by Bank of England are the important factor which affects the forward price in gold market.

The third is that, in 1998, UK established the Financial Service Authority to participate in the formulation of standards of professional behaviors of gold market participants and supervise over the implementation of such standards. The self-discipline of practitioners is achieved under strong regulation, and not the results of laissez faire.

The gold market of UK has a close relationship with "visible hand", and it is the same with the gold market of Japan. Brazil Futures Exchange is the main market for trading of gold futures and options in Brazil, which is regulated by Brazil Securities Regulatory Commission and is also an independent member-system institution established by the Ministry of Finance in Brazil. Therefore, it is not a special case that the China's gold market is guided and regulated by the central bank, and the China's gold market has its own characteristic. This characteristic is that, because more attention has been paid to the guidance and normalization in advance, there is a basis for in-process regulation and post-handling, so that the randomness has been avoided. It should be pointed out that, after the outbreak of USA financial crisis in 2008, many countries have further strengthened the regulation on financial market (including gold market), regarded it as a strategic choice, and gradually began to form the international consensus and general principles.

4.3 Top-level design: Chinese solution

Though the intervention of "visible hand" in market has become an extensively-existing reality, there is also criticism. The criticism mainly focuses on the fact that the wrong intervention and random intervention from "visible hand" will cause loss in economic development. This is one of the reasons why the theory school of free market economy still has great influence. With respect to the question about how to avoid the random intervention from "visible hand", the Chinese economic circle has made its own theoretical contribution by putting forward the concept of top-level design.

4 Top-level Design of China's Gold Market

What is top-level design? It means that, before intervening in the market, the government should make full survey and study, and on this basis correctly prepare the work program and design the path. What the government can do and what it can't do should be clearly defined. The government should exercise its power with restraint, and avoid random and wrong intervention in economy. This is necessary for ensuring that the behavior of "visible hand" is correct, and is the precondition for "visible hand" to intervene in economy. However, some persons believe that, the development of human society is a continuous process of trial and error, and the correction can be made only through practice, so that there does not exist the so-called top-level design. This is actually a claim that the "visible hand" can't play a role and should do nothing. The correction of behaviors of human beings is not only the result of practice, but also the result of culture correction. As a culture correction, the top-level design can reduce the wrong behaviors of human beings, even if it cannot eliminate the wrong behaviors. Therefore, the top-level design is necessary and meaningful, and the development of China's gold market is just the product the implementation of top-level design.

The People's Bank of China is the central bank of China, and is also the department responsible for the management on foreign exchange. In the work system of gold control, it is the specific implementer and manager of unified collection and distribution of gold. In the process of preparation and construction of gold market, it is the leader for implementation. After the gold market is established and put into operation, in accordance with the provisions of the *Bank Law*, it is still responsible for regulating the gold market. Therefore, the central bank is responsible for guiding and managing the development of China's gold market. When the gold market was established, there were also many free market theorists in China. They believed that the gold marketization was the liberalization of gold market and advocated the withdrawal of central bank from gold market, which once became the dominant policy orientation. However, the lessons from the establishment of silver market made the policy makers in central bank a little more cautious. China has

Chinese Gold: From Following to Surpassing

imposed the control on silver and gold for a long time. In 1999, the silver control was lifted firstly. The establishment of silver market took the road of full liberalization and marketization, but it was not successful. In order to prevent the gold market from following the old road of silver market, the central bank must undertake the task to re-design the path and mode for gold market, and on this basis to promote the construction of gold market. This is the origin of the top-level design for China's gold market.

The intervention of central bank in China's gold market is not the intervention in operation of gold market, but is mainly achieved through top-level design for development of gold market. This is a kind of non-direct-intervention soft management from "visible hand" on development of gold market, and the top-level design runs through the whole process of development of China's gold market. This constitutes a prominent feature of development of China's gold market.

In China, the central bank is the regulator for operation of gold market and the director of development, but is not the leader of market operation. The relevant leader of central bank once expressed: "The central bank will continue to support the continuous and sound development of the China's gold market. By further improving the laws, regulations and rules and achieving the standardization of market, the central bank will create the favorable external environment for innovation and development of gold market." This indicates that the boundary of the intervention from central bank in gold market is creating the favorable external environment for innovation and development of gold market, but not interfering in internal operation of gold market. Every market participant is an independent self-developing economic entity. Specifically, the government ensures the transparency and fairness of trading process through regulation. The theoretical source of top-level design for the development of China's gold market is neoclassical economics, so that China is the practitioner and innovator of market economy rather than the alternative of market economy.

The connotation of top-level design for China's gold market is to grasp the development direction of gold market and select the development mode. After comparison, we select the development road suitable for our specific situations. The significance of top-level design for China's gold market is that, it avoids the repeated trial and error, so that the China's gold market as a latecomer can learn widely from others and become a surpasser.

4.4 Central Bank: practitioner of top-level design

The neoclassical economics has established the theory of necessity of intervention of "visible hand" in market, but how to carry out intervention is still a controversial question. In the course of continuous trial and error, the program proposed by China is top-level design, while the China's gold market is the product of top-level design.

4.4.1 Top-level design in the preparation period of gold market

In the design phase for preparation program for China's gold market, the top-level design from the central bank mainly involved the following aspects.

■ **Where and who will build the gold market ?**

Based on the need to support the urban construction of Shanghai as the financial center, the State Council decided that the gold market would be established in Shanghai. Shanghai was immediately faced with the problem who should build the gold market and how should it be built. After obtaining the approval from the State Council, Shanghai immediately set up a preparatory team for gold market and started to carry out specific work. Later, however, under the guidance that importance would be attached to location rather than ownership, the team quickly withdrew from the preparatory work, and the work was undertaken by the relevant personnel of Shanghai White Platinum & Silver Exchange which could not be deemed as successful. The occurrence of this change was the product of gold commodity theory. Since the gold foreign exchange theory was the theoretical foundation of gold control, in order to break the gold control and promote the gold marketization, it was necessary to abandon the gold foreign exchange theory and establish a new theoretical foundation, so that the gold commodity theory emerged accordingly. In the international trend of gold demonetization, the gold commodity theory advocated that the gold had lost its financial attribute and achieved the regression of commodity attribute. Therefore, according to the thinking of gold commodity theorists, since the silver control had been released under the guidance of commodity theory, Shanghai White Platinum & Silver Exchange had been established, and gold is the precious metal as silver, it was unnecessary to build an independent market. As a result, the reform program for establishment of a gold trading market in Shanghai White Platinum & Silver Exchange was formed. This program was considered to be able to minimize the funds required for establishment of market and was once recognized and put into practice, so that the Shanghai preparatory team withdrew, and the preparatory team for Shanghai gold trading market was reorganized with most members coming from Shanghai White Platinum & Silver Exchange.

    This program was accepted owing to the great influence of good commodity theory at that time. At that time, many people had the opinion that "gold" was the common commodity just like Chinese cabbage and radish stored by Beijing residents in winter. However, this program guided by gold commodity theory was finally abandoned, and the relevant policy makers decided that a preparatory team set up by central bank would establish an independent gold market on the basis of the trading platform of Shanghai Foreign Exchange. Today, it can be said that this decision undoubtedly laid the foundation for the development of Shanghai Gold Exchange. Without this decision at that time, there would be no Shanghai Gold Exchange. The decision of the policy makers on where and by whom the Chinese gold trading market would be built

4 Top-level Design of China's Gold Market

was proved to be correct by later development and has withstood the test of time.

■ Can the tax preference policies be shifted to the market?

To a large extent, the reason why Shanghai White Platinum & Silver Exchange did not achieve the expected success is that there is something wrong with the design of tax system for silver. While the silver control was lifted and the silver marketization was promoted, the original tax preference was not applicable to silver trading any longer, and the silver VAT was levied, so that the silver market lost the advantage as a low-laying land for the purpose of taxation. As a result, a lot of silver was traded out of the market rather in the market, and a market without trading was surely an unsuccessful market. In 1994, China implemented the tax system reform and established the commodity VAT system, but the State Council approved the exemption of gold and silver VAT on the ground that the gold and silver were still subject to unified collection and distribution. After the control is lifted and the gold market is established, the ground for exemption of gold VAT will not exist any longer, so that the tax authority will levy the gold VAT. However, the lesson of silver market made the gold market organizer in the central bank deeply understood the significance of shift of tax system to market. Therefore, after undertaking the establishment of gold market, they took the shift of gold VAT policies to market as the precondition for opening of market, and carried out the continuous coordination and communication with tax authority. We don't know the contents of communication, but the communication was surely very difficult, because the cancellation of preferential tax system for silver and gold was the reform principle as determined in the Document No. 63 issued by the State Council in 1993. The originally-determined opening time, namely November 28, 2001, was postponed for near one year. On October 16, 2002, the Ministry of Finance and the State Administration of Taxation issued the Circular No. 142, achieving the shift of gold VAT policies to market. The establishment of this tax system satisfied the precondition for

Chinese Gold: From Following to Surpassing

the development of Shanghai Gold Exchange, and Shanghai Gold Exchange which obtained the advantage as a low-laying land for the purpose of taxation quickly became the gold trading center in China, and now the concentration ratio has exceeded 95%. In 2003, the production of mineral gold reached 200.6 tons, while the gold trading volume of Shanghai Gold Exchange was 235.3 tons, namely 1.17 times the production of mineral gold. The Ganwang gold market in Liaoning, which once became the focus of the society, was soon closed. Today, it can be said that, insisting on the shift of VAT policies is the key to the success of the China's gold market, and the shift of such policies becomes the systematic element which ensures the success of Shanghai Gold Exchange.

In the social atmosphere dominated by gold commodity theory at that time, the gold marketization was gold commoditization. A basic policy orientation of the State Council for promoting the gold marketization was that, the gold-related preferential economic policy system gradually formed since the 1980s would be simultaneously cancelled, and the gold would be brought back under the management as an ordinary commodity. After 1994, the VAT exemption policies became the core content of such preferential economic system, the shift of VAT to market was achieved, the inertia thinking was broken, and an ideological breakthrough was completed. As a result, the theory that gold is special emerged, which recognizes that, the gold entering the market still has special financial attribute and the gold market is a financial market rather than an ordinary commodity market, so that VAT, a tax levied in commodity market, should not be levied in gold market as a financial market. This is the basic logic of shift of gold VAT to market.

Since then, there were doubts and controversies on the exemption of gold VAT in the society, but the implementation of VAT exemption policies in gold market has basically become a consensus. When the gold commodity theory was dominant, the shift of VAT policies to market was regarded as a heresy, and the heresy theory was broken by the introduction of UK's "special tax system plan for gold".

The reason why the new logic of design of this gold tax system

4 Top-level Design of China's Gold Market

could be established in China is that the World Gold Council acted as a helper. It entered China in 1994 when the gold marketization reform in China was just initiated, so that it not only jointly organized the activities such as special symposium and training with the Gold Economy Development Research Center (now the Beijing Gold Economy Development Research Center) of the Ministry of Metallurgy at that time, but also established a connection with Chinese gold production and processing enterprises, became the window for Chinese gold enterprises to contact with international markets, and actively cooperated with the gold management department of central bank. After 2000, the provider of information consulting service of China's gold marketing reform promoted by central bank was the active participant of the period, so that it became the consulting service provider for the gold marketization reform promoted by central bank, and was also the active participant in the establishment of China's gold market. The World Gold Council firstly introduced the documents about special VAT plan of UK London gold market into China, and then made arrangement for Beijing Gold Economy Development Research Center to carry out sorting-out and summarization and publish the study results on the *Chinese Gold Economy*. The conclusion of such study is that, the exemption of gold from VAT is not a special case of planned economy, but a common international practice. The UK gold market is an internationally-dominant gold market and implements the special tax system plan, so that it can provide a reference for China to shift the gold VAT policies to market. If we say that the gold VAT policy is an important factor for the success of Shanghai Gold Exchange, then the introduction of special gold-related tax system plan of UK into China by the World Gold Council is a contribution made by the World Gold Council to the gold marketization reform in China.

■ **Would the exchange adopt the corporate system or the member system?**

After the 1970s, with the lifting of gold control in various

Chinese Gold: From Following to Surpassing

countries, a peak period of development of gold market appeared in the world, but most markets adopted the corporate system, and only a few adopted the member system. A gold market which adopts corporate system is not only a trading platform, but also a profit-making platform, so that it has the nature of private interests. There is a deviation between fairness and private interests, and in order to pursue private interests, the fairness is often sacrificed. However, a market which adopts member system is a sharing trading platform, which can better reflect the fairness of market platform. The establishment of Shanghai Gold Exchange indicated a huge opportunity for many commercial institutions, so that they actively advocated the establishment of a gold market which adopts the corporate system. Either the gold market program proposed by Beijing or the gold market program submitted by Shanghai White Platinum & Silver Exchange adopted the corporate system mode which took commercial institutions as main body of market.

For the sake of ensuring the fairness of market, the policy makers in central bank denied the market program based on corporate system. In order to maintain the fairness of platform, they brought forth another idea, namely establishing Shanghai Gold Exchange as a public institution directly controlled by the central bank. This program could ensure the trading fairness of market, but was not in line with the general direction of reform and was really not feasible under the background that the streamlining of public institutions was being carried out.

In light of the basic requirement and objective condition that the market fairness should be ensured, the central bank did not select the corporate system adopted by most international gold markets or our unique public-institution system, but selected the member system. The first batch of 108 members of Shanghai Gold Exchange mainly included gold producing enterprises, gold using enterprises and commercial banks. However, this member structure mainly focused on the transformation of gold trading from unified collection and distribution mode to free trading mode. With the transformation to gold financial market and the expansion of scale, the structure of

4 Top-level Design of China's Gold Market

members was adjusted and the number of members was increased. By 2018, Shanghai Gold Exchange had 260 members, including 157 general members and 103 special members. 74 members participated in the trading on international board, and 186 members participated in the trading on main board. Shanghai Gold Exchange has developed itself into an internationalized gold exchange, and now, near 30 commercial banks, financial institutions, gold processing enterprises and gold refining enterprises from more than 10 countries have become its members, participating in the trading on main board or international board. The member system ensures the fairness of the market, so that in its 16 years' operation till 2018, Shanghai Gold Exchange has not been involved in any scandal and has grown continuously. In 2018, Shanghai Gold Exchange achieved the (two-way) trading volume of 67,500 tons, becoming the second largest floor-trading gold market in the world. It has become the spot gold trading market with the largest trading volume in the world since 2006, which shows that the member system has led to the high stability of Shanghai Gold Exchange.

■ **Market mode: over-the-counter market or floor trading market**

The market trading modes adopted by international gold markets can be divided into over-the-counter market maker mode and floor matching trading mode. These two modes have their respective advantages and disadvantages, and the markets adopting these two modes develop in parallel. Which mode would be selected by Shanghai Gold Exchange as a latecomer? This should be determined in light of the actual situation of China.

The over-the-counter market maker trading mode is represented by London gold market in UK. The London gold market has a history of 300 years, and is an over-the-counter intangible market dominated by large commercial banks. Through the competition in its long-term development process, a special market maker system has been generated for the purpose of maintaining the trading continuity in market. The market maker is a special market participant that offers

Chinese Gold: From Following to Surpassing

both the bid price and offer price in the market. The market makers play an important role in over-the-counter gold market. They are the leader of trading and the undertaker of obligation to maintain the continuity of trading in over-the-counter market, and need the strong capacity to deal with market risks and the high market integrity, so that the market makers are the product of mature market. The advantages of over-the-counter market maker gold market include flexible service, personalized service and good confidentiality, but its transparency is poor, so that trading integrity may be fatal. In 2013, the international gold price manipulation scandal broke out in over-the-counter gold market in London.

The floor matching trading mode is represented by USA gold market. The USA gold market is a tangible market, and its trading object is standard futures contract. The advantages include high efficiency, low cost and open and transparent information, and the disadvantage is that the personalized service can't be provided and the confidentiality is low. The floor gold trading market is the product of lifting of gold control in the 1970s, its birth time is later than that of over-the-counter market, but these two trading modes have developed in parallel over recent decades. The trading volume of London over-the-counter gold market was always higher than that of floor trading market before 2008, but the situation was reversed after 2008. Especially when the UK over-the-counter market was troubled by gold price manipulation scandal, the trading volume of floor trading market exceeded that of UK London over-the-counter market, the difference was increased gradually, and the growth of floor trading volume was obviously higher than that of over-the-counter market. In 2017, the floor trading volume of gold futures all over the world reached 304,400 tons, while the over-the-counter trading gold volume of London Bull Market Association (LBMA) was only 160,700 tons. To a certain extent, this change reflects that, with the strengthened market regulation and the development of electronic technologies, the floor gold market has more advantages. The change in floor gold trading volume and over-the-counter gold trading volume around the world is as indicated in Figure 4-1.

4 Top-level Design of China's Gold Market

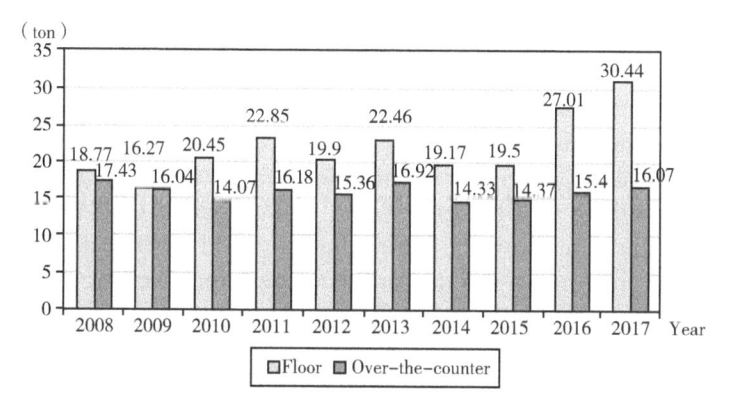

Figure 4-1 Change in Floor Gold Trading Volume and Over-the-counter Gold Trading Volume

Source: *China Gold Yearbook 2018.*

Based on the financial attribute of gold market, the commercial banks in China should play a key role in the operation of gold market, and should be the main force in the construction of China's gold market. In 2000 when the construction of China's gold market was just initiated, however, our national situation was that all commercial banks except Bank of China had not participated in gold business and were lack of experience and talents. Under such situation, it was unrealistic to let such commercial banks assume the responsibility of establishing and operating the gold market. In addition, there was no qualified market maker, so that if we selected the market maker trading mode, a huge risk would be generated, and high requirements would be imposed on the regulation of gold market. This was exactly a short board of work of central bank, because the market management level should be gradually improved in practice, but at that time the gold market was still under planning. Considering from many aspects, we could only build a floor trading market. This selection was a low-risk selection, because the floor trading market has the advantages such as high information transparency and easy management. Starting with the floor trading market, we can achieve the stability of reform and improve the success rate

Chinese Gold: From Following to Surpassing

of reform. This is the advantage of this selection. In the gold marketization reform of China, however, the delayed development of over-the-counter market has given rise to the fake "market maker", and the emergence of various precious metal trading platforms under the banner of market maker has become a disaster area of financial chaos.

The opening of Shanghai Gold Exchange in October 2002 changed the situation that China had no gold market during the past more than half a century, and become a major event attracting attention from all walks of life. This event was reported in the *News Broadcast* of that day. Although I didn't go to Shanghai to witness this historical moment, I was interviewed by the *News Broadcast* of CCTV in Beijing, and shared this historical moment with all other people. I was transferred to the Gold Economy Development Research Center of the Ministry of Metallurgy in 1991 to engage in gold economy research work. At that time, the discussions on the reform of gold management system had begun. This was also the first gold project for which I undertook the research task. From then on, I was linked with gold marketization, and observing and studying the development of China's gold marketization reform became the direction of my work. The opening day of Shanghai Gold Exchange is 10 years away from the completion of my first research report on China's gold marketization reform in 1992, so that I was somewhat excited and moved by the finally-achieved result of gold marketization reform. However, I was not a participant in the decision process, so that I don't know such process. Today, Shanghai Gold Exchange has been in operation for 17 years, and we realize the importance of top-level design for China's gold market when we discuss the reasons for its development. The top-level design determined the principles and directions of the development of China's gold market, and the successors just followed the direction determined by top-level designer and acted under the established principles.

The top-level design of policy makers has given the China's gold market a unique Chinese DNA (deoxyribonucleic acid) from the date of its birth, namely starting from the reality of China and taking

4 Top-level Design of China's Gold Market

our own road. The China's gold market did not copy the dogma in the so-called market economy textbook, and also did not adopt the existing mode of international gold markets. Instead, starting from the national conditions of China, we learned from the existing international experience and selected the development path and mode suitable for the national conditions, so that our disadvantage became an advantage, because we could advance on the basis of previous experience without repeated trial and error. This is the decisive element of the development of China's gold market. We shall fully recognize the value of the top-level design of the policy makers who promoted the development of China's gold market. They are the people who shape the DNA of China's gold market. Their contribution should not be forgotten due to the passage of time and the change of work posts.

4.4.2 Top–level design for gold market in growth period

In 2010, the six ministries and commissions including the central bank, the State Development and Reform Commission and the Ministry of Industry and Informatization jointly issued the *Several Opinions on Promoting the Development of Gold Market* (hereinafter referred to as "*Opinions*"). At that time, Shanghai Gold Exchange had been in operation for 8 years, the over-the-counter gold market in commercial banks had been in operation for 6 years, and the Shanghai gold futures contract had been listed in Shanghai Futures Exchange for 2 years: The trading scale of China's gold market was increased from 42.49 tons in 2002 to 14,000 tons, nearly 330 times; the task of transformation from commodity market to financial market was completed, and the trading volume of T+D deferred contract and gold futures contract accounted for more than 80% of total trading volume. Before the issuance of the *Options*, the State Council discussed the *Regulations for Administration on Gold Market (Draft)* in 2008, but it was set aside because of its immaturity. Therefore, the *Opinions* should be a substitute program issued for the purpose of promoting the issuance of the *Regulations*

Chinese Gold: From Following to Surpassing

for Administration on Gold Market.

The *Opinions* include 6 parts, involving the aspects such as market management, product innovation and opening up to the outside world. The top-level design of central bank has imposed the profound impact on issuance of policies and regulations relating to China's gold market. The *Opinions* summarize such impacts, and give the instructions for future development.

■ **Establish a multi-market system**

The *Opinions* determine that the China's gold market is a market system composed of multiple markets, rather than a professional physical gold trading market. The *Opinions* point out that: "After the cancellation of unified collection and distribution policies, the China's gold market has developed rapidly, the pattern that the gold business of Shanghai Gold Exchange, the gold business of commercial banks and the gold futures business of Shanghai Futures Exchange jointly develop has been basically formed, and the good situation that the gold market and gold industry achieve coordinated development has appeared." This is a summary and recognition of the reality of 8 years' development of China's gold market, and has also laid the legal foundation for multi-market, because the *Opinions* has made it clear that the China's gold market is not a single market, but a market system composed of multiple markets. This orientation distinguishes the China's gold market from the mainstream traditional international gold markets, because most countries in the world have single markets, and this difference also indicates that the development road of China's gold market is its own selection.

The *Opinions* make clear the functional orientation of each market in this multi-market system: "Shanghai Futures Exchange should make full use of the functions of futures market to identify price and manage risks, continuously strengthen the construction of market infrastructure, and steadily promote the sound development of China's gold market. In addition, Shanghai Futures Exchange should bring the market functions into full play, continuously improve the gold futures contract and business rules, intensify and refine the gold

4 Top-level Design of China's Gold Market

futures business, and improve the ability to support the development of national economy." The orientation of gold business function of commercial banks is "The commercial banks should focus on the whole industrial chain involving gold mining, production, processing and sales, innovate the financial products, make efforts to improve the financial services, make efforts to improve the service effectiveness, and provide the multi-directional financial services for the gold industry".

It is set forth in the *Opinions* that, in this market system, the function of gold futures market is to properly manage the risks, and the function of gold market in commercial banks is to provide the financial services for development of gold market. However, the function orientation of Shanghai Gold Exchange, as the first established and the most basic market became suspense. Therefore, the *Opinions* require that "Shanghai Gold Exchange should determine the future development direction and market orientation as soon as possible". Why the function orientation of Shanghai Gold Exchange has become suspense after 8 years' development? According to the top-level design given by the People's Bank of China before the birth of Shanghai Gold Exchange, Shanghai Gold Exchange would be a gold commodity market, and its function orientation is clear. On the basis of this function orientation, the membership structure with physical gold trading as main body is determined. Thereafter, the goal of Shanghai Gold Exchange to be transformed into financial market was basically completed in 2008, but the completion of this transformation task did not solve the problem about function orientation of Shanghai Gold Exchange, because there are several gold markets in China's gold market system, and the financial attribute of gold is the commonness of various exchanges, rather than the characteristic of Shanghai Gold Exchange. How will Shanghai Gold Exchange of which the future development direction and market orientation are unknown develop? This may become a problem. More confusingly, such an important suspense subsequently disappeared and was rarely discussed, becoming a conclusion without conclusion. The reason why the social function of Shanghai Gold Exchange can't be orientated easily is that its development has not taken a traditional path, so that it is difficult to determine the orientation with a single professional function. Shanghai Gold Exchange has developed into a gold market involving several trading modes (bidding, inquiring, pricing), several time/space modes (spot, spot deferred, forward), several metals (gold, silver, palladium) and several objects (gold ingot, gold coin, gold derivatives), so that it cannot be defined by traditional function orientation. The special functions of Shanghai Gold Exchange are attributable to its own effects. On the basis of gold spot trading, a great drama of innovation and development has been staged. The script of this drama is from the top-level design of central bank.

For the purpose of developing the market economy, it is necessary to oppose monopoly, because the monopoly sacrifices the fairness and violates the basic principles of market economy. The way to break monopoly is to advocate competition, but the distributed competition, which always causes the waste of social resources, should also be avoided. The China's gold market is not a unity structure but a multi-structure, and the multi-structure itself is the structure of competition. Due to the different function orientation of each market, however, this function differentiation also makes it possible for multi-markets to achieve cooperation and co-win. Therefore, it is required by the *Opinions* to strengthen the communication and coordination and establish the cooperation and coordination mechanism between Shanghai Gold Exchange and Shanghai Futures Exchange. The rapid development of China's gold market is the result of coordination, so that the multi-structure has opened up a new mode for development of gold market, which is one of the characteristics of the China's gold market.

■ Promote the reform of over-the-counter market maker system

The market maker system is a system innovation which achieves the continuity of market trading. This face-to-face trading mode has the characteristics such as high flexibility and confidentiality, but the low transparency of trading information is its disadvantage. The occurrence of gold price manipulation scandal of London gold market characterized by market maker system in 2013 indicates that there is defect in this market system. Therefore, they began to reform the market maker system which has lasted for 100 years. In fact, before the scandal broke out, we proposed the Chinese program, namely the proposal put forward in the *Opinions* for Shanghai Gold Exchange to introduce the market maker system and start our reform for over-the-counter market maker. It is this top-level design that opened the reform for diversification of social functions of Shanghai Gold Exchange. In 2014, Shanghai Gold Exchange and Shanghai Foreign Exchange Trading Center jointly launched an inter-bank gold inquiry market and established a Chinese-style market maker system. This greatly advanced the transparency of market maker trading information, and extended the platform to achieve the connection among gold market, currency market, foreign exchange market, stock market and bond market. Five years after this reform was carried out, it became the fastest-growing trading mode among three trading modes of Shanghai Gold Exchange, and the inquiry platform became the main trading platform of Shanghai Gold Exchange. In 2018, the trading volume on market maker inquiry platform of Shanghai Gold Exchange reached 45,600 tons, accounting for 67.56% of total trading volume of Shanghai Gold Exchange. This indicates that this market innovation has brought great impetus to the development of Shanghai Gold Exchange.

  The market maker system is an important market system appeared at the beginning of 20th Century. The development of market maker system made London gold market become the central market in the world. Over recent years, however, London gold market has initiated reform owing to the frustration in development. Letting over-the-counter market makers enter the floor trading is a Chinese program proposed by us for reform of this traditional market system. Its success is of great significance for reform of market maker system not only in China's gold market but also in international gold market.

■ **Highlight the regulation, and protect the investment from investors**

The *Opinions* take strengthening the regulation of gold market as a priority, and all relevant departments take carefully performing the regulation on gold market and preventing the risks of gold market as the top priority. After the outbreak of USA financial crisis in 2008, one of the actions taken by human beings through reflection is that, the governments of all countries generally strengthened the regulation of financial market, and took the prevention of risks as the top priority. We did the same in this trend, but the practice that we regard opening as the driving force of development could not be understood by everyone. The balance between strengthening the market regulation and expanding the opening scale is a big issue. The practice in development of China's gold market reveals that, the reform and opening-up is not laissez faire and also needs regulation. To achieve orderly opening, the market environment should be kept sound, so as to achieve the sustainable development of market and the largest protection on interests of investors. Therefore, the central bank has always adopted the principles that priority shall be given to risk control, and provided the room for innovation under the precondition that the risks are controllable. This is an important experience generated through the development of China's gold market. In the large environment with strengthened regulation, the development of China's gold market is a gradual and open process. In this process, the combination of continuous development and effective innovation has been achieved, and with a large number of non-normalized trading platforms delisted, the mainstream normalized markets have got more room for growth.

4.4.3 Top–level design for gold market in consolidation period

In 2018, namely 8 years later after the *Opinions* was issued, the central bank issued three policy documents: the *Circular on Issues Relating to Gold Asset Management Business*, the *Interim Measures*

4 Top-level Design of China's Gold Market

for Administration on Gold Deposit Business and the *Interim Measures for Administration on Internet Gold Business of Financial Institutions*. 2018 is the 17th year of development of China's gold market. In this year, the trading volume of China's gold market exceeded 100,000 tons for the third time. The new pattern of global gold market with tripartite confrontation composed of London, New York and Shanghai has been formed. Now, the top-level design of development of China's gold market is to settle the issue about how to achieve greater development and avoid the risks of development, especially to prevent the global risks caused by local risks. Therefore, preventing risks is the theme and purpose of this top-level design.

After the scale of China's gold market is expanded to the world level, its social influence will also increase greatly, and the risks occurring in gold market may also spread to other levels. After the gold market has the risk-multiplying effect, every problem occurring will be a big problem. Therefore, the focus of these 3 documents is placed on risks in gold market, namely the risks in the following two aspects.

The first is how to prevent the risks of gold market from spreading to currency market and thus resulting in the risks in the whole financial market. Gold is a kind of quasi currency. Gold and currency are highly interchangeable. Especially in the virtual gold trading process, the capital has very strong liquidity, and gold is also a kind of commodity. Therefore, some people take advantage of this feature of gold, hold the banner of trading of commodity gold and carry out the trading of currency, so as to seek for improper profits by avoiding the financial regulation. This illegal speculation often contains great risk of uncertainty. Once such risk happens, it seems that such risk happens in the gold market, but it will soon spread to the currency market, and even lead to the occurrence of financial crisis. This risk is not imagined, but has happened in reality, especially on some precious metal trading platforms. The amount involved often reaches billions of RMB and even tens of billions of RMB.

The second is that, there are many new technologies, and many new means, new tools and new paths for information communication are emerging. Therefore, the new requirements are put forward for financial regulation while the circulation efficiency of trading information is improved and the mode of information circulation is changed. The information management is the core of financial management, and the financial regulation is achieved through the regulation of information, but the progress of regulation means and tools and the use of new technologies are not synchronized, which forms the regulation blank area. In addition, some new technologies appear as the substitute of financial regulation, so that the application of new technologies becomes the reason for avoiding financial regulation. In fact, the technologies are a tool used by human beings, the new technologies are a new tool created by human beings, and the new tool may also become the potential source of financial risks. The fraud scandal in digital currency field represented by decentralized bitcoin prompted central bank to close the door and issue a ban. In December 2018, the central bank expressed that: "The Internet finance and financial technologies do not change the attribute of financial risks, and the risks arising from Internet, technologies, data and information security even become more outstanding. In this sense, the Internet finance or financial technologies shall be subject to stricter regulation." These 3 documents were issued against such a large background.

How will the central bank prevent such two risks? My interpretation of these 3 documents is as follows: clarify the boundary of financial gold, define the orientation of Internet-based technical tools, and implement the financial regulation with universal coverage.

The gold assets management and gold deposit businesses are defined as the businesses carried out by financial institutions and regulated by central bank. The regulation path and form of central bank for specific products vary in light of actual situations.

The gold asset management business which can be carried out is that, the financial institutions invest the entrusted properties in physical gold or gold products (which are, relatively speaking, paper gold). The establishment of products shall be filed with the central

4 Top-level Design of China's Gold Market

bank, and Shanghai Gold Exchange shall set up the independent gold account for gold assets so as to carry out the special management, and shall report the information about holding of physical gold by gold assets management products to central bank on the 15th date of each month, and publish such information on a regular basis.

The gold deposit business is a liability business wherein the financial institutions which have the bank deposit business open the gold account for customers and record the gold deposited by customers in a certain period in accordance with the agreement signed with customers. The regulation on gold deposit business is to incorporate the business into the balance sheet for management. Basically, when carrying out the supervision and management, the central bank regards this business as RMB deposit business.

The Internet technology changes the life of Chinese people, and the Internet gold as a commercial form appears, that is, the Internet enterprise uses Internet tool to carry out gold deposit and loan business. The Internet gold business is to borrow gold from the people and then lend out such gold by taking Internet technology as the means. The central bank separates the Internet technology from gold business, and the *Interim Measures for Administration on Gold Deposit Business* stipulates that: the Internet gold business of financial institutions is the activity of financial institutions carried out through their own official websites, mobile terminals or Internet institutions for selling the gold products developed by them. In this business, the financial institutions provide the gold account service, but the Internet institutions may not provide any customer account service. From then on, the Internet gold enterprises came to the end, because the online gold trading business may only be carried out by financial institutions, and the Internet gold enterprises can only act as business agent of gold products of financial institutions.

The issuance of such 3 documents in 2018 is the preventive measure taken by central bank, because the stability of financial market is extremely important, and the development of gold market must also be carried out under the precondition of stability.

Chinese Gold: From Following to Surpassing

Nowadays, the financial risks broken out repeatedly, especially after the outbreak of USD crisis in 2018, the disadvantages exposed by the international monetary system make human beings realize, in a market system with unreasonable structure, the top level design is urgently necessary. This impact makes the role of "visible hand" more recognized, so that the central bank basically has a positive evaluation on the intervention of gold market through top level design, and believes that this is the only way for development of China's gold market.

4.5 Eliminate the defective DNA from top-level design

In the eyes of outsiders, the development of China's gold market was under favorable conditions or was at a good time, because China just joined into WTO (World Trade Organization) and got fully integrated into the world economy when the gold control was released. However, people have neglected an important reason, that is, the relevant personnel eliminated the defective DNA in top level design before the birth of China's gold market, kept high vigilance in the course of development of gold market, and eliminated the new defective DNA found in time. Since the defective DNA was eliminated, the China's gold market developed smoothly and rapidly after its birth, and basically no big setback or fluctuation occurred. This is in sharp contrast with the development of Chinese stock market and futures market. The development of such markets has encountered setbacks and gradually embarked on a sound road after repeated trial and error. Which defective DNAs have been eliminated by top-level design for China's gold market?

4.5.1 Abandon the ordinary commodity theory and recognize the special commodity theory

The gold marketization in China is promoted in the trend of return of commodity attribute of gold. Therefore, the thought to equate the gold marketization with gold commoditization, completely open the market and establish an ordinary gold commodity market through competition had a large market room, and was also a dominant trend of thought in the early stage of the China's gold market. Finally, the top-level designers abandoned the ordinary commodity theory, and decided to take the special commodity theory as the guidance and retain the leadership and guiding right of the central bank for the construction of gold market. They decided to promote the construction of Shanghai Gold Exchange on the platform of Shanghai Foreign Exchange Trading Center, so as to ensure the fairness of trading platform, and also lay the foundation for the smooth transformation of Shanghai Gold Exchange from commodity market to financial market.

4.5.2 Abandon the over–the–counter market and decide to establish the floor trading market

With the longest history and the most far-reaching effect, the London gold market is the main reference for construction of China's gold market. The London gold market is an over-the-counter market which centers around market makers, and the market makers are special market participants that offer both the bid price and offer price in the market. However, the market makers which can undertake this special function are generated in long-term market competition rather than self appointed. Since there was no qualified market maker in China, the basic condition for establishment of over-the-counter gold market was not satisfied. If the market makers were generated in market competition, then there would be a lot of uncertainties. Therefore, the over-the-counter market was abandoned, and it was decided to establish a floor trading market, use the floor trading market to drive the development of over-the-counter market, and take a development road different from traditional road, so as to avoid the chaos caused by disordered competition and achieve the smooth development.

4.5.3 Abandon the free competition, and select the orderly competition

Just like the worship of market, we adore competition so infinitely, and regard competition as a panacea to activate the market vitality and eliminate the market defects. In fact, the disordered competition has led to a lot of social problems such as waste of resources. Therefore, how to avoid the disordered competition and achieve the orderly competition is the important content of top-level design. The central bank has established the gold market, abandoned the over-the-counter market and selected the floor trading market, but has not abandoned the market maker system. However, the growth road selected for market makers in China is different: the road for abandoning the free competition and actively seeking for orderly competition is to, on one hand, introduce the market maker system of over-the-counter market into the floor trading market so as to ensure that the market makers can grow in a relatively transparent and regulated environment, and on the other hand, adopt the restraining policies for over-the-counter market maker market, be highly vigilant against possible illegal activities in over-the-counter market maker market and crack down on them. The China's gold market still adheres to the bottom line of this policy even under the challenge in various names to this policy. Though crisis frequently occurs on the over-the-counter gold trading platform, the mainstream gold market still maintains the rapid and stable development.

4.5.4 Abandon the corporate system, and ensure the fairness of trading platform

With the release of gold control, the society saw a huge business opportunity. They scrambled for the right to speak in the construction of gold market, and put forward various programs for different reasons, but they all wanted to establish a corporate-system trading platform for the purpose of profit making. The trading needs fairness, so that the greatest danger of corporate system which acts as referee and athlete simultaneously is that the future gold market may lose the trading fairness. In order to ensure the trading fairness and eliminate disturbance, the top-level design of gold market abandoned the corporate system and adopted the member system, so as to ensure that the market participants will carry out trading fairly in an equal trading environment and thus lay the foundation for sound development of the China's gold market.

4.5.5 Abandon the thinking "development foremost" and establish the thinking "risk control first"

The understanding of human beings on market risks is gradually intensified with the accumulation of market risks. The 1980s was soaked with market liberalization, and the persons who supported financial innovation did not put the risk control first. Nowadays, under the threat of market risks, many people finally get the cognition that the development should be achieved under the precondition that the risks are controllable. After entering the new century, the human beings have increasingly put risk control before development. This does not mean that no development will be carried out when there is any risk, but means that the risk control ability should enhanced in order to achieve development. The development without risk control is only an accidental luck-based success. There have been adventurers proud of taking risks, but the development can't be based on luck. The so-called thinking of high risk and high income is not the right way of development. Therefore, in the new century, we have placed the risk control for economic development on an increasingly important position.

In 2007, the global economic crisis triggered by the US subprime mortgage crisis brought the global economic development into a turbulent period. Opportunity and risk coexist in development, so we need to establish the first thinking of risk control and clarify that the effective risk control is the precondition for development. The top level design of China's gold market focuses on implementing risk control and eliminating risks in time, and basically follows the work

Chinese Gold: From Following to Surpassing

ideas of developing the floor trading market, moderately developing the over-the-counter market and cracking down on illegal markets. As a result, we can maintain the overall stability of market and remain the development momentum unchanged under the condition that the risks in over-the-counter market frequently occur.

5

A Latecomer's Pursuit and Surpassing

Owing to the fact that the defective gene was eliminated through top level design, though the China's gold market started late, it took a road with Chinese characteristics. In other words, the development of China's gold market is not achieved through competition and continuous error correction as described in traditional textbooks, but through following and surpassing under the guidance of top-level design from "visible hand" on the basis of experience of predecessors.

After about two years of preparation and through the 3 phases including approval of preliminary program, composition of preparatory team and trial operation, Shanghai Gold Exchange was opened in October 30, 2002. This indicates that the China's gold market made the breakthrough from zero to one. Thereafter, it took only 6 years for China to build the gold market system composed of several markets. The development of China's gold market has entered a historical new stage.

The formation and significance of gold market system composed of several markets has gone beyond the gold market itself. The greater significance of the birth of gold trading market system is to make up for an important link in financial system which has missed for more than half a century in China. As a result, the financial system of China could become complete and the function could be improved, so as to improve the stability of financial market of China. In addition, the development road of China's gold market with top-level design has provided a different perspective for the human beings to understand the market development. This may be another great value of the development of China's gold market.

Chinese Gold: From Following to Surpassing

5.1 A real latecomer

The gold market is old, and is also young. The gold market is old, because it is the origin of modern financial market, and its existence is far earlier than the core market of modern financial market, namely the currency market; the gold market is young, because after the outbreak of World War II, all countries have successively implemented gold control that the circulation of gold has been blocked and the function of gold market has shrunk seriously. USA was the country which implemented the strictest gold control. In 1933, the President Roosevelt issued a gold ban, so as to expropriate the gold stored by every family, prohibit the private trading of gold, and require all gold to be sold to the Ministry of Finance. The violators would be sentenced to 10 years' imprisonment or fined USD 250,000, and the military, police and security departments were also used for this purpose. After the outbreak of world war, except for a few countries, most countries implemented the gold control, so that the gold became a special asset monopolized by government, and the gold control in China even lasted to the beginning of the new century. Under the conditions of gold control, the circulation and trading of gold also became a business between central banks of various countries. Under the conditions of gold control, the market trading became a forbidden zone for common people. In 1954, the London gold market resumed its operation. It was a market among central banks of various countries. Until the 1970s, due to the promotion of demonetization of gold, all countries gradually lifted up the control. In the middle and late period of the 1970s, there was a high development period of gold market, which was less than 50 years from now. Therefore, we also can say that the gold market is very young. However, even among the young gold markets, the China's gold market is still a latecomer.

In modern times, the China's gold market started not too late. In 1905, Shanghai gave birth to the first gold exchange in China, namely the Gold Industry Office, and in the late 1920s, with the trading volume reaching near twenty thousand tons, it became the third

5 A Latecomer's Pursuit and Surpassing

largest gold market in the world, only next to London and New York. Thereafter, however, the development of gold market was interrupted. After 1949, the special international situation also made us miss the golden period in the 1970s for the development of international gold market. At that time, owing to the planned economy and the economic blockade implemented by the western world, China's foreign exchange was in extreme shortage, and gold, as a rare foreign exchange, was strictly controlled. The contradiction that China was lack of foreign exchange was not alleviated until the middle of 1990s, and was basically settled only after China became the largest foreign exchange reserve country in the world in the new century. At that time, China released the gold control, and thus the condition for establishment of market for free trading of gold was satisfied. Therefore, from 2002 to 2018, the history of the China's gold market was only 16 years. As compared with the history of the main gold markets in the world, the China's gold market was a real latecomer.

In the contemporary gold market system, London gold market has the longest history of 300 years. However, it was closed in 1939 due to the outbreak of World War II, and was not reopened until 1954. Even calculated from 1954, it still has a history of 65 years, and is 48 years older than Shanghai Gold Exchange.

Just like London gold market, New York gold market is also the backbone market in the international gold market system. It was born in 1975, has a history of 44 years, and is 27 years older than Shanghai Gold Exchange.

Japan is a regional gold market in Asia, and Tokyo Gold Exchange was established in 1981, has a history of 38 years, and is 21 years older than Shanghai Gold Exchange.

The Swiss gold market is now the global gold logistics center. This is an intangible market which takes Switzerland's three international banks as main body, and is an international gold logistics center formed when London gold market was temporarily closed in 1968. It has a history of 51 years, and thus is 34 years older than Shanghai Gold Exchange.

The Istanbul gold market in Turkey is an emerging market, which

Chinese Gold: From Following to Surpassing

was founded in 1995 and is 7 years older than Shanghai Gold Exchange. Of course, there are also emerging markets which are younger than Shanghai gold market, such as India Multiple Commodity Exchange which was established in 2003 and Dubai Gold & Commodity Exchange which was established in 2005, but they are basically the markets born in the same period.

In 2002, when the China's gold market started from scratch and achieved a breakthrough from zero to one, the pattern of the international gold market system had been formed. For the international gold market, we, as a latecomer, were only a new player, did not have high expectations, and also did not cause great international reaction. The gold market born in a country lacking of gold culture had no natural advantage of development. When the China's gold market was born, the London gold market for spot over-the-counter trading and the New York gold market for forward floor trading were already moving forward rapidly. At that time, the two markets achieved nearly 90% of the global trading volume, possessing an unparalleled gold-absorbing force. As a result, all large international banks around the world opened branches in New York and London, so as to participate in the trading on these two markets. Though many gold markets appeared in every continent in the 1970s, none of them could catch up with these two markets, even those gold markets which had been operating for many years were still small in size as compared with these two markets, and the scale of most markets was less than 1/10 of them. However, the China's gold market, with only a short development history of 17 years, unexpectedly changed people's expectations. It not only achieved a breakthrough in the Chinese history, but also changed the pattern of international gold market. The performance of the China's gold market as a latecomer is really eye-catching.

5.2 The China's gold market is rewriting the history

As a latecomer, the China's gold market did not possess the historical advantages for development, and its largest advantage is

5 A Latecomer's Pursuit and Surpassing

that, as a latecomer, it could learn from the experience of predecessors, without repeating the process of previous trial and error. The China's gold market obtained good genes through top-level design, so that it had the right development direction and development path at the beginning. Today, the financial market is highly different from the traditional financial market, and the development of gold market also needs rethinking and restarting. Because of the new development issue currently encountered by gold market, namely the transformation from demonetization to re-monetization of gold, we need to re-orientate the social function of gold market. Therefore, learning is important, but carrying out adjustment in light of actual situation is more important.

The resumption of operation of London gold market is required for maintaining the stability of the international monetary system with USD as the center. The trading function of market has been alienated, it is USD rather than gold dominates the liquidity in the market, and endorsing the usefulness of USD is the core feature of its operation. Nowadays, however, when the USD is declining and multi currencies are emerging, such pattern is out of date. In addition, the development of international gold market occurred in the middle and late of the 1970s, and in the 1980s, the large environment was that the financial regulation was relaxed, the financial innovation was advocated, and the development of virtual economy was supported, so that the gold market inevitably bore the mark of that era. However, now we are in an era when the regulation is strengthened for the purpose of risk control, and for us as a latecomer, learning is to draw lessons rather than copying, and catching up is to surpass rather than follow the old path. We do not simply repeat the road that our predecessors have taken, but learn from the experience of our predecessors, climb up on the shoulders of our predecessors, and leave the Chinese mark in today's development of international gold market.

5.2.1 The Chinese factor will rewrite or has rewritten the pattern of international gold markets

Before the emergence of Chinese factor, the international gold market system was a binary structure, namely the pattern that the spot gold over-the-counter trading market represented by London gold market and the forward gold floor trading market represented by New York gold market developed in parallel. These two markets have different functions and equivalent scale. The binary market structure is derived from unitary market structure development, while other gold markets are regional markets.

■ Social function and evolution of unitary market

The gold market was born in Europe in the 18th Century, but Amsterdam in the Netherlands was once the European gold trading center. With the completion of industrial revolution in UK in the 19th Century, London became the largest international gold market in the world. The historical background for its development is that, at that time, UK occupied the central position in international gold standard system, so that London gold market surely became the central financial market in the world. The gold coins used at that time had three characteristics, namely free casting, free payment and free import/export, so that the London gold market was the gold trading and logistics center in the world. In 1939, it was closed due to the outbreak of World War II. In 1954, the economic background for resumption of operation was the USD gold exchange standard established after World War II. The social function of London gold market when its operation was resumed was to balance and stabilize the USD exchange system through the supply and demand of gold and thus achieve the stability of international monetary system, so that the object of transaction on London gold market was standard gold ingot, and it was still a spot gold delivery market. In essence, London gold market was a global gold logistics center and the balancer for adjustment of USD value, and was the basic tool for stabilizing the international monetary system at that time, and Bank of England was the market participant. However, as required by USA, the London gold market under the impact of gold run was closed for 15 days in 1968. During the closure of London gold market, the two largest gold producing countries, named South Africa and the

5 A Latecomer's Pursuit and Surpassing

Soviet Union[1] transferred their gold trading to the Swiss market, thus London lost its position as a global gold logistics center. In addition, the USD was decoupled from London gold market, and the stable USD exchange rate was no longer the indicator of supply-demand balance of gold, but became a fixed official gold price among central banks. What should the London gold market do? Under this situation, the London gold market launched the London Gold, which was not physical gold, but a kind of paper-based gold voucher. The trading based on this gold voucher eliminated the delivery of physical gold, made the gold trading become a convenient investment mode, and attracted many international commercial banks to participate actively. The trading volume of London Gold exceeded the trading volume of physical gold very soon, and then the London gold market changed from global gold logistics center to global gold investment center. The liquidity of London gold market is embodied in the replacement of gold logistics by currency flow, so that London is still the center for formation of global gold price, the price of London Gold is still the guiding price and basic price of global gold trading, and the London gold market maintains the position of the core market in the international gold market system. The transformation of London gold market means that a new kind of market has appeared in the international gold market system — paper gold trading market, so that the binary market structure composed of physical gold trading market and gold voucher trading market has been formed. The former is represented by Swiss gold market, and the latter is represented by London gold market. Both of them are spot trading market, only the form of trading object has changed, but the nature of market trading has not changed. Therefore, they are still the unitary spot gold trading market. The qualitative change of gold market happened only when the USA gold futures market appeared, but the change from unitary market structure to binary market structure is a gradual process.

---

1 At that time, the Soviet Union kept gold production secret and could not be ranked accurately.

Chinese Gold: From Following to Surpassing

■ Emerging binary market structure

The transformation of London gold market promoted the virtualization of spot gold trading, and the spot gold trading has been the champion in the global gold trading volume for a long time. From 1997 to 2017, the annual average trading volume of London gold market accounted for 54.09% in global total trading in average, reaching 170,400 tons. In 1997, its annual trading volume accounted for 87.63%, reaching 289,700 tons. In such year, the global trading volume of gold futures and options was only 38,100 tons, and the trading scale of London over-the-counter gold market was 4.47 times that of USA floor gold market. This is the binary structure of spot gold trading market. In 2008, the trading volume of New York gold market exceeded that of London gold market.

The New York gold market is a latecomer as compared with the London gold market, and is the product of USA's lifting of gold control. Over recent years, however, its trading scale has exceeded that of London gold market, becoming the largest gold market in the world. The London gold market is developed in the environment of gold standard and gold exchange standard, while the development environment of USA gold market is gold demonstration, so that it does not repeat the story of London gold market, but embarks on a development road with USA characteristics for serving the national strategy of USA. This is the basic feature of development of USA gold market. As a result, the binary structure of international gold market is deeply branded and influenced by USA strategy. However, this USA strategy has long been covered up for long time. For us, the inspiration of development road of USA gold market is that, the selection of development road for China's gold market must also have a national strategic view, which is an issue that must be paid attention to.

The London gold market was re-opened in 1954 in the period of USD gold exchange standard. Although the gold was no longer the payment currency, it was the basis for stability of currency, and the USD and gold were linked with each other at a fixed exchange rate,

5 A Latecomer's Pursuit and Surpassing

so that the main responsibility of London gold market was to achieve the value stability of USD through the supply-demand balance in gold market, and then achieve the stability of international monetary system. The London gold market is a physical gold trading platform, but in 1975 when the USA gold market was born, the USD had been decoupled from gold, so that USA did not establish a spot physical gold market like London, but took its own road and established an emerging gold futures contract market.

Just like the London Gold, the gold futures contract is a kind of gold voucher, is a kind of paper gold, and is a kind of gold derivatives rather than real gold. The difference is that, the London Gold is paper gold traded at spot price, while the gold futures contract is paper gold traded at forward price. In 1971, the USD was decoupled from gold, but the USD was still the international central currency, and maintaining the authority, namely usefulness, of central currency was extremely important, because the extensive usefulness is the manifestation and foothold of authority. Therefore, the usefulness of USD rather than the stability of USD value became the pursuit of USA.

Where does the usefulness of USD come from? Petroleum, as an important consumable energy commodity, has become a daily necessity of people and a strategic resource of a country. Using USD as the tool for settlement and payment can not only greatly increase the usage of USD, but also improve the usefulness of USD. Therefore, the petroleum settlement right of USD becomes the tool for USA to suppress its competitors. However, making USD the settlement currency for global petroleum trading was only an important step to expand the usefulness of USD, and the efforts made by USA to expand the usefulness of USD were comprehensive, among which, developing the USD-priced gold market has become the approach to expand the usefulness of USD.

After USA announced the decoupling between USD and gold in 1971, the International Monetary Fund ("IMF") also began to promote the gold decentralization, and the gold was no longer the direct basis for issuance of USD, so that USA obtained the right to

Chinese Gold: From Following to Surpassing

freely issue USD, which led to the random issuance of USD. Since the value of USD needed the support of gold, USA did not abandon the gold, but bought a gold insurance policy for USD, so as to deal with the possible collapse of USD. USA still retains 8,134 tons of gold reserves. Not only USA, but also many other countries in the world have bought gold insurance for their currencies. Most countries have gold reserves, but USA has the largest number of gold reserves, which is 4.39 times that of China in 2018 (1,853 tons) and accounts for 23.9% of global official reserves (34,000 tons). Many countries have increased gold reserves, and under the situation that the annual growth of gold reserve reaches the highest level in history, USA still holds the physical gold of nearly 1/4 of global official reserves as the reserve fund for occurrence of special situation to USD. The greater strategic purpose of USA for gold market is to promote the virtualization of trading, so as to change the function of contemporary gold market. As a result, the dominant liquidity generated by trading is USD rather than gold, and the gold trading platform becomes a tool to improve the usefulness of USD.

Under the banner of financial innovation, the virtualization of trading in gold market has developed continuously. Now, more than 99% of trading in international gold market is not gold trading, and only less than 1% is gold trading. Just like petroleum trading, the international gold trading is priced by USD and uses USD as trading settlement tool. Therefore, more than 99% of trading in international gold market is the trading of gold derivatives priced at USD, the gold market has become the USD trading market, and the international gold price has changed with the adjustment of USD value. The gold futures contract is a gold derivative with the maximum liquidity and can form a large-scale market using USD, so that making great efforts to develop the gold futures market is in line with the need of USA national strategy. Though USA is a main gold producing country in the world, it has no large-scale physical gold trading market, and its physical gold trading is mainly completed by using international gold market. Therefore, if we look at the USA gold market from the perspective of international politics, it also has

5 A Latecomer's Pursuit and Surpassing

top-level design.

In 2017, the global trading volume of gold was 469,000 tons, and the trading volume of gold futures accounted for 64.9%. As the representative of gold futures markets, the New York Commodity Exchange was first established and has the largest scale. In 2017, its trading volume accounted for near eighty percents (77.07%) of global trading volume of gold futures and accounted for 50.02% of global trading volume of gold, becoming the largest gold market in the world. At the beginning, the trading volume of gold forward contract was not high, and in the binary structure composed of spot market and forward market, the spot trading was dominant. In 2006, the forward trading volume reached the 100,000-ton scale, equivalent to that of spot gold trading market. In 2008, the forward trading volume reached 187,000 tons, exceeding the spot trading volume which was 174,300 tons. Thereafter, the difference was increased continuously. Therefore, the international binary market pattern has been formed for only 41 years.

Firstly, the formation of a binary structure of international gold market conforms to the need of USA national strategy. From the perspective of objective development requirements of gold market, the gold forward market embodies the requirement on expansion of function of gold market arising from the transformation from gold standard to gold demonetization. It is not only the requirement for completion of delivery of gold, but also the requirement for avoidance of price risk, so that the development of gold forward contract market can meet such requirement. The market risks are also mainly caused by uncertainty in change of USD value, and since USD changes from stable to fluctuant after getting rid of the constraint from gold, the trading of gold forward contract can provide a tool for USD to avoid uncertainty risk. However, this function of gold futures market is gradually understood, and is not immediately accepted. For a long time, the forward gold market was only a supplementary market. The gold futures markets of Canada and UK came to permanent end quickly, and the trading volume of New York Commodity Exchange as a successful one wad only

Chinese Gold: From Following to Surpassing

1,223.84 tons in the first year, less than 1/3 of that of Shanghai Futures Exchange in the first year after its gold futures contract was launched. However, New York Commodity Futures Exchange is the market with the fastest growth of gold futures trading over recent years. In 2016, its trading volume reached 185,700 tons, higher than that of London gold market (165,600 tons). In 2017, with the trading volume of gold futures reaching 234,600 tons, it achieved the self surpassing and created the history of market development. This is the result of more than 40 years' development of New York gold futures market born in the 1970s. The emergence of binary market structure has its political and economic background. Now, owing to the hope placed on it for changing the binary pattern of international gold market, the China's gold market, as a latecomer, has attracted attention from all over the world.

■ Chinese factor in ternary structure of gold market

The gold market of human beings has developed from the unitary structure of spot physical gold over-the-counter trading market to the binary structure composed of spot over-the-counter gold trading market and floor forward contract trading. After the Chinese factor entered the market, there is the trend that the binary market pattern will develop to the ternary market pattern.

The China's gold market born in 2002 was only a marginal existence in international gold market in the early stage of development, and was an unknown follower. However, after 14 years' development, its trading volume was increased by 2,000 times by 2016. Its two-way trading volume exceeded 100,000 tons in the market, reaching 125,900 tons, and its one-way trading volume reached 62,900 tons in the unilateral trade volume. From the perspective of trading scale, it is the third largest gold market in the world, only next to London and New York. After the two-way trading volume of China's gold market reached 125,900 tons in 2016, it was decreased by 19.38% to 101,500 tons in 2017. In 2018, the gold trading volume of Shanghai Gold Exchange was 67,500 tons, the gold futures trading volume of Shanghai Futures Exchange was 32,200 tons, and the gold trading volume

5 A Latecomer's Pursuit and Surpassing

over counter of commercial banks was 8,000 to 10,000 tons, so that total trading volume was about 110,000 tons. The two-way trading volume of China's gold market has exceeded 100,000 tons for 3 consecutive years, which means that although the trading volume of China's gold market is not a constant value, it has been stabilized at the 50,000-ton level at single side. The trading volume of other main gold exchanges in Asia in this year is as follows: 10,800 tons for Turkey, 6500 tons for Japan, 5100 tons for India, and 300 tons for Dubai. The China's gold market is the leader in Asian gold market. The trading scale of China's gold market is 2.2 times the total trading scale of several gold markets in Asia, so that it can be said that the China's gold market is the leader in Asian gold market.

In the international gold market dominated by virtual gold trading, the trading volume of physical gold is more authentic. It is the true reflection of flow direction of gold wealth, and is the real gold demand rather than the demand serving the usefulness of USD. The development of China's gold market has a strong foundation of gold industry, which is not possessed by London and New York gold markets. With the support of gold industry, the trading volume of physical gold in China has exceeded 2,000 tons since 2013, occupying the first place in the world till now. The actual gold demand in China accounts for more than 40% of global demand, and there is potential for improvement. It is highly probable that China will become the global gold logistics center, and the China's gold market has become the global champion in four aspects, namely gold demand, gold production, gold processing capacity and gold import volume. It takes the lead in the international physical gold trading market, and has become a unique pole in the international gold market system.

Japan was originally the central gold investment & trading market in Asia, but now its role has changed. The trading scale of Shanghai Gold Exchange only reached hundred-ton level in its first year. The trading volume of gold futures of Tokyo Commodity Exchange reached 26,600 tons in such year, but was only 6,500 tons in 2017, decreased by 75.56%. The demand of physical gold also dropped from

Chinese Gold: From Following to Surpassing

258 tons in 2003 to 99.1 tons in 2017, decrease of 61.59%. In contrast, the trading volume of China's gold market grew by 214.7 times during this period, from 235.5 tons to 50,800 tons. The trading scale of China's gold market is 7.82 times that of Japan. The demand on physical gold in China reached 1,507 tons in 2017, namely 15.2 times that in Japan, so that China has replaced Japan as the central gold market and investment center in Asia.

The international influence of China's gold market is firstly embodied in the fact that it has upgraded from a marginal market to the central market in Asia. Though the current scale of China's gold market is still much smaller than that of world-class markets (one-way 100,000 tons), the China's gold market has an optimistic development prospect, has the potential to reach the 100,000-ton scale, and is the only emerging market that can challenge the binary structure of international gold market. Scale is only a representation. The unique DNA of China's gold market poses the greatest challenge to the binary structure of international market. It sets an example for the reform to be carried out for international binary market, and thus becomes the Chinese factor for reform of international gold market. Therefore, in the future, the China's gold market will become the formulator of market rules. For the international gold market, the rise of the China's gold market means that the binary structure will be replaced by the ternary structure, because China is no longer a follower, but has become a partner for equal dialogue and a model for learning. This is a historical change.

When the global gold market system was developed from unitary structure to binary structure, the number of markets increased, and a new kind of market, namely forward contract trading market, also came into being after the competition between two markets of same nature. Therefore, the function of gold market was also developed from the single delivery function to market uncertainty risk management function. The change from binary structure to ternary structure is mainly attributable to the emergence of Chinese factor. The development of China's gold market brings a series of reflections on the future development of international gold markets:

5 A Latecomer's Pursuit and Surpassing

the first is the reflection on human nature, and the self-discipline must be based on regulation; the second is the reflection on development mode, and the risk control must be given priority; the third is the reflection on behaviors of participants, and the trading must be based on real demand.

The reason why the development road of China's gold market is different is that, as a latecomer, the development environment of China's gold market is greatly different from that of two forerunners, namely London and New York, and each has its own brand of the times: the development of London and New York gold markets benefits from the financial market environment in the 1980s in which the regulation was ignored and the innovation was emphasized. However, after more than 30 years' development, the virtualization of trading has become increasingly distorted and divorced from the actual trading demand, and these two markets have become the place for market tycoons to speculate and provided the ground for breeding of fraud. The development of China's gold market started in the first 10 years of the 21st Century, and the development environment had changed that the regulation was emphasized, the service was enhanced and the leverage was controlled. As a result, the China's gold market has been endowed with the unique DNA since its birth, and shows the unique characteristics - the development starts with top-level design. It challenges the free market economy, grows in order competition, achieves self-discipline under effective regulation and puts the risk control in priority, thus achieving the low-risk development. Therefore, the directing and guiding role of Chinese experience in future development system of international gold market will be increasingly apparent.

5.2.2 The allocation pattern "flow of gold from the west to the east" in the world is determined

As a kind of currency metal and the absolute wealth of human beings, the gold is the symbol of prosperity or strength of a region or country. Therefore, in modern times, Europe set off a boom in

Chinese Gold: From Following to Surpassing

searching for gold in the whole world, and finally found the gold in America. The European colonists plundered the gold and silver of America to Europe, so that Europe became the richest area in the world. In addition to being consumed by emperors in Europe, the gold wealth became the material foundation for Europe to establish the gold standard, so that Europe was the most concentrated place of gold before the 19th Century. The two world wars in the 20th Century broke out in Europe, and USA, which was far away from the war, pulled the chestnut out of fire. Therefore, a lot of gold of Europe flowed into USA during World War II. The USA government gathered 75% of official gold reserves around the world (namely 40% of global gold at that time) by means of foreign trade and internal compulsory levy, and the quantity was as high as 22,000 tons. By holding gold in its hands, USA was able to promise to keep the value of USD stable on the basis of gold standard, so as to win the trust for USD and make USD replace the British pound and become the new central currency in international monetary system. Thereafter, USD was called as US gold, which means that USD is a paper currency with stable value like gold. However, the practice has proved that, only the gold is the physical asset with intrinsic value, while USD is only colored printed matter with value given by the country. Gold and USD are two different substances, and USD can't substitute gold. The Europeans were aware of this, so that they set off a gold run in the 1960s by using the USD obtained from the post-war reconstruction. Gold also flowed back to Europe, and they rebuilt the national gold reserves. Now, among the top-10 countries with official gold reserves, 6 are in Europe, ranked at the second, third, fourth, fifth, seventh and ninth place respectively. The official gold reserves of six countries including Germany, France, Italy, Russia, Switzerland and the Netherlands reach 11,300 tons, accounting for 1/3 of global official gold reserves. However, USA still holds the largest number of gold reserves (8,134 tons) among all countries, and its gold accounts for the largest proportion (75%). In general, Europe and USA are still the regions with the largest number of gold in official possession today, but a trend "flow of gold from the west to the east"

5 A Latecomer's Pursuit and Surpassing

has appeared over past 20 years, and this is mainly due to the effect of gold demonetarization. The common people have become the new leading buyer of gold, while the government has become the non-leading buyer. Due to the cultural differences in consumption in different countries, the people in different countries have different preferences for gold, and Asia has become the continent with the most gold consumption. Although Europe is the gold smelting center and logistics center in the world today and most of the gold minerals in the world enter Switzerland for initial processing or enter UK market for trading, Europe has no high gold demands. Therefore, most of the finished gold in Europe enters Asian market through market trading and is deposited in Asia. This is the so-called phenomenon of "flow of gold from the west to the east".

Now, Switzerland is the largest physical gold trading market in the world, is the gold logistics center in the world, and is also the largest gold importing country in the world. In 2017, Switzerland imported 1,367 tons of gold and exported 1,477 tons of gold. In other words, in such year, Switzerland not only converted all imported gold to exported gold, but also exported 110 tons of inventory gold previously held by it. According to the statistics of Swiss customs, from 2000 to 2017, Switzerland imported 17,260.6 tons of gold, and exported 19,926.9 tons of gold. During this period, the export volume of gold from of Switzerland was 2,666.3 tons more than the import volume, which means that the inventory gold in Switzerland decreased (the national gold reserve of Switzerland was reduced by 50%), and the gold in the west flowed to Asia in the east. Recently, more and more American gold has been directly exported to Asia, because Asia is the continent with the highest gold demand today, and its market demand accounts for about 60% of global demand. In 2017, the total gold demand of Asia was 2,318.9 tons, accounting for 59.29% of global demand (3,911 tons), while the gold production of Asia was only 673.9 tons, and the gold recovery was 414.6 tons. Therefore, the total gold supply in Asia was 1,088.5 tons. After deducting the total supply in Asia from the total demand, the import volume of gold was 1,230.4 tons. The imported gold has become

Chinese Gold: From Following to Surpassing

the largest supply source of Asia. The import volume accounted for 26.76% of gold supply, which means in such year, about 1/4 of global gold supply was deposited in Asia, becoming the inventory of gold wealth of Asia.

Asia is now the largest gold using area in the world, while China and India are two major supports for gold demand in Asia. Before the Chinese factor appeared, India was the largest gold demanding country in Asia, and was also the largest gold demanding country in the world. Because there is no gold mine in India, India basically has no gold production, and all the gap between supply and demand is filled with the gold imported. According to the *GFMS Gold Survey 2018*, in 2017 in India, the physical gold consumption for investment purpose was 164.2 tons, the gold consumption for industrial purpose was 11.2 tons, and the gold consumption for production of jewelry was 570.7 tons, so that the total demand was 746.1 tons. Except for recovered gold, all other gold supply for meeting the demand was imported. Over the past 10 years, the annual gold import volume of India has ever reached 1,100 tons, and stayed at 800 tons normally. China was a gold exporting country because of its gold industry with the highest gold production in the world, so that it had a strong capacity to allocate the gold supply. However, after the release of gold control, the private gold demand has grown rapidly, and there has been a gap between supply and demand, which makes China become a gold importing country to achieve the balance of supply and demand by importing gold. In 2007, China imported 28.77 tons of gold, accounting for 7.28% of supply, which means that the import was still a supplementary supply factor. Since then, the import volume has grown continuously, and reached 1506.5 tons in 2013, creating a historical record and making China surpass India and become the largest gold importing country in the world. Thereafter, though the annual import volume decreased slightly, it still exceeded 1,000 tons in average, and the imported gold had become the largest source of gold supply in China. In 2017, China imported 1,110 tons of gold, accounting for 58.11% of total supply of whole country and accounting for 24.75% of total supply (4,484

5 A Latecomer's Pursuit and Surpassing

tons) of the whole world, so that China became the largest gold importing country.

Owing to the increase of demand in China's gold market, the gold demand in Asia has changed from "solo" of India to "two male competition", so that the gold demand of Asia is improved and the pattern "flow of gold from the west to the east" is consolidated. The pattern "flow of gold from the west to the east" has emerged under the situation of gold demonetarization. The people in Europe and USA have a long history of gold standard and the deep gold coin culture, and their estrangement from gold shows that, their gold culture has changed from currency to ordinary commodity, so that the gold's sense of usefulness and sacredness is greatly reduced for European and American people. In addition, as the substitute of USD, the gold is in competition with USD, and in order to establish the authority of USD, it is necessary to belittle gold. These are the reasons why the people in Europe and America are estranged from gold. However, the gold culture of Asian people represented by Chinese and Indian is different from that of European and American, because there is no gold standard in China and India. As a result, the people in China and India have a weak concept of gold currency, while they have a profound concept of gold wealth. In addition, the demonetization of gold does not mean that the gold is not a wealth. Therefore, the demonetization of gold has not kept the people of China and India away from gold. Furthermore, since China and India have become the locomotive of world economy, the economic development increases the income of people, and the increase of family wealth enables them to hold more gold wealth, so that the gold demand in Asia has grown continuously. This is the culture reason for the trend "flow of gold from the west to the east". Recently, however, there has been a trend of "gold re-monetization" in Europe and USA, and the idea of gold monetization has been awakened again. What kind of effect will this have on "flow of gold from the west to the east"? We should wait and see. However, we should understand that "flow of gold from the west to the east" will not remain unchanged for ever. It is an opportunity window that may be closed at any time. As soon as 2019 started, the news came that USA sold the Eagle gold coins equivalent to half of total sales volume of 2018 in one day, and Sam Zell, a 77 year old billionaire, bought the gold for the first time in his life. This shows that, people in Europe and USA have begun to change their attitude towards gold.

The trend "flow of gold from the west to the east" is consistent with the requirements of RMB internationalization. Just like the internationalization of pound and the internationalization of USD, in order to achieve the internationalization of RMB, enough gold reserves should be established, because the value of paper currency can be supported only when it is linked with physical substance. The trend "flow of gold from the west to the east" provides a strategic opportunity for us to establish the gold support force for internationalization of RMB. We should cherish this opportunity, and complete the construction of gold support force for internationalization of RMB within this strategic opportunity period. If the trend "flow of gold from the west to the east" disappears, the difficulty in building the support for RMB gold will be increased, and the costs will also be increased greatly. Therefore, we must take precautions.

5.2.3 The domination of USD in formation of gold price is broken

The cross-regional gold trading is continuously carried out round the clock, and the price is formed in London. The USD London gold price formed in secret room after several rounds of quotation becomes the international gold price, and becomes the price basis for cross-regional gold trading around the world. Since the gold is a special commodity which has financial function, the international gold price is not only used in gold trading, but also in bulk commodity trading and in financial market. Therefore, the USD gold price formed in London is not only the settlement standard for spot trading of gold, but also the pricing standard of financial derivatives. The international gold price is very important not only for marketing trading of gold, but

5 A Latecomer's Pursuit and Surpassing

also for pricing of financial products. Therefore, the London gold price has extensive influence, and becomes the important factor which can affect the price of commodities and financial products.

On the surface, London gold price is the gold price generated on the supply-demand equilibrium point according to the multiple quotations of the market, so that it has fairly run for a hundred years without any problem. However, the London gold price, which is decided by a few people in secret room, lacks the supervision from third party, and also lacks the open and transparent mechanism, so that fraud may occur easily. Eventually, in 2013, the scandal about manipulation of gold price by Barclays Bank broke out, and the public opinion was in a great uproar. The formation mechanism of gold price was forced to reform, and the aftereffect has not been solved. However, this is only a problem at the operational level, and the deeper problem is that caused by USD pricing. The fair price should be generated at the market supply-demand equilibrium point, but international London gold price is based on USD. Therefore, the formation of international London gold price includes not only supply-demand factor, but also USD factor. The value of USD is not fixed but changeable. The change of USD and the change of gold price are in reverse motion under many situations. The gold price will drop when USD rises and will rise when USD drops. Of course, the gold price does not always keep inverse movement with USD. After long-term observation, people believe that the probability of reverse movement between gold price and USD price exceeds 70%, which indicates that the influence of USD does exist objectively. The value of USD is also determined by supply and demand, but the supply-demand change of USD is different from that of gold. Although the supply-demand change of USD is expressed on the market, it is not determined by the market but controlled by Federal Reserve, and is a result of human manipulation. This manipulation is based on the need of economic development of USA itself, which is unfair to other countries, because the interest demands of USA are not completely consistent with and even completely opposite to those of other countries. Fairness is one of the market trading

Chinese Gold: From Following to Surpassing

principles. However, the gold trading with USD pricing can't guarantee fairness, but becomes the tool for USA to obtain unfair interests. Especially after the establishment of USD hegemony, USA has taken USA interest first as an open rule of law. USD dominates the formation of international gold price, so that the voice of reform has been raised everywhere, which requires multi currency to play a role in the formation of international gold price. This is the pursuit of fairness by human beings.

The traditional international gold price mechanism not only has the defect in procedure, but also has the defect in USD pricing, so that the London gold price which was once authoritative has become the object of revolution. It is not easy to reform the formation procedure of London gold price, and it is more difficult to reform the current situation of single USD pricing. The reform on single USD structure in international gold price requires not only desire, but also strength. What kind of currency can become the new participating currency for international gold price? Can EURO, the second largest international currency, participate in? For the purpose of expanding the influence of EURO, Europe is not without will, but Europe has neither real gold demand nor urgent demand on deposit of gold wealth. On the contrary, Europe is the outflow place of gold wealth, so that it is only a market dominated by virtual trading. There are still a large number of official gold reserves in Europe, but the official gold reserves have a special function orientation, their liquidity is very low, and there is no turnover rate in the market. Therefore, EURO lacks the driving force and influence on reform of gold market. The EURO area has neither capacity nor strong desire to change the gold USD pricing mechanism.

Since 1954, the European gold market has been closely bound with USD. From the perspective of political choice, the Japanese yen and pound have no desire to challenge the USD pricing mechanism, which is an embarrassing reality.

RMB used to be a kind of marginal currency. With the promotion of reform and opening up, RMB has gradually entered the ranks of international currency. Now, it has been listed in the SDR (special

5 A Latecomer's Pursuit and Surpassing

drawing rights) package currencies of International Monetary Fund, and thus has the qualification of international currency. As a part of the process of RMB internationalization, RMB has both the great willingness and practical needs to enter the mechanism for formation of international gold price. For the purpose of stabilizing its value, RMB has the needs to get linked with gold in a certain manner. Therefore, the improvement of discourse power of RMB in the formation of international gold price is what we actively promote and are willing to see, but the increase of RMB's influence in the formation of international gold price needs certain basic conditions.

Firstly, China should have a strong voice in the international gold market and be able to have an equal dialogue with the main gold markets in the world. The China's gold market didn't have such condition when it was a follower, but now such condition has been obtained gradually. After the trading volume reached 50,000 tons, China became the third largest gold market in the world, and gradually possessed the bargaining power, because at that time the trading volume of China's gold market accounted for 15%-20% of global trading volume, the trading on China's gold market began to have enough representativeness, and the claim and willingness of Chinese gold investors in the aspect of trading price were increasingly international.

Secondly, there should be international product priced with RMB in the international market and such product should be able to become the substitute of product priced with USD and gold, so as to improve the proportion of RMB in international gold price. In April 2016, Shanghai Gold Exchange launched the Shanghai Gold which is priced in RMB and can be traded around the world. The Shanghai Gold not only is priced in RMB, but also can be internationally traded after the benchmark price is formed in Shanghai every day. Therefore, besides the USD pricing center for London Gold, there is another RMB pricing center for Shanghai Gold. This center becomes a channel for RMB to enter the formation process of international gold price.

The outbreak of London Gold scandal undoubtedly gives advice for the design of price formation mechanism of Shanghai Gold.

Chinese Gold: From Following to Surpassing

In the process of initial quotation, subsequent balance and final generation of trading price, there is no essential difference between RMB gold price and USD gold price. However, the large difference between Shanghai Gold and London Gold (There will be a third one after reform, but this mechanism has not been fully recognized) is that a third party, namely Shanghai Gold Exchange, will regulate and record the whole process, so as to prevent the price manipulation and ensure the fairness of trading. With the continuous expansion of trading scale of Shanghai Gold, the RMB factor in international gold price has increased continuously. Now, the investors participating in trading of Shanghai Gold are fully internationalized, covering domestic and foreign commercial banks, securities dealers, gold producers and gold users. The trading volume of Shanghai Gold was 569.19 tons in 2016, 3,476.47 tons in 2017 and 3,997.94 tons in 2018, growing year by year.

These effects can be said to be a step forward, but the ultimate goal has not been reached yet, and there is still a long way from the ultimate goal. However, a small step now is a big step in the future. The rise of China's gold market changed the pattern of gold trading in the world. The round-the-clock trading activity is divided into three time zones, and the three most active markets, namely London in Europe, New York in America and Shanghai in Asia, form the golden triangle of international gold trading. In the past, this role in Asia was assumed by Tokyo of Japan, and now it has been replaced by Shanghai. In the 24-hour non-stop trading around the world, this golden triangle constitutes the complete closed-loop of international capital flow, and the China's gold market becomes a node of this closed-loop. This is the location advantage of the China's gold market, and is also the results of natural selection.

5.3 The growth of market is a development process

From 2002 to 2018, the development of the China's gold market has gone beyond our expectation. The gold has successfully transformed from a subject collected and distributed by the People's Bank of China in a centralized manner into a subject freely traded between buyers and sellers. This is the initial motivation and appeal of China to promote the marketization of gold, and is not an ambition. However, Shanghai Gold Exchange became the largest spot gold trading market in the world in the fifth year after its opening, and this is a great progress. Shanghai Futures Exchange became the second largest gold futures exchange in the world 6 years after its gold futures contract was launched. Now, the total gold trading volume of China steadily occupies the third place in the world. This is the report card submitted by China's gold market after 17 years' development. The value and meaning of gold marketization in China began to be recognized by the Chinese people and draw more and more attention from the world. The appraisal obtained is even beyond our own expectation.

5.3.1 The starting point of development was not brilliant

In a short period of 17 years, the China's gold market quickly surmounted many pioneers, and began to approach UK and USA, the two internationally-leading gold markets. However, the starting point of China's gold market was not high. In the early stage of development, its performance was not brilliant. The average monthly trading scale in the first year was only at the 10-ton level, while the annual trading volume was only at the 100-ton level in the following four years and was increased to the 1,000-ton level, reaching 1,648.9 tons only in the fifth year. Shanghai gold trading market also became the largest spot floor gold trading market in the world. As compared with international markets, the one-way trading scale of Shanghai gold trading market was 824.45 tons, only accounting for 0.28% of total one-way trading volume of 295,800 tons in global gold market in that year. Therefore, Shanghai gold trading market was still a marginal market without importance among the international gold markets. The biggest driving force was the listing of gold futures contract in 2008. In such year, the China's gold market system was formed, and the total trading volume of China's gold market was

Chinese Gold: From Following to Surpassing

increased by 496.35%, reaching 13,975 tons and jumped up onto 10,000-ton level. This is a great step forward in our own view, but among all international markets, we were still a weak latecomer. The trading scale was only 3.7% of global trading scale (378,100 tons) in such year, was only 11.71% of trading scale (119,300 tons) of New York Commodity Exchange in such year, was only 8% of trading scale (174,300 tons) of London gold trading market in such year, was only 46.58% of trading scale of Indian Bulk Commodity Exchange in such year, and was only 42.51% of trading scale of Tokyo Commodity Exchange in such year. In other words, the scale of China's gold market in 2008 not only lagged far behind the gold trading markets in London and New York, but also lagged behind the regional gold markets such as Japan and India in Asia. The China's gold market was still a marginal force in the international gold market. In 2012, after experiencing 10 years of development, the bidirectional trading volume of China's gold market reached 21,500 tons, but its share in the global trading volume was less than 3%, still lower than that of Tokyo Commodity Exchange and Indian Bulk Commodity Exchange. Anyway, the trading scale of China's gold market has reached the 10,000-ton level. It can be said that, the China's gold market became a regional trading market through 10 years' development.

The breakthrough occurred in 2013. In this year, the gold trading volume was increased by 161.3% year on year, and the one-way gold trading volume reached 56,300 tons. In this year, the growth alone reached 34,800 tons (two-way), namely 1.61 times the trading volume in 2012. Unexpectedly, this extraordinary growth momentum continued, and during 2014-2016, the two-way trading volume was increased by more than 20,000 tons per year. Therefore, during this 3-year period, the trading volume of China's gold market successively went up seven 10,000-ton steps (namely 60,000 tons, 70,000 tons, 80,000 tons, 90,000 tons, 100,000 tons, 110,000 tons and 120,000 tons), and reached 125,900 tons, a historical peak, in 2016. In 2017, the trading volume was 101,500 tons and was decreased by 19.38%. In 2018, the trading volume of Shanghai Gold

5 A Latecomer's Pursuit and Surpassing

Exchange reached 67,500 tons, and the gold futures trading volume of Shanghai Futures Exchange was 32,200 tons, so that the total volume was 99,700 tons, and if the trading volume of OTC market of commercial banks was added, then the total volume was about 112,000 tons. Therefore, a historical record was created in 2016. Thereafter, the trading volume also exceeded 100,000 tons in 2017 and 2018. This indicates that the scale of the China's gold market has reached a new height.

Looking at the development history of China's gold market, the trading scale started at the 100-ton level, and after 10 years' development, the China's gold market was still a follower of international gold markets and was also not the leader in Asia. The trading scale was smaller than Tokyo Commodity Exchange and India bulk Commodity Exchange. However, it entered an extraordinary development period since 2013. Taking 2013 as the boundary, the China's gold market has two different development periods. 2002-2012 is low-speed development period, and 2013-2018 is extraordinary development period. The change in double-way trading volume of China's gold market is as indicated in Figure 5-1.

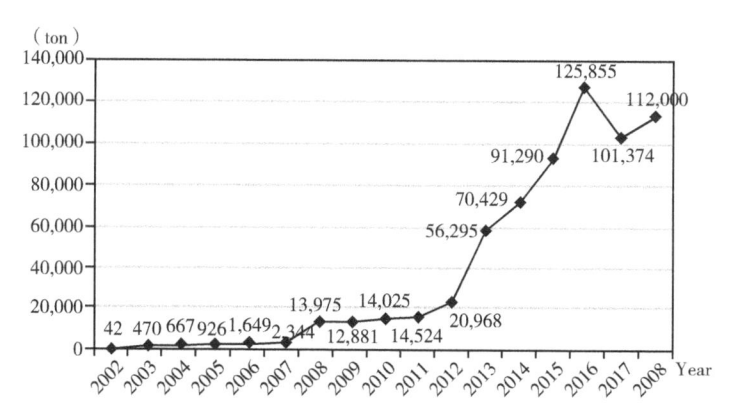

Figure 5-1 Change in Double-way Trading Volume of Chinese Gold Market
Source: *China Gold Yearbook (2009-2018)*.

Chinese Gold: From Following to Surpassing

The boundary between these two historical stages is 2013. During the ten years before 2013, the trading scale grew from 100-ton level to 10,000-ton level, and from 2013 to 2016, the annual average growth of double-way trading volume exceeded 20,000 tons, and the trading scale even reached 125,900 tons. Though the trading scale dropped slightly in 2017 and 2018, it was still higher than 100,000 tons. This is a new height in development of China's gold market. The trading scale of China's gold market was 4.49 times the total gold trading volume of four countries including Japan, India, Turkey and UAE in 2016, and 4.12 times in 2017. With the gap between it and other main gold markets in Asia increased by an order of magnitude and its proportion in global gold trading volume increased to more than 15%, the China's gold market has become the leading gold market in Asia and the third largest gold market in the world, and, together with USA forward gold trading market and UK spot gold trading market, constituted the tripartite confrontation. This naturally leads to a question: what happened in 2013? What made the development of China's gold market have a super high speed?

5.3.2 Culture is the instruction for action

2013 is a breakthrough year. In such year, the growth of trading volume of China's gold market exceeded the total growth achieved in previous ten years. From 2003 to 2012, the total growth of trading volume of China's gold market was 20,900 tons; in 2013, the growth was 34,800 tons, namely 1.67 times the total growth in previous nine years; from 2014 to 2016, the annual average growth was 23,200 tons, namely 1.07 times the total growth in previous nine years (2003 to 2012). Therefore, during this period, the trading volume of China's gold market successively went up seven 10,000-ton steps (namely 60,000 tons, 70,000 tons, 80,000 tons, 90,000 tons, 100,000 tons, 110,000 tons and 120,000 tons), and reached the historical peak in 2016. Thereafter, the trading volume was decreased by 19.38% in 2017 and was increased by about 10% in 2018, remaining at the 100,000-ton level. As a result, after 2013, the China's gold market

5 A Latecomer's Pursuit and Surpassing

entered a new stage, gradually changing from an international marginal market to an international important market, becoming the third largest market in the world, only next to London and New York, leaving other regional markets far behind and having the ever-increasing international influence. Where does the explosive power of China's gold market come from?

There are many answers to this question, but from the perspective of development logic of market, we find that the essence of market scale expansion is the growth of demand, and the growth of demand originates from the behavior of people. Demand is a kind of selective behavior. In a market with diversified supply, the human beings have the problem of selection, and what will be selected or will not be selected is determined by the behavior instruction of human beings. Different behavior instructions will lead to different demand, and behavior instruction is the essence of culture. Therefore, in the final analysis, the explosive power of China's gold market should be found from the culture. What happened to the gold consumption culture of people at that time?

Because of the gold shortage which has lasted for one thousand years in China, the gold has not sufficiently participated in our real economic life. At the turning point of modern history of the world, the Chinese gold also lacked the discourse power, so that our gold culture is not so profound. In particular, under the gold control of more than half a century, the Chinese people have been isolated from gold for at least two generations. As a result, when the market is open and we achieve the zero-distance contact with gold, we are unfamiliar with gold and our understanding is superficial. Most of us still stay in the story about gold in troubled times, and are at a loss about the essence of value of gold. Therefore, in such a cultural environment, it is not surprising that the starting point of China's gold market is not high, and the low-speed growth in previous 10 years can also be understood. Obviously, the rapid development since 2013 is attributable to change in behavior instructions of people, namely change in culture. Then, what change has taken place?

Chinese Gold: From Following to Surpassing

I believe that the cause of the change in gold culture of Chinese people is that, the US subprime mortgage crisis broke out in 2007, and the world entered a period of continuous economic turbulence caused by USD crisis. Its seriousness was described by some authoritative people as the once-in-a-century crisis. This crisis has uncovered the mystery of international monetary system with USD as central currency, and exposed the disadvantages of international monetary system. The understanding was gradually deepened. When approaching the truth of USD step by step, the human beings awaken the gold complex through comparison and reflection, and further understood the gold. The gold demonetization started from the 1970s stopped abruptly and there came the era of gold remonetization. And some people predict: "The currency war has become obsolete, and the battle of gold is the future." In order to protect their wealth against the inflation of paper currency and in order to ensure a stable life, people begin to take gold finance as an appeal for reforming today's international monetary system. The lesson of reality is the best teaching material. The Chinese people of our generation begin to observe the essence of gold, see the eternal value of gold through comparison of wealth of human beings, and understand that the gold with eternal value is the absolute wealth and the highest form of wealth of human beings. As a result, more and more Chinese people become "fans" of gold, and the gold becomes the first choice of people who pursue the value preservation and inheritance of wealth. This is the difference of gold culture before and after 2013. This difference in gold culture leads to the change in people's behavior for configuration of family assets.

In 2018, Guangfa Bank, together with Southwest University of Finance and Economics, conducted a survey on family wealth in Chinese cities. The results show that, the total assets of Chinese family was RMB 1.617 million in average, including RMB 55,7000 used for investment and ranked second in the world. How is the type of assets selected? The survey report indicates that, in the total assets of family, the real estate accounted for 77.7%, and the financial assets accounted for 11.8%. In the financial assets, nearly

5 A Latecomer's Pursuit and Surpassing

half was bank deposit, while the stock was less than 1% of the total assets. The result of survey carried out ten years ago must be highly different from this result. At that time, the proportion of equity assets would be much higher than that of today. The reason why people begin to stay away from stocks is that they realize that under the threat of currency devaluation, the preservation and inheritance of assets are more important, and thus they are vigilant about the security of financial assets. Therefore, nearly 90% of people selected real estate, a half of financial assets were bank deposit, and then the gold was selected. The most typical representative event is that, at the beginning of 2013, the Chinese middle-aged housewives who knew nothing about the advanced financial theory created a sensational event in financial history. By taking advantage of the sharp fall in gold price in 2013, they bought a large number of gold in the markets of Mainland China as well as Hong Kong and Macao, making the short sellers lose money and surprising the world. Their behavior was called as "irrational blind movement" by some financiers, and thus was questioned and ridiculed. In fact, their behavior is a kind of asset replacement rather than speculative profit-making behavior. Their behavioral logic is based on the maintenance and inheritance of family assets, and has nothing to do with profit making.

Just in such year, the demand scale of the China's gold market started entering the fast lane. In such year, the trading volume of China's gold market increased sharply by 168.48% or 35,300 tons. Since 2013, China has always maintained the high level of gold demand, because the Chinese people completed a reconstruction of gold culture, the core of this reconstruction was that the Chinese people completed the functional transformation of gold from commodity to assets, and this transformation met the demand of people on value preservation of gold. Therefore, in the process of value preservation of family wealth, the demand on gold wealth was vigorous, and the gold marketization enabled the Chinese people to obtain gold at the lowest cost and in the most conventional manner, which greatly excavated the potential of people's gold demand, and

Chinese Gold: From Following to Surpassing

gave a strong driving force to the development of gold market after 2013. The emergence of strong gold wealth demand on the basis of reconstruction of gold culture is the culture condition for strategic success in scale of China's gold market. The gold culture, namely the creation, consolidation and development of behavior instruction for gold demand, is the fundamental power source for development of gold market. The cultivation and maintenance of gold culture is the top priority for development of any gold market. However, we often ignore the existence of this important issue.

6

An Encounter on the Road to Internationalization

The development of China's gold market is aimed at internationalization in an open environment, so that the China's gold market, as a latecomer, is full of enthusiasm and inclusiveness in learning the experience of international gold market, which enriches the connotation of the China's gold market. We pay attention to the rhythm of opening up, but also do not oppose the goal of internationalization, which is an important feature of the internationalization of China's gold market. The top level design of China's gold market takes the international gold market as the comparative coordinates, and is the product of internationalization. In the process of internationalization of China's gold market, the China's gold market met and cooperated with the World Gold Council. Therefore, the World Gold Council has played a different role in the development of China's gold market, becoming a participant in the whole process of the development of China's gold market and leaving some memorable anecdotes, which constitutes a part of the internationalization process of China's gold market.

6.1 World Gold Council

The World Gold Council was established and registered in Switzerland in 1987, with its current office in London, UK. It can be said that the World Gold Council was born from the self-redemption of gold producers. In the second half of the 20th Century, though the international monetary system still took gold as standard, the mighty USD has become the substitute of gold, and was even

Chinese Gold: From Following to Surpassing

called as US gold. The authority of gold was challenged in the international monetary system, the use of gold was compressed, the social function of gold shrank, and the usefulness of gold was challenged, so that the pressure was placed on gold producers. At that time, South Africa, as a large gold producing country, started its action first. In 1967, the South Africa Mining Association launched a kind of gold coin named Kruger. The gold coin was 1 ounce and contained 22K gold (about 91.6%). In fact, it was a small gold nugget with pattern, and appreciated very quickly. The purpose of South Africa Mining Association to launch Kruger gold coin is to fight back against the gold demonetization, and to provide the gold that can be bought and sold by ordinary people, so as to increase the demands of people on gold. It believed that people's acceptance of gold coin is also the recognition of gold standard. However, under the situation that the gold control was implemented in most countries in the world, the issuance of gold coin was actually an "edge ball" played by gold producer in order to break through the control. The implementation of double track system for gold price in 1968 provided liquidity for this gold product. As a result, the gold coin issued by South Africa achieved success. In 1984, South Africa sold 40 million Kruger gold coins. The success of South Africa led to the competition from other gold producing countries. USA, Australia, Canada and other countries successively issued their own gold coins. China issued Panda Gold Coin in 1979. The world entered the era of gold coin. At that time, 15%-20% of mineral gold was used for production of gold coins. At that time, in the control system, the absolute big buyers of gold were central banks of various countries, so that the gold had no marketing problem. However, the producers of gold coin had to face the highly dispersed individual demanders and the fierce competition from various gold coins, so that they had to carry out marketing activities for their gold coins. As a result, there came the intervention from gold producers into market for the purpose of promoting their gold coins, and this is also the reason why the World Gold Council set up by international big gold producers actively enters market and promote the gold.

6 An Encounter on the Road to Internationalization

In 1978, the gold demonetarization was finally confirmed at the legal level, and the central banks of various countries withdrew from the gold market successively. For gold producers, this means that they have lost the largest customers of their own products, and also means that the single buyer of gold has become the diversified buyers and the single demand satisfaction has become the diversified demand satisfaction, so that the promotion and marketing should be expanded from gold coin to the gold. As a world-class product, the gold has the nature of high grade and popularity, and this puts forward higher requirements for its marketing mode. Therefore, it is necessary to integrate the scattered resources so as to form a professional global expansion platform for gold producers. As a result, the World Gold Council was born in 1987. The World Gold Council is a member-system international institution mainly composed of gold mining enterprises, and its purpose is promoting the application and demand of gold.

The initial members of the World Gold Council were 67 gold production enterprises. Since there was no strict restriction on qualification of members at that time, several mine enterprises under a company could become members. Later, it was specified that a company could only have a member seat, so that there are 27 members now, all of which are top gold mining companies in the world, including all main large gold production enterprises such as Barrick, Newmont and Anglo. China Gold Group and Shandong Gold Mining Group also are members of World Gold Council, with the production ranked first and second respectively in China. These 27 members have more than 500 mine development projects and more than 100 gold mines in excess 45 countries, and their gold production capacity is about 1,500 tons, accounting for 56% of total industrial gold production and 36% of total production of the world respectively.

The fund of the World Gold Council comes from the membership fees paid by members on the basis of production. However, after the listing of the largest ETF (exchange traded fund) in the world in 2003, the World Gold Council, as a director unit, also has the income of trading management fees. This becomes another important source of funds for the World Gold Council, and also supports the World Gold Council in promoting the application of gold market around the world.

6.2 World Gold Council and China

In 1994, the World Gold Council entered China, and set up the representative office in Beijing. For the Chinese gold enterprises which were under control at the time, the World Gold Council was spending its own money on other people's wedding dresses. The reason why the World Gold Council wanted to enter China is because it found that, China had a large population, the market was not yet open, and the potential demand was huge, so that it was a final and promising "virgin land" which could drive the global gold demand. Today, more than 20 years later, China has became the largest gold demanding country, the largest gold producing country, the largest gold processing country and the largest gold importing country in the world. It can be said that, the goal set by the World Gold Council when it entered China has been achieved beyond expectation, or even far beyond expectation. Therefore, it is reasonable that China has become a country to which the World Gold Council pays great attention.

In1993, namely the year before the World Gold Council entered China, the Document No. 63 of the State Council was issued, the goal of gold marketization in China was just proposed, and there was still a blind spot in understanding on gold marketization. This provided an opportunity for the World Gold Council which just entered China to play a role as consultant, and thus it becomes a unique presence in the gold marketization history of China. At that time, China only resumed the market supply of gold jewelry, and the gold was still under control rather than in the state of free trading. Under the policy environment of China at that time, the work focus of the World Gold Council was initially placed on Hong Kong, and in Mainland China, the main work was to expand the consumption of gold jewelry. With

6 An Encounter on the Road to Internationalization

the progress of gold marketization reform in China, the focus of the World Gold Council has gradually shifted to Beijing. In 1999, the People's Bank of China initiated the preparatory work for construction of gold market, and the decision for promotion of gold market reform was in line with the purpose of the World Gold Council, so that the World Gold Council gave active cooperation. In order to promote the gold marketization reform and build the gold market, the People's Bank of China also needed to understand and learn from the experience of development of international gold markets, and thus needed a channel to connect with international gold markets. Therefore, the World Gold Council took on the right role and got connected with the gold marketization reform in China at the right time.

The supporting works carried out by World Gold Council in the preparation period of China's gold market involve the following three aspects: The first is establishing the work relationship with the relevant personnel of the People's Bank, and bringing forth suggestions and carrying out discussions on a regular basis for the establishment of China's gold market; the second is providing the intellectual support for gold marketization reform in China, and assisting the Development Research Center and the National Economy Research Institute under the State Council submitting the special research reports; the third is helping to introduce the London gold tax system plan so as to lay a theoretical foundation for the shift of VAT policies in China. In 2002 when Shanghai Gold Exchange was opened, the consulting and communication services of the World Gold Council were terminated.

Thereafter, the role of World Gold Council was changed to assist the transformation of gold jewelry processing and retail industries in China and upgrade the quality of gold jewelry products. This is because that, in the early days of the new century, with the development getting frustrated, the Chinese gold jewelry industry suffered "cold winter", and in order to get out of trouble, their products would be improved and upgraded. Therefore, by making use of its advantage in internationalization, the World Gold Council

Chinese Gold: From Following to Surpassing

which has established the close cooperation with many Chinese gold jewelry enterprises began to help the Chinese gold jewelry enterprises make the gold jewelry fashionable. In this process, the World Gold Council played an enlightening and leading role.

The USD crisis in 2008 caused the global economic crisis, and the international environment was changed greatly. The market expansion work carried out by World Gold Council started to shift from gold consumption to gold investment, and meanwhile, the internal management mechanism was also adjusted. As a result, in 2011, the World Gold Council adjusted its representative offices in China, weakening the work in China. In 2015, Wang Lixin, who once served as the general manager of China District of World Gold Council, returned to World Gold Council as the managing director of China District. The work of the World Gold Council in China returned to normal. At that time, the China's gold market entered a new development stage, so that the cooperation between the World Gold Council which always paid attention to the development of China's gold market and the relevant parties of the China's gold market was raised to a new height.

China Gold Group became a former member of World Gold Council in 2017, and Shandong Gold Mining Group also became a member in 2019. In 2018, the World Gold Council specially established the China Committee, with Song Xin, the chairman of China Gold Group, acting as the chairman. This further strengthens the interaction with the gold industry of China. The World Gold Council and the China Gold Association jointly hosted the biennial China International Gold Conference, which has been held for three times; in 2018, they also jointly hosted the annual Shanghai International Gold Investment Conference. The platform for communication between China's gold market and international markets was established through the holding of these conferences. Since 2008, the uncertainty arising from USD crisis has triggered a huge change in the financial market, so that at the China International Gold Conference in 2018, the World Gold Council issued a special report on the development of the China's gold market in the following 5 years. In March 2019, the first place that the new CEO David Tait visited after assuming such post was China, and he visited Shanghai Gold Exchange, Shanghai Futures Exchange, China Gold Group and Shandong Gold Mining Group successively. After learning about the contact between the World Gold Council and the China's gold market over the past more than 20 years, we can understand why Aram Shishmanian, the former CEO of the World Gold Council, paid special attention to the development of China's gold market and made a high appraisal.

6.3 An international perspective

In April 2017, Aram Shishmanian's speech in Shenzhen started as follows: "Looking back to the Millennium, there was almost no sign of China in the international gold market. The gold output of mines and smelters in China was about 200 tons, while the gold manufactured and consumed in China was about 200 tons, and the scale of recycling market was very small. China's import & export volume was very small, there was little connection between the domestic gold market and other regions around the world, and few foreigners cared about the gold market here. Today, China is no longer what it was, and the significant change has taken place. Over the past 15 years, China's gold market has achieved great development. Thanks to the prudently-formulated strategy and the clear policies, the gold industry has been promoted to its present position from an industry which was strictly controlled and lack of liquidity."

The rapid development of the China's gold market is really an obvious characteristic, and the positive appraisal given by Aram Shishmanian for development of China's gold market is also based on this, so that it is not surprising. What is surprising is his expectation on future development of China's gold market. He believed that: "China is about to enter the new development stage - it is ready to take over the leading banner of global gold market and grasp all opportunities and responsibilities arising therefrom. On the

Chinese Gold: From Following to Surpassing

basis of this leading position, China will help the global gold market determine its future structure and composition."

Obviously, Aram Shishmanian gave the China's gold market a great praise, but this praise did not immediately get a warm response from the domestic industry. Though catching up with or surpassing the traditional London gold market or the emerging New York gold market is not the goal put forward by us publicly, it is really an invisible goal. In 2016, the two-way gold trading scale in China exceeded 120,000 tons, setting a historical record of the China's gold market. In term of one-way trading, its trading scale of 62,900 tons was not of the same order of magnitude as the trading scale of London gold market and New York gold market. In such year, the trading volume of London gold market was 154,000 tons, and the trading volume of New York Commodity Exchange exceeded that of London gold market and reached 185,600 tons. Therefore, the trading scale of China's gold market was only 40.8% of that of London market and only 33.9% of that of New York Commodity Exchange. From the perspective of trading scale, the China's gold market still lagged far behind them, and was even not at the same level as them, so that the China's gold market was still a follower, how could it be said as a "leader"? Therefore, many people regarded Aram Shishmanian's speech as flattering China. It is likely that, we had seen so many foreign skeptics about China, so that we were not used to and even felt suspicious of the affirmation from Aram Shishmanian.

To this end, in July 2017, I, together with other professionals, held a symposium about innovation in gold market in Capital University of Economics and Business. The theme of this symposium is "Is China ready to be the leader of gold market?" The holding of this symposium is a response to Aram Shishmanian's speech and an answer to "Is China ready?" At that time, I had such a basic understanding that, first of all, we should make clear what the connotation of leader is. I believe that, the conclusion drawn by Aram Shishmanian that "the China's gold market is a leader" is the results of international comparison. Therefore, we need an

6 An Encounter on the Road to Internationalization

international perspective. From the international perspective, we may have the different feeling; from another perspective, we may have a new understanding on us. This is obviously a useful discussion.

At the symposium, I pointed out in my speech that, the China's gold market should form its own core competitiveness, namely its irreplaceable uniqueness in international gold market system. The trading scale is replaceable, so that it is competitiveness but not core competitiveness. Therefore, I believe that Aram Shishmanian's focus is not placed on scale. What is that? He pointed out in his speech: "Today, all people's eyes are firmly locked on China. The world is focusing on China, where there is the largest market for gold ornaments, gold bars and gold coins; the gold ETF has been issued; Shanghai Gold Exchange set up the international board to encourage overseas institutions to participate in the gold market, and published the gold benchmark price in RMB at this time last year - 'Shanghai Gold'. In addition, a series of new gold businesses have also been launched in China successively. This year, we witnessed the cooperation between ICBC and Tencent to launch the innovative product 'WeChat Gold', with 800 million WeChat users becoming the potential gold buyers. Shanghai Gold Exchange has set up a reliable online platform 'E-jintong (Common People's Gold)' to help people buy gold more easily."

Here, Aram Shishmanian expressed his concern about the China's gold market. What he focused on was not the trading scale of the China's gold market, but the following three directions: The first was the largest physical gold market in the world; the second was the emergence of RMB factor in gold market; the third was the application of new technologies promoted the innovation of products. From the respective of international comparison, why did Aram Shishmanian pay attention to the development of the China's gold market in such three aspects? What is their value? As a matter of fact, Aram Shishmanian's praise for the China's gold market is more a reflection of Aram Shishmanian in the face of development crisis of international gold market. What happened to the international gold market?

6.4 "Our teachers" are meeting their "Waterloo"

London gold market and New York gold market are the backbone markets of the contemporary international gold market system. They are the two markets that support the binary pattern of international gold market, and are our models and catch-up goals. However, with the setback in development, they are now meeting their Waterloo.

6.4.1 London gold market is beset by scandals

London gold market is an over-the-counter market, and it is market maker who supports the continuous trading in this market. The market maker provides continuous buying and selling prices, and carries out two-way trading of buying and selling. The trading price takes the price of London Gold generated in secret room as basis, and now the basis goes wrong. This pricing system was born in 1909. After one hundred years' erosion, this pricing system was full of flaws, and finally the crisis broke out in 2013. The cause of crisis is that, in 2004, the person in charge of precious metal trading of Barclays Bank, which bought the London gold market maker seat from Roth-child Bank at a "cabbage price" of USD 1 million, signed a gambling agreement: If the gold price exceeds USD 1,558.96 per ounce, Barclays Bank has to pay USD 3.9 million to customer; if the gold price is lower than USD 1,558.96 per ounce, Barclays Bank is not required to pay such amount. Therefore, the person in charge of precise metal trading of Barclays Bank falsified a large number of short orders to decrease the gold price before pricing, and then threw the false short orders in the pricing process. Finally, he not only won the gambling, but also made the improper profits of USD 1.7 million. However, he was caught in the act and the bank was fined USD 290 million. Barclays Bank is not the only perpetrator. In 2014, the financial authority of Germany conducted an investigation on fraud of Deutsche Bank in the gold pricing process. In order to prevent the spread of negative impact arising from such investigation, Deutsche Bank reached a settlement with the financial authority of Germany

6　An Encounter on the Road to Internationalization

and announced its withdrawal from the formulation of benchmark price of London Gold as of 2015. The scandals exposed may be just the tip of the iceberg. Swiss Credit Bank and the pricing chairman UK Roth-child Bank withdrew from this hotbed of scandals in 2002 and 2004 respectively. At the end of 2014, UK Intercontinental Exchange beat London Metal Exchange and Chicago Commodity Exchange in competition, and won the management right of London gold price. The new pricing mechanism is that, Intercontinental Exchange will provide the electronic price platform, and then the trading and accounting settlement will be carried out according to the pricing procedure. The traditional way of pricing in secret room by telephone has been abolished, and the traditional London gold pricing mechanism has completed its historical mission.

　　The pricing reform of London Gold has not made the London gold market out of trouble completely. The opacity of the London gold market has not changed fundamentally, and it has been criticized that the reform for improving the transparency and standardization of the market is much said and little done. The investors' distrust of the market has not been completely eliminated, and the number of market makers is decreasing. Barclays Bank and Industrial Bank have exited. Scotiabank Bank also is preparing for exit. Now, there are only 12 market makers left. Since its trading volume has been exceeded by that of New York, London gold market gave up the first place and took the second place. The glory of London gold market as the world leader is dim.

6.4.2　New York gold market also fails to keep its nose clean

　　Established in 1975, New York gold market is the product of abolishing gold control and promoting gold marketization, and is a floor trading market. The floor trading market is more transparent and more strictly-regulated than over-the-counter market. Now, the trading scale of New York gold market has exceeded London market and become the largest gold market in the world, and it seems that it will hold high the banner of leader of global gold market. However, New York market, which grew up in the environment during

Chinese Gold: From Following to Surpassing

the 1980s in which the regulation was ignored, the leverage was increased and the scale was emphasized, also fails to keep its nose clean.

New York gold market is different from London gold market. Its main function is to manage the risks in gold trading risk rather than deliver the gold, and it serves the expansion of usefulness of USD, so that the main participants are large investment institutions and hedge funds. These large investment institutions and hedge funds have no background for actual use of gold, but use the change in gold price to make speculative profits, and they mainly achieve the profit-making purpose by creating the fluctuation of market price through long short contract game. For the sake of profit making, some market participants collude with each other to create false trading so as to influence or manipulate the change of gold price in the direction in favor of themselves, which constitutes a crime.

In 2015, the judicial department of USA, in cooperation with Commodity Futures Trading Commission, initiated the investigation into more than 10 institutions mainly engaged in gold trading, including large international banks such as Deutsche Bank, Standard Chartered, Barclays, HSBC and Scotia as well as large investment institutions such as UBS, Morgan Stanley and Goldman Sachs. In 2018, the Commodity Futures Trading Commission of USA finally held that three banks, namely UBS, Deutsche Bank and HSBC, conducted the illegal acts such as fraud and gold price manipulation, and imposed a fine of millions to tens of millions of USD.

There were also gold price manipulation and fraud in New York gold futures market, which indicates that New York gold market also has structural defect in market system. The design of New York gold futures market itself is a market that has nothing to do with the actual demand of gold and a gaming platform for gold price, and the success or failure of gold price game is determined by intelligence of human beings. Since it is a game, there must be rules of the game and the game must be bound by rules. However, the human beings often do not consciously accept the constraints, and in the absence of external constraints, the human beings will deviate from the original game rules and make mistakes or crimes based on the instinct of seeking profits. Therefore, the absence or weakening of regulation is the reason for deviant behaviors. This is also the system defect of gold futures market. The cause of such system defect can be traced back to the financial innovation period in the 1980s.

6.4.3 Why Aram Shishmanian gave the thumbs-up to China ?

Aram Shishmanian's praise for the China's gold market must be based on international coordinates, and the attention was paid to China only after problems occurred to the international dominant markets. While visiting China for the first time, the current CEO of World Gold Council unabashedly expressed his disappointment with the slow pace of adjustment and reform of such traditional trading markets, and pinned great hope on advancement of China's gold market. Against this big background, we can understand why Aram Shishmanian, the former CEO of World Gold Council, said that China will lead the future of international gold market.

The development of international gold market has to face up to the historical events that will take place. There are many causes of change, such as the modification of policies, the modification of consumers, the modification of capital market and the emergence of new technologies, but the core modification is the modification of market structure. The international gold markets are developed in the international monetary system with USD as the central currency, and the function of gold markets is to serve the smooth operation of this currency system, so that the USA government has become the "visible hand" for development of international gold markets: in the period when the gold was linked with USD, the function of gold markets was to achieve the stability of USD value through the balance of supply-demand relationship in gold markets; after the decoupling of gold and USD, the function is to expand the using scope of USD through the pricing of gold and USD, so as to achieve

Chinese Gold: From Following to Surpassing

the sustainable usefulness of USD. However, the contemporary international center currency is changing from unitary to pluralistic, so that the macro environment for development of international gold markets has changed or is about to change. This change is a fundamental change, and its essence is that the power center of the world is changing from unitary to pluralistic. In order to adapt to this change, the further development of gold market needs reform, and the reform needs a leader. The development of China's gold market has taken its own unique road and has good performance. It also means that the development of China's gold market has provided an actual case for the reform of international gold market. Therefore, "All people's eyes are firmly locked on China".

In order to strengthen the function of USD usefulness, the contemporary gold markets have continuously promoted the trading of gold derivatives, and thus the trading function of gold markets has been seriously alienated. Only 1% of market trading is real physical gold trading, while 99% is currency flow dominated by USD. The traditional gold markets in Europe and USA are the promoters of this trend, and have lost the function to gather gold wealth. Therefore, in the eyes of the World Gold Council, the emergence of China as a new RMB physical gold trading center may be a leader to inhibit and resist the virtual trading of USD gold and promote the return of gold trading function, which is in line with the restructuring of social wealth pattern. This may be the reason why Aram Shishmanian first pays attention to the growth of physical gold trading in China!

The gold products priced with RMB promote the opening up and internationalization of China's gold market, so that from our own perspective, this is required by RMB internationalization, but from the perspective of the World Gold Council, this is a move to break the domination of USD in gold market. Therefore, the China's gold market is the leader for international gold markets to get adapted to the multi-center currency development trend, and thus Aram Shishmanian pays special attention to the International Board and Shanghai Gold. Because the launch of RMB-priced gold products

6 An Encounter on the Road to Internationalization

and trading platform is the actual measure taken for promoting the multi-currency pricing reform for international gold market, it still has the meaning and value of directional indication, even if it is only a preliminary exploration.

The emergence of new technologies changes the social life of human beings, and also changes the trading mode of human beings. Therefore, the World Gold Council is very concerned about the impact imposed by new technologies on development of gold market. However, any new technology has a process of development and maturity, and the use of new technology also involves risks. Therefore, the People's Bank of China is prudently supporting the application of new technologies in gold trading, which means that it allows trial and error, but will, if any problem is found, immediately stop the trial or settle such problem. At present, the world is full of the noise and temptation of new technologies, but not so many can take root. As a result, Aram Shishmanian pays special attention to the innovation of "WeChat Gold" and "E-jintong" products in the China's gold market. What he saw is the example the China's gold market has provided the example of application of new technologies, so that from the point of view of the World Gold Council, the China's gold market is a market with innovation vitality, and can play a demonstration and leading role for the future of international gold market.

The conclusion drawn by Aram Shishmanian that the China's gold market will lead the development of international gold markets is based on his strong dissatisfaction with the fact that the traditional gold markets have lost their development direction and their weakness in reform. When visiting China for the first time, the newly-appointed CEO David Tait also expressed his disappointment towards the old gold markets without any hesitation: They are conservative and unwilling to reform, the information is not transparent, and the fraud occurs one after another. Therefore, the World Gold Council places its hope on the China's gold market. This shows that the two CEOs of the World Gold Council have the same understanding, and this consistency also comes from the same

Chinese Gold: From Following to Surpassing

perspective.

After the frequent occurrence of scandals in trade gold market, the reconstruction has began, and the reconstruction is now still in the initial exploration stage. In the sense of reform, the traditional markets and the emerging latecomers are on the same starting line. In this transformation time, whoever has innovation ability can get adapted to change as soon as possible and thus occupy the commanding point of future market and decide the structure and composition of future international gold market. Therefore, the China's gold market with innovation ability will be the leader of future market development mode. This is the basic connotation of "leader" in the speech of Aram Shishmanian.

6.4.4 How should we understand ourselves?

The appraisal from the World Gold Council gives us an international visual angle, and we also should re-understand ourselves from this international visual angle. We have pointed out that the China's gold market is a product of top-level design from "visible hand", which is the most important Chinese feature. At present, however, there are serious differences in the evaluation of role of "visible hand" and "invisible hand" on economic development, so that there are different evaluation standards for how to evaluate the development road of China's gold market, and the different evaluation standards will lead to different conclusions. Not only in international community, but also in China, there are two opinions. Especially, the public opinion that denies the development road with Chinese characteristics is rampant, and attacking China is regarded as the fashion. The attack focuses on the strict regulation on financial market by China, and the economic development road under the control of strong government is a wrong way. For the free market economic theorists in western countries, it is an unacceptable way. If we get developed by taking this way, we deny the western free market economic development road, so that the western countries feel unprecedented pressure on their selection of development road. However, they

6 An Encounter on the Road to Internationalization

can't ignore the fact that the western free market economic road does have problems and need reform and innovation. The London gold market and the New York gold market is the learning model of the China's gold market as a latecomer, but over recent years, the fraud scandals broke out one after another, and their great image collapsed. They have learned from the bitter experience that the "invisible hand" cannot cure all kinds of diseases, there are defects in system, and self purification efficiency of market is very low, so that they need the "visible hand" to play a role. Internationally, the market regulation system has been rebuilt and the market regulation has been strengthened. To a certain extent, this shows the self salvation carried out by western countries after the outbreak of global economic crisis in 2008. The *Basel II* finally reached by them through repeated discussions proposes to strengthen the regulation of banks and stabilize the finance. Therefore, the said agreement upgrades gold to the class-1 asset of banks. The *Markets in Financial Instruments Directive* implemented as of January 2018 also expands the regulation on financial market. In contrast, in the development of China's gold market, we have put risk management in the first place from the beginning, ensured the openness and fairness of trading as well as the transparency of trading information, and eliminated the unhealthy DNA, so as to ensure the health of market and avoid the same mistake. Therefore, when the international gold markets are still groping out of crisis, the China's gold market has embarked on the rapid development road. This contrast is impressive. The fact in development of China's gold market proves the necessity and effectiveness of top-level design from "visible hand", and provides the experience for establishment and strengthening of international gold market regulation system. In this regard, we are changed from a student to a teacher, so that we are valued by those who understand that the development of western free market economy needs reform. The development results of the China's gold market, which has not taken the development road of free market economy, are affirmed in the eyes of western reformers. This makes us more confident in our system. Of course, the self-confidence of system is not the reason for

Chinese Gold: From Following to Surpassing

stagnation, but the driving force for continuous development. This is my understanding. Maybe it is beyond the original intention of the speech given by Aram Shishmanian, but I want to tell the story about Chinese gold in accordance with my understanding.

7
A Diversified Market System

China's gold market is undoubtedly impressive for its speed of development, the trading scale has ranked among the world's top three in just 17 years, thus rewriting the dual market pattern of the international gold market, at the same time the structure of China's gold market itself also has transformed from single market into multiple market. The reason for the formation of the structure of our country's gold market itself is a "system" problem, in the international perspective of observation, multiple market system is also one of the Chinese characteristics of the country's gold market, it constitutes a scale element of the country's gold market and is the driving force to support the country's expansion of gold scale. The gold market of all countries in the world today has two different structures, one is the specialized single market structure, the other is the specialized multi-market structure. The former indicates that a country only has a single-function specialized gold market, and the latter is that a country has more than one specialized gold markets with different functions.

7.1 Specialized Single Gold Market Structure

The entire international gold market is a multifaceted market system, but it is not necessarily so when it comes to a specific country.The international gold market system gradually forms in the background of division of labor based on specialization, so each country's gold market is a specialized market, even if there are two markets, there is always a market that exists temporarily, or as a marginal market, and the other market is the dominant one, and the dominant market function is a single function of specialization, and its deficient function is made up through the international market, because this market structure is a result of international competition and a product of global resource allocation.

The most heavily traded gold market is currently the New York Mercantile Exchange (NYMEX), with a trading volume of 226,900 tonnes in 2017. It is an on-market gold futures contract trading market and a forward trading market for gold derivatives. The Chicago Mercantile Exchange in the U.S. also had gold futures contract trading from 1975 to 1988, after which there was no longer gold futures trading. The United States used to be the world's first gold-producing country and is now the fourth gold-producing country, but there is no active real gold spot trading market in the country, physical gold trading is completed through participation in the international market, and the transaction of most of the mineral gold is completed through the Swiss market, so the U.S. gold market is a single gold derivatives forward trading market.

The trading volume of the London Gold Market was once the first in the world and is now the second. It is an over-the-counter spot gold trading market, trading through the market maker quotation (Both buying price and selling price), but London also once had an floor gold exchange - the London Metal Exchange, but its gold trading had stopped in the 1990s. On the occasion of the gold price manipulation scandal of London over-the-counter market, the floor gold forward trading products are released, but from the current point of view, this practice is still difficult to shake the original market pattern, and the London Gold Market will still maintain the single market pattern dominated by the original over-the-counter spot gold market.

Based on global resource allocation, the gold market established thereafter are basically specialized single function markets. Although Japan and India do not have a strong gold production capacity, they have a strong gold processing and consumption capacity, and they do not have a well regulated independent gold spot trading

7 A Diversified Market System

market, but only floor gold futures markets which are important gold trading center markets in Asia. However, the trading volume of Japan's gold futures market in 2017 was less than 10,000 tons, and that of India was less than 5,000 tons. Japan and India have not made any progress in the gold market despite more than 20 years of development, they have retrogressed instead and cannot be compared with the gold market in China. The gold markets in Dubai and Istanbul have only a few hundred tons of trading volume, so the Asian gold market group with China's gold market as the center has been initially formed. From a global point of view, each year, the 300,000 to 400,000 tons of trading volume is mainly concentrated in the three gold markets in New York, London and Shanghai. In 2017, the total trading volume of global gold markets was 469,000 tons, an increase of 9.58% over 2016, the highest record in history. The trading volume of New York Gold Market was 234,500 tons, accounting for 50% of the total trading volume, the trading volume of London Gold Market was 165,600 tons, accounting for 35.31% of the total trading volume, the trading volume of Shanghai Gold Market was 50,700 tons (Unidirectional), accounting for 10.81% (14.71% in 2016). The total proportion of the above three markets was 96.12%, which shows that these three markets are the leading markets in the international gold market system in terms of trading scale. In these three markets, New York and London adopt a specialized single market structure, only Shanghai Gold Market chooses a specialized multi-market structure, and this unique market structure is an important reason for the rapid growth in trading scale of China's gold market. There are comparisons before there is a judgment, so the development of China's gold market has drawn so much attention. The fast development is an aspect of concern, more importantly, we take a path that is different from the international gold market, as mentioned above, many countries in the international gold market follow "single corps" professional development, or a single market structure, and we favor "multi-corps" gold market professional development, or a market system composed of multiple markets. Whether a single-market structure or multiple-market structure is more conducive to the future development of the gold market will be assessed by future practice, but the emergence of this kind of alternative gold market in China provides a comparative coordinates for the two kinds of development paths.

7.2 Segmented Development of Our Gold Market

Ours is a multi-market gold market system not formed at the very beginning, but a product of a market constantly segmented. There were two main reasons for the segmentation of our gold market: One was the demand; the other was the existence of "system" conditions. The development of China's gold market was not pulled by free competition, but by demand. Because China's population was large, the demand was diversified, in order to meet the diversified needs, the gold market functions gradually diversified, the products gradually diversified, requiring more than one corresponding professional markets. But the establishment of an all-round gold market was not an option that had been ruled out from the beginning, China's sector-based financial management system forms constrained on this option, this was because of multiple system reasons of China's multiple gold market forms, so China's gold market was not constantly concentrated, forming a monopoly, but continuously segmented as driven by the demand. The multiple specialized markets coped with diversified demands, and eventually formed a gold market system consisting of multiple specialized markets.

In 2002, Shanghai Gold Exchange was opened, it was a gold commodity exchange, and the main purpose of this market was to complete the transformation of the gold trading mode from the uniform collection and distribution of the People's Bank of China to free market trading, but the marketization of the gold commodity was only a small part of the gold marketization because the trading volume of gold with commodity properties in the total trading volume of the international gold market only accounted for less than

7 A Diversified Market System

1%, so the operation of Shanghai Gold Exchange meant that only less than 1% of the gold trading was marketized and the rest 99% of financial gold trading was not. After Shanghai Gold Exchange opened, the People's Bank of China requested it to transform to the gold financial market after the transformation of the gold trading method was stabilized. After that, the People's Bank of China requested China's gold market to realize three transformations in 2004, and the transformation to the financial market was one of them. So in 2004, after two years of operation, Shanghai Gold Exchange began to transform into a financial market, and thus launched gold spot deferred products, which were gold financial products serving institutional investors. This change in the percentage of products traded signified the extent to which Shanghai Gold Exchange has transformed itself into a financial market. In 2008, Au (T + D) series products accounted for 72.5% of the total, becoming the dominant trading variety and marking the transformation of Shanghai Gold Exchange from a commodity gold market to a financial gold market. However, from an overall perspective, the financial transformation of China's gold market needed to be further deepened - from institutional participation to the participation of the general public, thus creating the demand for the establishment of a gold retail market. The construction of a gold trading platform for the general public started at the same time as the transformation of Shanghai Gold Exchange in 2004, because at the end of 2004 the CBRC approved the four major state-owned commercial banks to carry out gold investment business for the general public, so the gold investment products for the general public were also pushed to the market one after another. That was the first segmentation of China's gold market, that was, the segmentation from the commodity gold market and the financial gold market. The segmentation presented a commercial bank over-the-counter gold trading market. Because the commercial bank gold business was supervised by the CBRC, forming a difference from Shanghai Gold Exchange supervised by the central bank, the market segmentation realized not only the segmentation between the gold commodity market and the gold

Chinese Gold: From Following to Surpassing

financial market, but also the segmentation between the gold retail market and the gold wholesale market.

After the successful financial transformation of the spot gold market of Shanghai Gold Exchange, it was necessary to promote the launch of gold futures contracts, a more important gold financial forward product. Shanghai Gold Exchange put the launch of this product on the agenda in 2007. Because the market price of gold is floating up and down, and has great uncertainty, this uncertainty brings speculators profit opportunities to buy low and sell high, but also brings investment risk to investors. Market risks will not be eliminated, but can be locked or avoided, and locking and avoiding market risks is mainly realized in the forward market using derivatives transactions. Based on the need for market risk management, promoting the development of the forward gold trading market is necessary and reasonable. Originally, the gold futures contract was only listed on Shanghai Gold Exchange as a new product, but because the futures market was under the supervision of the CSRC, the gold futures contract would be out of bounds if it was listed on Shanghai Gold Exchange, and finally, on January 8, 2008, the gold futures contract was traded on Shanghai Futures Exchange, which marked the completion of the second segmentation of China's gold market, that was, the segmentation of the gold spot market and the gold forward market. The segmentation also advanced the segmentation of the real gold spot trading market and the gold forward contract trading market. Therefore, in addition to the spot gold trading market of Shanghai Gold Exchange and the over-the-counter gold trading market of commercial banks, there was another gold forward trading market that operated in Shanghai Futures Exchange.

In 2010, the central bank and other six ministries and commissions jointly issued *Opinions on Promoting the Development of the Gold Market*, which described the development of the gold market as follows: "After the abolition of the policy of unified collection and distribution, China's gold market has developed rapidly, and initially formed a pattern of common development of the gold business of

7 A Diversified Market System

Shanghai Gold Exchange, the gold business of commercial banks and the gold futures business of Shanghai Futures Exchange and a good situation of synergistic development with the gold industry."

Some people have doubts about China's market development environment that is gradually opened up and with a top-level design, they believe that this will exclude competition and make the development of the gold market lose momentum, they advocate that China's gold market development shall introduce more sufficient competition. However, the multi-specialized market system formed under China's "system" conditions is not without competition, instead, it turns the homogeneous competition in the same market competition into competition among multiple markets with parallel development, reduce resource depletion caused by excessive disorderly competition, increase the positive energy of competition, thus promoting the service functions of China's gold market. Compared with the current state of the international gold market, China's gold market has the richest product supply, the most diverse trading methods and the most convenient gold logistics, which is the positive effect produced by China's diversified and specialized gold market system and is increasingly producing an international demonstration effect. The conversion from one market to multiple markets is not only an increase in quantity, but also forms mutually influencing market systems with different functions and parallel development. So our gold market has the richest forms, the most perfect functions, enriching the form the international gold market system exists and creating a new era of the development of the gold market.

7.3 Moving forward in a Complementary Manner

Shanghai Gold Exchange, Shanghai Futures Exchange and commercial banks' over-the-counter gold trading market are the three major trading platforms of China's gold market system, because each of these three trading platforms has its own service function positioning and participation groups, and China's gold market has formed a complementary development pattern.

7.3.1 Shanghai Gold Exchange: The Core Market that Promotes China's Gold Marketization Reform

Shanghai Gold Market was established in 2002, or 17 years ago, as the first gold market in China. At the beginning of the establishment, it was a gold commodity trading platform, although now it is China's physical gold transaction center, from the structure of the trading volume, it is already a financial attribute dominated spot multi-metal trading market. Shanghai Gold Exchange is the core market of China's gold market system, the reason why it is the core market, not only because it is the basic market of China's gold market system and bearing the main responsibility of China's gold transaction and circulation, but also because it is the main promoter and leader of China's gold market reform. It almost became the source of China's gold market reform since 2002, and has constantly released new reform and innovation projects. The Shanghai Gold Exchange has not only promoted its own development, but also won international reputation for China's gold market. It is the product of the top-level design of China's "visible hands" and a market directly supervised by the central bank, so it is deeply marked with Chinese characteristics.

■ Scale Expansion of Shanghai Gold Exchange

Since Shanghai Gold Exchange opened for business on October 30, 2002, the trading scale has continued to grow and showed an accelerating trend. In the first several years since its operation, or from 2002 to 2005, the trading scale was only at the level of 100 tons; in 2006, it rose to the level of 1,000 tons, or 1,249.6 tons specifically. After seven years of development, the scale made a breakthrough and the trading volume exceeded 10,000 tons in 2013, amounting to 11,600 tons. Although Shanghai Gold Exchange is now China's largest gold trading market, the world's second-largest spot gold trading market and the world's third-largest gold

7 A Diversified Market System

market, its performance was not outstanding from 2002 to 2013, and every year after 2013 the growth in trading volume was almost at the 10,000-ton level, so between 2014 and 2018, the scale of gold trading ascended to five tonnage steps of 20,000 tons, 30,000 tons, 40,000 tons, 50,000 tons and 60,000 tons respectively, and the trading volume in 2018 was 67,500 tons, which was 143.6 times the trading volume of 470 tons in 2003, the average annual incremental growth rate from 2014 to 2018 was as high as 45.5%, and such extraordinary development made Shanghai Gold Exchange the star drawing global attention. The change in the trading volume of Shanghai Gold Exchange is shown in Figure 7-1. The change at the cultural level is that the Chinese people have completed a re-creation of the gold wealth culture against the backdrop of the dollar crisis, resulting in strong gold consumption and investment behavior, which has led to a continuous high level of gold trading after 2013, especially benefiting Shanghai Gold Exchange, which has a background in physical gold transactions.

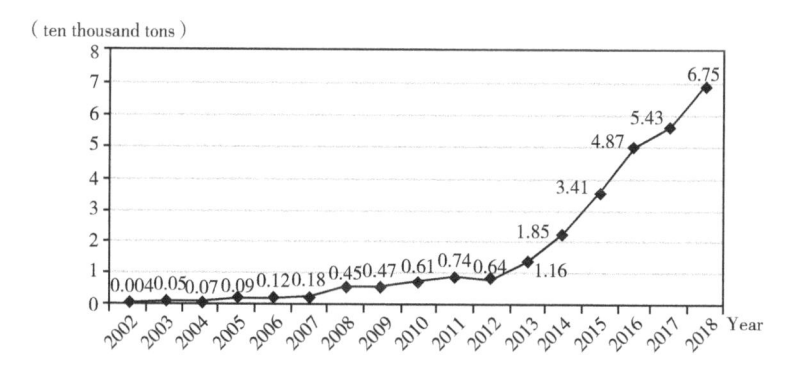

Figure 7-1 Changes in Trading Volume at Shanghai Gold Exchange
Source: *China Gold Market Report (2002-2018)*.

Scale is a factor of competitiveness, though not the core competitiveness of development. It is because of the continuous expansion of the trading scale that Shanghai Gold Exchange has turned from an unknown marginal market into an increasingly concerned market:

Chinese Gold: From Following to Surpassing

In 2006, Shanghai Gold Exchange became the world's largest spot trading floor market with a trading volume of 1249.6 tons; in 2013, the trading volume exceeded 10,000 tons and reached 11,600 tons, making it one of the central markets in Asia and starting the super-long growth period with an annual growth of trading volume of over 10,000 tons; in 2017, the trading volume of Shanghai Gold Exchange, which was 54,300 tons, exceeded that of Shanghai Futures Exchange's gold futures contract, or 39,000 tons, becoming China's largest gold market. In 2018, this momentum was maintained, with a year-on-year growth of 24.31%, making it the world's second largest gold trading floor market after New York. It can be said that Shanghai Gold Exchange's gold trading scale is already world-class, the further expansion of its scale has enhanced the position of Shanghai Gold Exchange in China's gold market system as an important symbol of the development of China's gold market. Moreover, the process of expansion in the trading volume of Shanghai Gold Exchange is also the process of its overall development and maturity, and it has gradually developed its own core competitiveness.

■ **The Market Development doesn't Stop at Scale**

The expansion of the trading scale of Shanghai Gold Exchange is an important symbol of its development, but its development does not stop at scale. The expansion of the scale of Shanghai Gold Exchange has become increasingly rich in connotation, and the process of its expansion is also a process of continuous enrichment and development of its social service functions. The expansion of the scale of Shanghai Gold Exchange presents the possibility of a qualitative breakthrough in the accumulation of quantity, so the expansion of the trading volume of Shanghai Gold Exchange has begun to transcend its own significance, created an increasing social radiating effect, led to the reform of China's financial market, made the gold market increasingly closely linked with the commodity, financial, securities and foreign exchange markets as an important factor in the reform and innovation of these markets. The greatest

7 A Diversified Market System

significance of the development of Shanghai Gold Exchange is that it has gradually turned China's gold market from a marginal market in the financial market into a fundamental market, which means that China's gold market has become an important part of the financial market. For the gold market, this is a qualitative change.

Shanghai Gold Exchange started from a commodity market, serves the central bank to complete the requirements of gold marketization, that is, the gold trading method changes from unified collection and distribution to free market trading, but this is only the primary goal of the gold market reform, and the return and strengthening of the financial properties of gold is deeper challenges brought by gold marketization. The long-term gold control make gold basically lose its liquidity, the financial properties of gold seriously shrinks, in more than half a century, gold has almost disappeared from China's financial market and the gold market has become an absentee even in college finance textbooks. How the gold market, previously an absentee, plays a role in the finance market is still a problem. Even if the gold control has been lifted, this problem will not be solved naturally. How the gold market integrates with the financial markets including the foreign exchange market, the monetary market, the fund market, the futures market and the insurance market is the key issue facing the development of the gold market, especially in China's separately managed financial markets, this integration is facing institutional obstacles. In 2004, Shanghai Gold exchange proposes to develop from a gold commodity market to a gold financial market, which not only indicated the direction of development of the gold market, but also presented an opportunity to address this issue thanks to the reform practices that began to integrate with the financial markets.

The institutional environment for the transformation of Shanghai Gold Exchange into a financial market is a separated financial market management system in which banks, securities, insurance, foreign exchange and currencies are under the supervision of different management departments. The transformation of Shanghai Gold Exchange into a financial market faces cross-border issues and sectoral barriers. Therefore, Shanghai Gold Exchange must first increase the liquidity of the existing spot trading market, that is to say, increase its own liquidity and the financial nature of gold spot trading, which is the background of the launch of the spot deferred Au (T+D) product and the first step towards the integration of the gold commodity market into the gold financial market.

The spot deferred Au (T+D) product is a kind of spot gold contract with a deferred delivery function and belongs to category of physical commodity gold trading, because of the deferral function, it is provided with the financial function of transferring and managing market risks, thus expanding the range of participation groups of market spot trading, and improving the liquidity of gold. The gold deferred product was launched in 2004, and the kinds of product have increased from 1 to five. In 2008, Shanghai Gold Exchange's trading volume of physical commodity gold fell from 100% to 27.1%, while the trading volume of gold deferred contract rose from 4.65% to 72.5%, or from 665.3 tons to 4463.77 tons, an increase of 5.7 times, and in 2017, the proportion of the trading volume of gold deferred contract further increased to 87.75%. This marks the improvement of liquidity of Shanghai Gold Exchange and the strengthening of its financial attributes.

The launch of the gold spot deferred contract is the first cornerstone of Shanghai Gold Exchange's innovative development, and the decisive factor in the transformation of Shanghai Gold Exchange into a gold financial market. However, the gold market remains an isolated market without a high degree of integration with the financial markets. After the successful launch of the spot deferred gold contract, a more significant move was the launch of the gold futures contract in 2008, which extended Shanghai Gold Exchange from spot trading to forward trading, and this extension was suspected of overstepping the boundaries in the system of separated management and met with institutional resistance, which finally frustrated Shanghai Gold Exchange. This event demonstrates that the separate management system is a prerequisite for the integration of the gold market and the financial markets, and any

7 A Diversified Market System

development is done under this system. The financial system of separate management has two sides, one is restraint and the other is protection. Under the conditions of this system, Shanghai Gold Exchange does not stop pursuing development, instead, it adjusts the path of development from product innovation to platform innovation, so that financial products under the supervision of different departments can be traded on the gold market trading platform built by Shanghai Gold Exchange, and Shanghai Gold Exchange becomes a common market trading platform, thus dissolving the fetters of separate regulation.

The platform innovation is an effort of Shanghai Gold Exchange to create a personalized trading platform for investors to meet their individual needs. Investors can trade freely on this platform according to the rules, and Shanghai Gold Exchange endorses the legality and fairness of the transactions. The cross-border flow of gold under the conditions of separate management system has increased the social service capacity and social radiation of Shanghai Gold Exchange, which has now established a market maker inquiry and trading platform, an offshore Renminbi gold international trading platform and a "Shanghai Gold" pricing and trading platform in addition to the competitive trading platform. The gold market with a single trading platform has become a gold market with multiple trading platforms. The birth of the gold market with multiple trading platforms is of international leading significance, because so far, except for China, other gold markets in the world are all single trading platforms, so Shanghai Gold Exchange's multiple trading platform structure is one of the Chinese characteristics of China's gold market.

The opportunity and risk co-exist, so the reform is not only the reform direction and the choice of reform goals, but also to achieve the reform of risk control, construction characteristics of the trading platform to promote the reform of one reason is to enable the reform can start from a partial rather than comprehensive at once, which makes the reform of the risk is limited to a manageable range, so as to provide a comprehensive reform of the opportunity to trial and error, can not be done before. The Shanghai Gold Exchange can be the first to try it out on the special trading platform, so the Shanghai Gold Exchange has quickly strengthened its links with the money market, foreign exchange market, securities market, bond market and capital market through the construction of the special trading platform. Therefore, the participants of the Shanghai Gold Exchange are not only the supply and demand sides of gold, but also an increasing number of securities companies, currency companies, trust companies, financial service companies and commercial banks. They become members or special members and participate in gold trading, and gold becomes the tool and means of risk management and asset allocation for these non-gold institutions, and provides the benchmark for the design of market derivatives, thus China's gold market is beginning to become the fundamental market of the financial market system. The transformation of the Shanghai Gold Exchange into a gold financial market began with product innovation, and platform innovation is an upgrade of this transformation.

■ Gradual Internationalization of the Markets

Today, any gold market in pursuit of development should promote internationalization because gold is a global and continuously traded financial subject matter, and has the natural attribute of internationalization. China adheres to the implementation of the opening up policy, so the development of China's gold market should also take the road of internationalization. As early as in 2002 when Shanghai Gold Exchange opened for business, the central bank leadership put forward "to make China's gold market really an important part of the global gold integration market", that was to achieve internationalization. However, China's gold market is not suddenly internationalized, but in a gradual manner. The reason why internationalization is gradual is because it is related to the "system", and the transformation of China's economy to a market-oriented track is gradual. Shanghai Gold Exchange did not open to the public until 2008, when it began to attract members from foreign financial

7 A Diversified Market System

institutions. There are now eight foreign financial institutions trading on the main board of Shanghai Gold Exchange. In 2008, after six years of development, Shanghai Gold Exchange already became the world's largest spot gold trading floor market, and the trading scale was basically shaped.

Another bigger international initiative was the launch of Gold Exchange International Board in Shanghai Free Trade Zone in 2014, and the International Board allowed foreign institutions to use offshore Renminbi to participate in main board trading. By this time the Shanghai Gold Exchange had been in operation for 12 years, with a market size of 18,500 tonnes, and had developed into Asia's central gold market, while by 2018, Shanghai Gold Exchange International Board had 74 international members and 77 international clients in addition to its members. 6,500 tons of gold was traded annually, an increase of 37.09%, and 21,800 tons of silver was traded, an increase of 195.31%.

The launch of "Shanghai Gold" pricing and trading platform in 2016 pushed the internationalization of Shanghai Gold Exchange to a new stage: from the opening up of the market for gold trading to the open export of trading rules. By 2018, there had been 26 members and 33 institutional clients participating in "Shanghai Gold" trading, and Renminbi gold price had become the settlement price standard for overseas gold derivatives, and Renminbi-denominated gold futures contracts had been officially listed and traded in Dubai Gold Market and various commodity markets. In 2016, when "Shanghai Gold" pricing mechanism was open to the outside world, the trading scale of Shanghai Gold Exchange exceeded 30,000 tons, reached 48,700 tons, making Shanghai Gold Exchange an important gold market in the world, so there were conditions and competitiveness to enhance the opening up to the outside world.

The internationalization of Shanghai Gold Exchange was an initiative to open up after it has established its own market rules on the basis of its own scale and experience, including "inviting in" and "going out". Therefore, when we opened our doors and invited foreign investors to enter the China's gold market, we had the ability to start a dialogue with them on an equal footing, and our relationship with international investors was that of equal business partners rather than a teacher and a student. The gradual internationalization has provided Shanghai Gold Exchange with a relatively favorable environment for its development. It did not immediately enter into international competition at the early stage of its development, thus, in the "early years", it received a relatively "peaceful" opportunity for growth and development.

The internationalization measure that goes hand in hand with "inviting in" is "going out", in which Shanghai Gold Exchange and international gold markets have jointly developed new international products of "Shanghai Gold" and explore new modes of cooperation. Concrete results of cooperation with Dubai Commodity and Gold Exchange have been achieved, and cooperation discussions have been held with Yangon Exchange, Moscow Exchange, Deutsche Börse, Malaysian Derivatives Exchange and other foreign exchanges, and a memorandum of cooperation has been signed with Budapest Stock Exchange. Cooperation with countries along the "Belt and Road" is a priority choice for Shanghai Gold Exchange to "go out".

The above are the preliminary results of the internationalization of Shanghai Gold Exchange. It will be a long-term task for Shanghai Gold Exchange to continuously expand and deepen the breadth and depth of its internationalization. Although the internationalization of Shanghai Gold Exchange cannot be said to have been completed, it has taken a step forward in its communication and integration with the international gold market, it is no longer an unknown orphan but has become part of the international gold market system. In this sense, Shanghai Gold Exchange has achieved internationalization, and now the main problem facing the internationalization of Shanghai Gold Exchange is not only to attract foreign investors, but also how to play a more leading role in the international gold market. The conversion from a follower to a leader is the advanced stage of the internationalization of Shanghai Gold Exchange, that is, the stage of innovation and development. The path of development of Shanghai Gold Exchange will no longer be an imitation of the international gold market, but an innovative leadership. This is the common development situation and common task that not only for Shanghai Gold Exchange, but also for all gold trading platforms in China. In other words, the internationalization of China's gold market is on the eve of a qualitative change and the market will enter a different stage of development, so a new development thinking and a new top design are needed.

7.3.2 Shanghai Futures Exchange: A Market for Managing Risks

Shanghai Futures Exchange was established earlier than Shanghai Gold Exchange and is the second largest futures market in the world, with 16 commodity varieties currently traded. During the preparatory period in 2000, Shanghai Futures Exchange did research and preparatory work to promote the launch of gold products based on the prospect of business development, so after the central bank decided to promote the launch of gold futures contracts on Shanghai Gold Exchange, Shanghai Futures Exchange also started the launch filing of gold futures contracts.

■ Twists and Turns for the Launch of Gold Futures

China's development of gold futures market was included in the work agenda of the president of the People's Bank of China as a task for Shanghai Gold Exchange to transform into a gold market, and the initiative failed ultimately, one reason was that Shanghai Futures Exchange proposed to launch gold futures contracts at the same time to the CSRC, so two institutions applied for the same product, and the CSRC could decide with its authority. Finally, gold futures were not launched on Shanghai Gold Exchange, and Shanghai Futures Exchange completed the process of launch, which was related to the financial system of China's separate management.

The central bank is the traditional legal administrator of gold, the identity has not changed since the advancement of the gold market reform, and was written into the Banking Law. The futures market

Chinese Gold: From Following to Surpassing

is regulated by the CSRC, which is legalized by the promulgation of the *Futures Management Regulations*. So the launch of gold futures came under two authorities - the central bank and the CSRC, and Shanghai Gold Exchange and Shanghai Futures Exchange belonged respectively to these two authorities. Shanghai Futures Exchange submitted an application to the CSRC for the launch of gold futures according to the provisions of the *Futures Management Regulations* that the transactions of futures products were regulated by the CSRC, and the compliance of gold futures launched on Shanghai Gold Exchange was challenged by the CSRC, so the gold futures were finally launched on Shanghai Futures Exchange. Subtle differences have since emerged in the presentation of the relevant documents, with Shanghai Gold Exchange being labeled as a gold market approved by the State Council, while Shanghai Futures Exchange is labeled as a gold market approved by the State Council.

As an outsider, to prevent monopoly, I opposed the unitary market structure system and advocated the establishment of a diversified gold market system. I voted in favor of the launch of gold futures contracts on Shanghai Futures Exchange and published a 10,000-character article titled The Previous and Present of Gold Futures in the China Gold News at that time, the article was widely disseminated, and probably because of that, I was invited to attend the gold futures contract launch ceremony on January 8, 2008, and witnessed an important moment in the development of China's gold market. So far the gold futures contract has launched on Shanghai futures market, and China's multivariant gold market system took shape.

By 2018, gold futures contracts has been launched on Shanghai Futures Exchange for 10 years, but its 16 online varieties traded within Shanghai Futures Exchange were varieties with a small trading volume, and did not have the advantage of scale in front of some large varieties such as nonferrous metals and energy. The trading volume was fluctuating, and was declining in the recent two years, but gold futures itself is still showing a growth trend, and Shanghai Futures Exchange is the best performing gold futures

7 A Diversified Market System

market in Asia: In the first year of launch, the two-way volume was 7,780.9 tons; in 2011, it exceeded 10,000 tons and reached 14,400 tons; in 2014, it exceeded 40,000 tons; in 2015, it exceeded 50,000 tons and reached 50,600 tons; in 2016, it reached 69,500 tons, the highest volume in eight years of trading; in 2017, the trading volume fell 43.88% to 39,000 tonnes, as shown in Figure 7-2. The trading volume continued to decline by 17.95% to 32,000 tonnes in 2018. Shanghai Futures Exchange has become the second largest gold futures market and the third largest gold market in the world since 2012, and its gold futures trading volume was surpassed by Shanghai Gold Exchange in 2017, but it remained the second largest gold futures market in the world, while its ranking in the gold market moved back one place to the fourth largest gold market in the world.

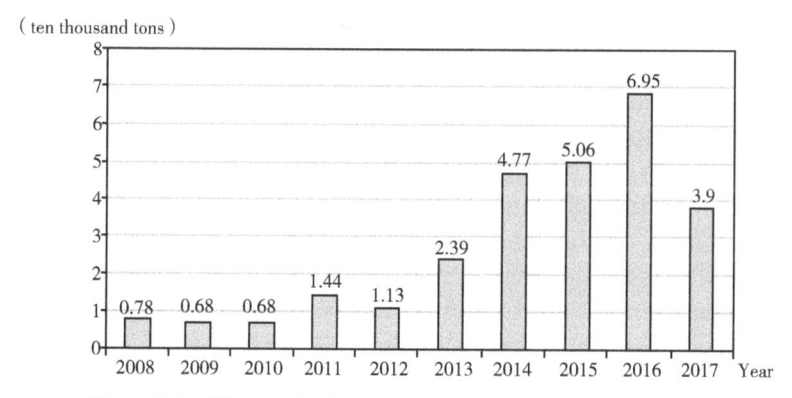

Figure 7-2 Changes in the Trading Volume of Gold Futures on Shanghai Futures Exchange

Source: *China Gold Market Report (2009-2018)*.

The launch of gold futures contracts on Shanghai Futures Exchange greatly boosted the growth of the trading scale of China's gold market, pulling China's gold trading volume to more than 10,000 tons in the first year of launch in 2008, reaching 13,975 tons, an increase of 496.35%. Although the proportion of gold futures in China's total gold trading volume has declined in recent years, it was China's largest gold trading market until 2017. The highest proportion was 67.2% in 2014, while in 2017 it fell to 38.85%. In the fixed thinking of pursuit of scale, trading volume has been the primary economic indicator of the development of Shanghai gold futures market, gold futures contracts have been fluctuating for more than 10 years since the launch, so how do we explain this phenomenon?

■ **Values of Launch of Gold Futures**

We need to understand the characteristics of gold futures to answer the question of what is the value of launching gold futures. Gold futures market is a new type of market that only appeared in the 1970s, it is different from the long-established spot gold market, of which the function is to complete the gold trading and transaction, realize circulation, produce gold logistics, and the gold futures market mains produces capital flow, and the resulting logistics generally accounts for only one thousandth of the total volume of transactions. So the function of the gold futures market is not to complete gold trading and transaction, but to manage price uncertainty risks through the capital flow adjustment, which is exactly why the gold futures market came into being when the gold price control was liberated and the fixed price system was changed to the floating gold price system. Once you have understood the characteristics of gold futures, you may also understand the value of gold futures contracts on Shanghai Futures Exchange. Its value is first of all to provide gold investors with the most convenient tool for risk management of market prices with the lowest transaction costs. The launch of gold futures contracts improves the ability of the gold market of China to transfer and avoid market risks, which plays an irreplaceable role in increasing the overall stability of China's gold market and protecting the development of China's gold industry chain. Gold futures trading market is a capital flow dominated market, with frequent capital flows. Shanghai Futures Exchange platform has multiple varieties of trading, and funds will find it very convenient to flow in and out the varieties and cause fluctuations of varieties in the trading. In the recent two years, gold prices are low

7 A Diversified Market System

and stable, there are few arbitrage opportunities, and the trading volume is naturally low. The frequent flow of funds in the futures market has also raised higher requirements on the ability of market investors to control their funds, making it a more suitable market for professionals to participate in. China's futures industry, which was born in the 1990s and witnessed 20 years of development, has provided a number of professionals to the gold futures market, so China's futures companies have become the main force in the gold futures market, with more than 80% of futures companies participating in gold futures trading every year.

■ Development Continues and Adjustment Is under Way

Our understanding of the peculiarities of the function of the gold futures market is gradually deepened in the course of practice, and with the deeper understanding of its characteristics, we also increase our ability to control the development of the market. In order to give full play to the gold futures market's function of managing market risks, Shanghai Futures Exchange begins to adjust its membership structure, explores and absorbs investment institutions and industry members, promotes links with industry to enhance the function of serving the gold industry. In 2017, 19 commercial banks and 4 large gold producers and processors have entered the market. Reform is continuing, the launch of gold futures and options has reached a critical momentum, and there are new initiatives for opening up.

Gold futures have been listed for 10 years, and the gold futures contract is China's first gold forward contract, a breakthrough, and another main force pulling the trading scale of China's gold market. Over 10 years, the development of China's gold futures market is steadily progressing, but in recent years the trading volume have shown a large decline, while in the international perspective, gold futures trading volume has been on the rise. International gold futures trading volume has grown from 187,700 tons to 334,400 tons over the past 10 years, an increase of 78.16%. In 2016, the trading volume of New York Board of Trade was 185,600 tons, while the trading volume of London spot trading market was only 154,400 tons, so London Gold Market walked off the championship for the first time. In 2017, the trading volume of New York Board of Trade widened this gap even further. In that year, the trading volume of New York Board of Trade increased by 26.4%, reached 234,600 tons, while the trading volume of London spot trading market only increased by 7.5% to 165,600 tons. The gap rose from 31,600 tons to 69,000 tons, showing the strong momentum of the development of the gold futures market. In China, an opposite scenario was shown. The gold futures market has developed in fluctuations, and the spot market has advanced significantly. 2016 and 2017 saw a sustained decline of nearly 40% and nearly 20% in gold futures trading volume, the contrast cannot be said to be scientific, but gives us a window to observe and compare.

7.3.3 Over-the-counter Market of Banks: A Multi-role Player

Due to the long-term gold control in China, before 2002, except for the Bank of China, which had the experience of overseas gold business, the gold business of other commercial banks was blank, so on the whole, the gold business of commercial banks in China as a member of Shanghai Gold Exchange started in 2002. Among the first 108 members of Shanghai Gold Exchange, there were 16 commercial bank members.

■ **From a Stranger to Market to an Active Participant**

Commercial banks have been participanted in the gold market from the date of the opening up of China's gold market, although they were not promoters of the gold market reform, their gold business started their self-managed or entrusted gold floor transactions as the first batch of members of Shanghai Gold Exchange. The over-the-counter self-managed gold business of commercial banks started from 2004 when the gold wholesale market was separated from the retail market as Shanghai Gold Exchange transformed into a financial market. The development of the gold business of commercial banks was synchronous with the development of China's gold market, but people maintained a wait-and-see attitude at the early stage.

As analyzed in the top design of China's gold market, China's commercial banks have been isolated from the gold business for a long time, they were lack of experience and talents, the unfamiliarity to the gold business made commercial banks very cautious when carrying out the gold business. There were far more onlookers than movers, so in 2004 the scale of bank counter gold business was only 2.2 tons. Although 16 commercial banks became the first members of Shanghai Gold Exchange, in 2003 the floor trading volume was only 171 tons, averagely only more than 10 tons per bank, the average trading volume was less than 1 ton per month, and what broke the deadlock was the two events that happened later.

Firstly, Industrial Bank actively entered the market, obtained the first pot of gold from the gold business and played a demonstration role. Industrial Bank was a private bank, and there was no competitive advantage to carry out the traditional financial business, so it found a new path and highlighted the Au (T + D) gold business of Shanghai Gold Exchange. The market was then a blue sea without many competitors, and Industrial Bank made a success and a profit of hundreds of million yuan. That might not be a big deal for a large-scale bank, but it was for Industrial Bank, which was an active participant in the trading of Au (T + D) products from 2008-2010. There is no limit to the power of example, this success of Industrial Bank was emulated by more banks, and Minsheng Bank's performance was also outstanding.

Secondly, ICBC set up an independent gold business unit. ICBC is the world's largest bank and has been the first major capital settlement bank since the opening of Shanghai Gold Exchange in 2002. In 2010, it took a step that attracted the attention of the community by forming an independent gold business department, which meant that the world's largest bank was paying attention to the gold business. Over the 40 years of gold demonetization, gold business has been marginalized in the banking business, the move by ICBC was seen as directional and has caused some banks to follow,

Chinese Gold: From Following to Surpassing

and they began to push forward and strengthen the construction of their gold business units.

By the end of 2014, 245 head offices of commercial banks and 588 provincial branches of commercial banks had carried out the gold business in China, the gold business has become a standard configuration of commercial bank business, it could be said that the gold business was basically popularized, which was a rare thing 10 years ago.

The gold business of commercial banks started in 2002 in the floor trading of Shanghai Gold market; in 2004, the bank over-the-counter trading market was established, and commercial banks became the dominant player in this market; in 2009, commercial banks entered Shanghai Futures Exchange and became a participant in gold futures trading; in 2010, China published for the first time the data of China's commercial banks participating in gold trading outside the country. In 2017, there were 36 commercial bank members in Shanghai Gold Exchange, including eight foreign banks; there were 19 commercial bank members in Shanghai Futures Exchange. Six Chinese commercial banks participating in overseas gold market trading had become full members of London Bullion Market Association as of the end of 2017, and they were Construction Bank, Bank of China, Industrial and Commercial Bank of China, Bank of Communications, Pudong Development Bank and Ping An Bank, with the addition of Minsheng Bank in 2018.

The depth and breadth of the gold business of China's commercial banks have seen a great development for more than ten years, and now China's commercial bank gold business is composed of three parts, namely the domestic gold market trading, over-the-counter bank trading, and overseas trading. Commercial banks overseas gold business is mainly over-the-counter trading and supported floor trading. The total volume of gold trading of commercial banks is the sum of the trading volume of the three parts, so commercial banks have played a variety of roles in the gold market.

Commercial banks are the main force of Shanghai Gold Exchange. In the process of growth, the membership structure of Shanghai

7 A Diversified Market System

Gold Exchange was originally based on the sellers and buyers of physical gold as the main trading body, and commercial banks were only service providers to ensure market liquidity. Shanghai Gold Exchange has gradually adjusted its membership structure and increased the proportion of commercial bank members to meet the need of transforming into the financial market. At present, there are 72 commercial bank members in Shanghai Gold Exchange, accounting for 26.7% of the total 270 members. Since 2010, the gold trading of commercial banks has been the first in this market, completing 39,600 tons of trading volume in 2017, or 72.93% of the total trading volume of Shanghai Gold Exchange, thus completing the transformation from a supporting role to a leading role, which was also a sign of the transformation of Shanghai Gold Exchange into a financial market.

Commercial banks are participants in the trading of gold futures contracts on Shanghai Futures Exchange, and the trading volume of gold futures by 19 commercial banks in 2017 was 1,399.58 tons, accounting for 3.59% of the total trading volume of gold futures on Shanghai Futures Exchange. In terms of the proportion of trading volume, commercial banks are still a marginal force within the gold futures market, and they have two options for the development of the gold futures contract market: one is that they can use gold futures contracts as a tool for speculative profit-making, and the other is that they can use it as a tool for transferring market risks.

Commercial banks are the master of the over-the-counter gold trading market of banks and the bearer of responsibility for operational safety, the over-the-counter gold trading market of banks is recognized as a legal over-the-counter market maker market, one of the three major markets in China's gold market system. The trading volume of the over-the-counter gold trading market of commercial banks that was born in 2004 was 8073.63 tons in 2017, an increase of 5.5%.

Commercial banks are increasingly important participants in the international gold market, in 2017 their gold trading volume in overseas markets was 16,200 tons, down 20.01% from 2016, but it was still higher than the domestic over-the-counter gold trading volume of banks, and the overseas trading volume of commercial banks in recent years has shown a rapid growth trend.

Based on the above 4 items, the commercial banks' gold business completed a trading volume of 65,300 tons in 2017, an increase of 3% compared to 63,400 tons in 2016, and the increase was mainly achieved by the growth in trading volume of Shanghai Gold Exchange.

■ **Over-the-counter Gold Market of Commercial Banks**

The over-the-counter gold market of commercial banks is an over-the-counter trading market, and commercial banks are the market makers who quote the buying price and also the selling price in this market, providing liquidity and continuity guarantee for the market and being the leading player in the development of this market. The over-the-counter gold market of commercial banks is one of the three major trading platforms constituting China's gold market system, and the market platform with the smallest trading volume. The gold trading volume of Shanghai Gold Exchange and Shanghai Futures Exchange has reached tens of thousands of tons, while that of the over-the-counter gold trading platform is still in the level of thousands of tons.

The background of the birth of the over-the-counter gold market of commercial banks was that in December 2004, the CBRC approved the four major state-owned commercial banks to carry out the gold financial services for individuals and families. In the background of the further opening up of the gold financial market, commercial banks were provided with the market space for independent research and development and sales of gold financial products, so when China's gold commodity market and gold financial market was separated, a new commercial bank over-the-counter gold market also developed, this process also promoted the separation between the gold wholesale market and retail market, and commercial banks who had a close connection with general public's assets and funds have naturally had the advantage of occupying the gold retail terminal

7 A Diversified Market System

market, and thus the commercial bank over-the-counter gold market occupies a dominant position in China's gold retail terminal market, although Shanghai Gold Exchange and commercial institutions are still undertaking this function.

The over-the-counter gold market business of commercial banks started from small gold bars, an investment product of the general public, and paper gold, which made personal investment more convenient, represented by gold passbooks and gold certificates of deposit. Accumulated deposits of gold that satisfied the gold investment demand of general public also appeared. The one taking the first place now is the gold market risk aversion products, such as swaps, sales in advance, etc., the participants of those products trading are mostly institutions, and the gold investment by general public is mainly realized with real gold subject matter and paper gold, only a few of those investors use gold derivatives. In 2017, the total trading volume of over-the-counter gold market of commercial banks was 8073.63 tons, of which the physical gold was 304.01 tons, only accounting for 3.78% of the total; paper gold was 2,130.8 tons, accounting for 26.39% of the total; and gold derivatives were 2,437.71 tons, accounting for 30.19% of the total volume. Others were gold loan and pledging, which totaled 2,995.48 tons, accounting for 37.1%.

From 2004 to 2017, the development of over-the-counter gold market of commercial banks in China has been more than 10 years old, and the trading volume started from 2.2 tons to more than 8,000 tons, an increase of several thousand times, which is highly impressive, and through analysis, we have found out the reason behind this.

The over-the-counter gold business of commercial banks went up a thousand times because the starting point was very low, but it never broke through the trading scale of 10,000-ton. Because the over-the-counter gold market of commercial banks dominated the retail terminal of the gold market, Chinese consumers became the biggest beneficiaries after entering the market to buy gold in 2013, and the volume of physical gold transactions reached a record high

Chinese Gold: From Following to Surpassing

of 521.77 tons, a surge of 1.65 times compared to 2012, 12% of the global supply of 4,340 tons of physical gold in that year. The the annual trading volume of the over-the-counter gold market of banks also reached 6,594.2 tons, an increase of 1.37 times compared to 2012, an increase of 3,809.8 tons, 1,000 tons more than the sum of the growth volume from 2004 to 2012, and in 2014, the volume fell by 2,479.8 tons, a decrease of 37.6%. The bank over-the-counter gold market thus entered a recovery period again, only surpassing the figure in 2013 three years later in 2017. Why did this happen? This exposed the problem of innovation capacity in this market. Chinese consumers bought gold in large quantities as a bottom-fishing behavior, they do not have higher requirements for the quality of gold products, basically traditional gold bars and gold jewelries, but after the disappearance of impulse buying, the market did not have a follow-up supply of higher quality products more suitable for the upgrading of the consumption to make this purchasing power continue. In fact, since 2013, the real gold products traded in the over-the-counter gold market of banks have been on the decline, which also indicated that gold product innovation was in urgent need of a breakthrough, especially when the development drive of China's gold market has gone from general product innovation to the stage of cultural innovation. There should be deeper thinking and newer explorations for the development of the over-the-counter gold market for better development.

■ Offshore Gold Business of Commercial Banks

In 2010, China officially made public the gold trading data of China's commercial banks participating in overseas markets, 12 Chinese commercial banks completed the trading volume of 3581.89 tons overseas in that year, which was certainly not the trading data of the initial year. It is said that Chinese banks became quite famous in London Market in the 1990s, but there was no official data released, so we can only rely on the data released in 2010 to analyze the gold business of Chinese commercial banks outside China.

The participation of Chinese commercial banks in overseas gold

7 A Diversified Market System

markets, both in depth and breadth, has continued to develop, and those banks, once a bystander, have increasingly become an important presence in the international gold market. In 2010, there were 12 Chinese commercial banks engaged in the international gold business, and by 2013, the number had increased to 25. As of 2018, seven commercial banks, namely, China Construction Bank, Industrial and Commercial Bank of China, Bank of Communications, Bank of China, Pudong Development Bank, Ping An Bank and Minsheng Bank, had become full members of London Bullion Market Association. After China Construction Bank and Bank of China became market makers, two Chinese commercial banks, Industrial and Commercial Bank of China and Bank of Communications, became the 13th and 14th gold fixers of the London Bullion Market Association. ICBC Standard Bank joined the precious metal clearing system of the London Precious Metals Clearing Limited and began to provide settlement services for gold transactions. This indicates that an increasing number of Chinese commercial banks are beginning to become regular armies from guerrillas in the international gold market, they have an increasing voice and are no longer just a market rule abider and user, and are beginning to transform into market rule makers. The increased presence of China's commercial banks in the international gold market is also manifested in the continued growth of the overseas gold trading scale, the annual trading volume has reached 10,000 tons from 1,000 tons, which is the trading scale that commercial banks have still not reached after 14 years of the development of the domestic over-the-counter gold market. However, in 2016 the overseas gold trading volume encountered a turning point after reaching 15,800 tons, in 2017 it fell by 20.01%, indicating the end of a sustained growth period. I think this reflects the interactive relevance of commercial banks' overseas gold trading and the domestic gold market. The overseas gold business of China's commercial banks is an important form of the internationalization of China's gold market, it has an important significance to further promote the connection between the international gold market and

Chinese Gold: From Following to Surpassing

the domestic gold market, and the international gold market has been the inevitable choice for the balance of the gold trading position of domestic commercial banks.

The product structure of commercial banks' overseas gold trading provides a key for us to analyze this correlation, and in 2017, for example, the first product of China's commercial banks' overseas gold trading was swaps, with a trading volume of 7,645 tons, accounting for 60.67% of the total trading volume of that year; another product was forwards, with a trading volume of 1,309 tons, accounting for 10.39% of the total trading volume; there were also futures and options, which was 77.95 tons, accounting for only 0.62%; spot trading volume was 3,449 tons, accounting for 27.37% of the total trading volume. Thus, the trading volume of swaps, forwards, futures and options accounted for 71.68%. Therefore, overseas gold trading commercial banks is dominated by gold derivatives, and the changes of gold trading volume of commercial banks overseas in China are shown in Figure 7-3. The main function of gold derivatives trading is arbitrage and risk hedging, which also determines that the main purpose of gold trading overseas by China's commercial banks is to arbitrage profits and transfer risks, then the arbitrage opportunity and the demand for risk transfer must come from both international and domestic aspects. The trading risks in the domestic market of commercial banks must be transferred to the international market, and also need to be transferred to the international market, because the risks in the local market can only be resolved in a larger market, and the arbitrage opportunities arising from risk transfer should also be materialized in the international gold market, which is the correlation between the domestic gold market and the overseas gold business of commercial banks. That is to say, any lack of synchronization between the domestic gold market and the international gold market may make the two markets produce arbitrage opportunities and promote the development of overseas gold trading of commercial banks, and the increase in the synchronization of the two markets will reduce overseas gold trading of commercial banks, of course this is only one of

7 A Diversified Market System

the factors, the reduction in overseas gold business of commercial banks is also related to relative stability and reduced speculation. But the development of the domestic gold market is an important factor influencing the overseas business of commercial banks, the more the development of the domestic gold market, the stronger its international influence, and therefore the overseas gold business of commercial banks is also the need for the development of China's domestic gold market. We should pay attention to the correlation between the two factors and this is a new issue arising from the internationalization of China's gold market.

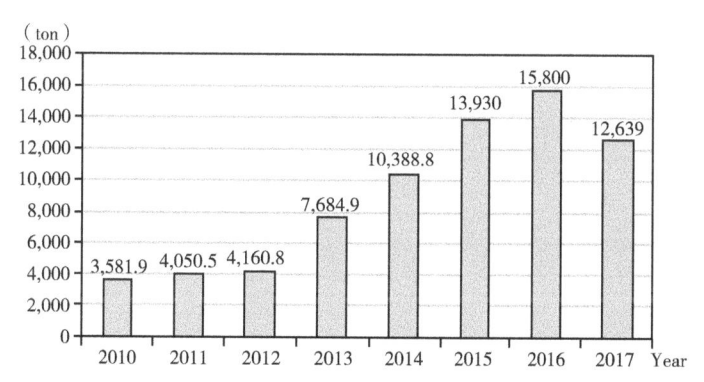

Figure 7-3 Changes in the Volume of Overseas Gold Trading of China's Commercial Banks

Source: *China Gold Market Report (2011-2018)*.

8

Innovative Gold Consumption Demands

After thousands of years of development, gold has become a kind of metal with both commodity and financial properties. The social properties of gold shaped by human culture has historical inheritance and permanence, so the dual properties of gold have not changed, what is changed is the gold management mode, that is to say, gold is either controlled or marketized. It is also the change of gold management mode that affects the circulation mode of gold, the direction of use of gold and the breadth and depth of use. Gold marketization changes the use of gold by the official monopoly into the sharing by government and people, thus expanding the social existence of gold, dramatically expanding the breadth and depth of the use of gold. Among them, the impact on the field of gold consumption is particularly profound, perhaps this is the biggest change brought by gold marketization to the social functions of gold.

Gold consumption demand is stimulated and developed with the lifting of gold control. The international monetary system uses the U.S. dollar as the central currency, so the dollar is used in social circulation instead of gold, but the dollar and gold are linked with a fixed exchange rate to achieve the stability of the dollar value. The gold is useful mainly because it supports the stability of dollar value, so gold becomes the financial asset and means of foreign exchange payment controlled by the Ministry of Finance (central bank), and the new increase of mineral gold must also be sold or handed over to the country. So even if the use of gold in the financial field is single and narrow, but when gold is released from the state control to become the metal free to be owned and traded by people, the use also expands to a broader social level, gold is no longer only the means of foreign exchange payment and the basis of currency issuance, and began to be used more widely in the field of commodity consumption of human beings to constantly enrich and beautify the life of the people, so that the gold consumption market is developed.

Although the advancement of China's gold market lags behind the world, it is consistent with the international development direction, so the realization of China's gold marketization also drive the development of the country's gold consumption market. China's gold consumption is mainly gold for manufacture of gold jewelry, gold for high-tech products and gold for manufacture of industrial raw materials. By 2018, although the gold marketization started only 16 years ago, China's gold consumption market has not only a number of varieties, but also a scale that has reached the international level, so the emergence of this world-class gold consumption market is also an important achievement of China's gold marketization reform.

8.1 Gold Demand for Manufacture of Gold Jewelry

Gold jewelry consumption has a long history in the consumption of gold by human beings. China's earliest gold jewelry was a pair of gold earrings unearthed in Huoshaogou, Gansu Province, dating back to more than 3,600 years ago. The history of gold jewelry at the international level dates back to at least one 1,000 years earlier. After the demonetization of gold, the currency demand for gold shrank and gold jewelry manufacturing become the largest consumer of gold. In the late 20th century, the amount of gold used in jewelry reached about 80% of the world's total gold consumption, with an average annual gold consumption of 3,497.8 tons between 1993 and 2000, accounting for 77.74% of the total global demand. The proportion of gold used in jewelry has declined in the new century, but still ranks first in gold use, with an average annual proportion of 52.48% between 2010 and 2017 and an average annual gold use of 1835.8 tons. The proportion decreased by 25.26 percentage points, and the amount of gold used decreased by 1662 tons. China's gold jewelry market opened up earlier than the gold market, but the development of the gold jewelry market benefited from the opening up of the gold market. After the opening up of the gold market, the gold supply constraints could be eliminated, and the growth in demand of gold jewelry accelerated significantly. In 2013, China's gold jewelry demand of 716.5 tons exceeded that of India, the multi-year champion, which was 634.3 tons. China became the new champion in terms of global gold jewelry demand and has held the title for six years through 2018.

8.1.1 Relaunch of Development of China's Gold Jewelry Market

The recovery of China's gold jewelry market was 20 years earlier than the establishment of the gold market, and the recovery of China's gold jewelry market was in 1982, while the establishment of the gold market was in 2002. The background of China's recovery of the gold jewelry market was that in 1979, China implemented the reform and opening-up policy, put the reform of rigid planned prices of commodities on agenda, but the reform to leverage marketization of commodity prices caused a two-digit inflation, so the suppression of inflation became a priority, and the recovery of the gold jewelry market was a measure to suppress inflation at that time, thus also opened up a new prospect of the development of China's gold jewelry market!

At the end of the Qing Dynasty, a certain number of branded gold jewelry manufacturing enterprises were gathered in the then central cities such as Shenyang, Beijing and Shanghai. However, the public-private partnership in the 1950s made most of these brand enterprises disappear, the jewelry production enterprises were merged into the arts and crafts industry, and there was not longer an independent gold jewelry industry.

In 1962, the interruption of the gold jewelry market led to the further shrinkage of the gold jewelry processing industry, so there

Chinese Gold: From Following to Surpassing

was an interruption for the development of China's gold jewelry industry. In 1982, the curtain of development was pulled open and China's gold jewelry industry was relaunched again, but we cannot say the timing was a good one. In 1982, the reason China resumed the supply of gold jewelry was to curb inflation, rather than to develop the gold jewelry industry. At that time, the development of the gold jewelry industry encountered two bottlenecks, one was the purchasing power bottleneck, which was a problem of the purchasing power of gold jewelry influenced by the income of the general public. Chinese people who were starting to properly feed and dress themselves had a low spending power and gold jewelry was still a luxury for them, for this reason in the early 1990s, China imposed a consumption tax on gold jewelry, in order to suppress consumption. The second was the bottleneck of raw materials of gold, and the raw materials for gold jewelry processing enterprises were in short supply. In 1985, the state put 100 tons of gold in circulation for re-circulation of currency, after that policy orientation of strict control of gold has never changed, and only a few tons of gold were supplied. The existence of these two development bottlenecks restricted the development of China's gold jewelry market.

In 1982, there were only 38 gold jewelry processing enterprises in China. At that time, the industrial output value of the jewelry processing industry as a whole was less than 80 million yuan (79.11 million yuan), of which 45.39 million yuan (57.4%) was export processing income, and the scale of the domestic market was only 33.72 million yuan. Therefore, China's gold jewelry market started on a very small scale. At that time, the gold jewelry retail industry mainly served foreign tourists and overseas Chinese. In 1990, although the number of designated gold jewelry processing enterprises grew from 10 to 95 and the sales income created reached 1.4 billion yuan, the average size of each enterprise was only 14.74 million yuan. According to a calculation based on the sale prices, the average processing scale of each enterprise was only about 100kg, so the gold jewelry processing industry after years of development

8 Innovative Gold Consumption Demands

was still in the stage of manual workshop. When a thing is rare, it becomes precious. Due to the influence of traditional gold culture, gold jewelry was defined as wealth, so gold jewelry was priced by weight rather than workmanship and style, and consumers emphasized on gold content and neglected craftsmanship, so it was not surprising that gold jewelry was of low quality at that time.

A new situation emerged in the development of China's gold jewelry industry in the middle and late 1990s. As one of the top ten industrial sectors in Hong Kong, China, the gold jewelry processing industry began to move inward and gradually formed a gold jewelry processing industry base in Shenzhen. Now the scale of Shenzhen's jewelry industry accounts for more than 70% of the country's total. The reasons why Hong Kong's jewelry processing industry moved inward were firstly the low labor costs as China's population dividend was released in the reform and opening up, and secondly the growth of demand for gold jewelry by Chinese mainland residents. The premise of the growth of gold jewelry demand was the growth of residents' income, and an important observation indicator of residents' income growth was residents' personal deposits. In 1980, the balance of household deposits was only 20 billion yuan, but by 1990 it had reached 800 billion yuan, an increase of 40 times. The conditions for the development of the gold jewelry market in mainland China began to mature. The jewelry industry in Hong Kong, China, discovered this business opportunity and began to set up factories in the mainland, and Shenzhen became the first choice for Hong Kong jewelry processing enterprises to settle in the mainland because of its geographical advantages. Many of the pioneers failed and winners were the outstanding ones among the latecomers, because of the gold control at that time, some enterprises engaged in disorderly conducts in obtaining licenses and raw materials. Another reason was that the gold price continued to fall and the external environment of development was relatively unfavorable. However, with the gradual maturity of the development environment of the gold jewelry market in mainland China, there were new entrants. Therefore, at the beginning of the

Chinese Gold: From Following to Surpassing

new century, two gold jewelry processing enterprises gathering areas were gradually formed in Panyu and Shenzhen, Guangdong Province. Panyu was a cluster of export-oriented enterprises based on the processing of supplied materials, while Shenzhen was an cluster of internally-oriented enterprises focused on the domestic market. When the conditions of the mainland market were immature, the export-oriented enterprises processing supplied materials had certain development advantages over gold jewelry enterprises in Shenzhen, but the internally-oriented jewelry enterprises were the biggest winners of the development opportunities in the mainland market. Therefore, the development of the gold jewelry industry in Panyu was far inferior to that in Shenzhen, especially after the lifting of gold control, the mainland market has made rapid progress, and Shenzhen has become the design, processing and logistics center of gold jewelry in the country. The gold jewelry industry has become a characteristic industry in Shenzhen, while the gold jewelry processing industry in Panyu began to shrink and lose its attraction.

In 2000, while gold control was still in existence, the people's Bank of China approved its Shenzhen branch to carry out gold consignment sales business,that was, using Shenzhen's own foreign exchange to import foreign gold and then selling it to gold-using enterprises in Shenzhen. The development of this business greatly alleviated the contradiction of the shortage of raw materials in the gold jewelry industry. Shenzhen attracted mainland gold jewelry enterprises because of the advantage in the supply of gold raw materials. This was the expansion period of Shenzhen's gold jewelry industry, it can be said that Shenzhen has harvested the "first pot of gold" of gold marketization in China. During the preparatory period of the gold market, Shenzhen did not actively fight for it, which may be due to the vested interests. After that, Shenzhen also expressed its willingness to bid for the gold market, and finally lost to Shanghai, which became the gold trading center of the country. However, as gold jewelry enterprises were concentrated in Shenzhen, 70% of the gold output eventually went to Shenzhen and 80% of the gold was processed in Shenzhen, so although Shenzhen was not the location of China's gold market, it was the gold logistics center of the country. The formation of the gold jewelry production base in Shenzhen constituted a transformation of China's gold jewelry industry, the layout of the gold jewelry industry was historically adjusted, and a world-class gold jewelry industry rose in Shenzhen, but the process was full of twists and turns.

8.1.2 The Gold Jewelry Market has Gone through a Cold Winter

When the supply of gold jewelry was restored in 1982, the country was still in the era of wealth shortage, and gold jewelry was endowed with the cultural function of showing off wealth, so consumers pursued the purity of gold jewelry. They were not satisfied with pure gold, they wanted 99.99% pure gold. Therefore, gold jewelry was sold by gram without paying attention to style and workmanship, which greatly weakened the cultural connotation of gold jewelry, although it met the public's consumption demand for gold jewelry from scratch. When entering the new century of building a well-off society in an all-round way, the wealth of the people was increasing day by day. After solving the problem of owning wealth, consumers expect something better. The gold jewelry market which could only satisfying the need of the general public for ownership was given cold shoulders. Therefore, the development of the gold jewelry market needs cultural reorientation, and the direct reason for the urgent relaunch of gold jewelry market culture was the rise of platinum jewelry.

■ The Rise of White Jewelry

Although there are many jewelry materials, gold is the base material of all kinds of jewelries and it is very widely used, so gold jewelry has been the big shot in the jewelry family in China, but this position was seriously challenged from in the late 20th century to the early 21st century. The rise of platinum jewelry brings China's jewelry market from the "golden autumn" into a "white-capped winter".

Chinese Gold: From Following to Surpassing

The Grants and Funding Management System (GFMS) has made a long-term follow-up observation on China's gold jewelry market and released such observation results, since 1999, China's gold jewelry demand has continued to decline for four years, the demand for gold jewelry fell from 243.3 tons in 2002 to 199.6 tons in 1996, a decline of 18%, and demand level of 1998 had not restored until 2006. At that time there was a sustained decline in gold prices, under the dual pressure of the demand and the market, the development of China's gold jewelry market presented a "V-shaped" curve, but China's overall jewelry market during this period showed a sustained growth trend, so why did the gold jewelry demand shrink? And what filled the resulting market space?

It was platinum jewelry that formed a reverse movement against the growth or decline of gold jewelry, filled the jewelry market space at that time, and pulled gold jewelry off the throne of wedding jewelry, so how did platinum jewelry do that?

Platinum jewelry has not made debut in the Chinese jewelry market until 1994, when the market demand was 0.47 tons, only 1% of the total global demand and 0.24% of the demand for gold jewelry in China that year. It was completely a marginal product on the market and was not immediately recognized by Chinese consumers, but surprisingly, the sales volume of platinum jewelry increased by 36.4 times from 0.47 tons to 17.58 tons, accounting for 23% of the global total. In 1998, China's platinum jewelry market was already second in the world behind Japan, and two years later, in 2000, the demand increased by 77.4% to 31.18 tons, the highest in the world, and reached 41.96 tons in 2002. This new type of white platinum jewelry generally spread in China's jewelry market, declaring the advent of the "white winter" in the jewelry hypermarkets . What is the reason to make platinum jewelry turn the table? The answer is culture.

■ The Cultural Positioning of Platinum Jewelry

Platinum jewelry was an authentic import, and the front runner was the World Platinum Council. The World Gold Sales Association

8 Innovative Gold Consumption Demands

was similar to the World Gold Council and was an international organization that promoted the use of platinum by platinum producers as members. But gold and platinum had different statuses in human society. After long-term cultural shaping by human beings, its commodity and financial attributes have been recognized, even if the Chinese people have been isolated from gold for more than half a century, the concept of gold as a monetary metal was still very profound. Platinum was different, although it was rarer than gold, it was mostly used as catalysts for industrial applications, the general public did not have much direct contact with platinum, which was more regarded as a metal like stainless steel to which human beings did not have any cultural links. How could the public be made to accept platinum jewelry? The first thing was to establish a cultural link between platinum jewelry and human beings. Different from the World Gold Council that promoted the formation of China's gold marketization policy first, the World Platinum Council publicized the platinum consumption culture first, started from the cultural positioning of platinum jewelry and opened up the demand situation of the platinum market in China.

World Platinum Council compared platinum to purity and water for its color in order to change the cold feeling of platinum. In order to improve the noble sense of platinum, they combine platinum and diamonds, they resorted to famous celebrities for endorsement and make the most perfect interpretation of human love with platinum and diamond jewelry: Purity, flawlessness, tenderness like water, and eternity. This cultural creativity became fashion through the delivery of a lot of advertisement, "diamonds are long-lasting like love" became a popular slogan at that time, moving new couples ready to enter the marriage hall, so that the cold platinum once rejected was accepted, and became the first choice of wedding accessories, while gold wedding jewelry was an embodiment of wealth and discarded by the increasingly affluent population who believed gold was tacky and a symbol that love was for sale. So some retailers turned to vigorously promote the sale of gold and diamond wedding jewelry and focused on platinum jewelry, they also adjusted the store

Chinese Gold: From Following to Surpassing

layout, so the "yellow harvest" disappeared, into the "white winter". In fact, the development of the global platinum jewelry market was not popular, and only China and Japan had a relatively large consumption of platinum jewelry. China's platinum jewelry market reached 53% of the global total in 2002. But the World Platinum Council has successfully created a new platinum demand market which had a global impact on the global platinum production, accordingly in 2001 the platinum price rose by 33.1% compared to 1996, while the price of gold fell by 30.12% over the same period. In 1996, platinum price was 1.02 times the price of gold, while in 2001 the price of platinum has risen to 1.95 times the price of gold, thus creating a golden age for platinum.

The success of the World Platinum Council also benefited from China's market-oriented promotion. Shanghai Gold Exchange opened to business in October 2002, in August 2003 platinum became a variety traded in Shanghai Gold Exchange, in June of the previous year, China announced the exemption of platinum trading links of the value-added tax, thus platinum jewelry production did not suffer either short supply of raw materials or policy barriers, so in the absence of any platinum traditional cultural accumulation, a new platinum jewelry market soon emerged in China. This case showed a powerful cultural force-a force that can shape human consumption behaviors.

World Platinum Council did not go one step further and make bigger breakthroughs for platinum jewelry for further development of the market of platinum jewelry after the success in the creation of platinum and diamond wedding culture. On the contrary, the platinum jewelry began to shrink, so the success of a product did not necessarily mean a global subversion. After that, China's jewelry market restored the "golden autumn", and gold jewelry became the favorite of the jewelry market again. There were two reasons: one was that gold jewelry was in progress, and the return of the "autumn" was the result of its own progress; the other was that platinum jewelry would regress without new breakthroughs, and the result of stagnation was the loss of the market. After 10 years

8 Innovative Gold Consumption Demands

of stagnation, recently the World Gold Council launched platinum investment bars. However, expanding the social function of platinum and its commodity properties to financial properties would be a long cultural cultivation process, and there would be a huge uncertainty.

■ The World Gold Council was also on the Move

The World Gold Council entered China for the same purpose with the latecomer - World Platinum Council, and that was to explore the Chinese market demand. The two international organizations had many similarities, and the development of market demand for two different metals in the same market would inevitably result in competition. Although they did not comment publicly on their respective actions, there was a potential for comparison and reference. The change from "autumn" to "winter" in the Chinese jewelry market put pressure on the World Gold Council that had been in China for 10 years by then and regarded as their own family by Chinese practitioners, and it had also taken the affairs of Chinese practitioners as its own affairs. At that time, there were a number of international organizations that entered China to expand the precious metal market, but the one that was more closely connected with Chinese jewelry practitioners was the World Gold Council. Human effort was the decisive factor. Here I want to talk about two people in the World Gold Association, one is Zheng Lianghao, who was the general manager of WGC Asia and a director of the World Gold Council. He retired in 2017 and founded the Singapore Precious Metals Council; the second is Wang Lixin, who is a veteran of Beijing office of the World Gold Council. Wang joined the World Gold Council in 1995, left for three years in the middle for some reason, and returned in 2014. He is now the general manager of Beijing office of the World Gold Council. Their persistence, enthusiasm, seriousness, sincerity, responsibility and commitment were fully reflected in their actions in response to the recession in the gold jewelry market.

The recession of the gold jewelry market indicated that consumers began to abandon traditional gold jewelry products, so the gold jewelry

Chinese Gold: From Following to Surpassing

market must make innovations in gold jewelry products in order to regain the favor of consumers. That was the key for gold jewelry market to go of the recession, but they found it really puzzling to start gold product innovation. Earlier we have mentioned that China's gold jewelry market was restored to curb inflation. In the 20 years from 1982 to the beginning of the new century, China's gold jewelry market development was mainly focused on solving the public demand for gold from scratch. In the end of the 1990s, the gold jewelry market was in depression, the change of the general public towards gold jewelry reflected that the cultural consumption choice of China's gold jewelry consumers changed, and marked the beginning of the public's pursuit of "good gold". In face of such change, China's gold jewelry practitioners lacked experience, but the World Gold Council had an international vision and rich experience in response to the change in China's gold jewelry market, and acted as a guide and vanguard of China's gold practitioners.

If we say the World Platinum Council successfully launched platinum and diamond wedding ornaments, then the first gold jewelry product launched by the World Gold Council in the Chinese market was X-Forever gold ornament, which was a large-gram traditional pure gold product. The cultural positioning of traditional pure gold products was wealth, and the possession and wearing of pure gold jewelry was a sign of wealth, but this was disdained by consumers of wedding jewelry who were increasingly seeking spiritual fashion. Was wealth really not important anymore? Of course it was important, but it's no longer appropriate to over-declare it in a marriage. Therefore, instead of changing the cultural function of gold jewelry, X-Forever was a gift from parents to the newly married as a dowry. It expressed parents' feelings of apprehension and reluctance when their children grow up and go off on their own. This adjustment was intended to interpret the new story of gold, injecting new life into the pure gold jewelry. The biggest significance of the birth of X-Forever brand was that China's gold jewelry market began to take the first step in the cultural gold.

The second gold jewelry product launched by the World Gold

8 Innovative Gold Consumption Demands

Council was K gold fashion gold ornaments, or low gold content K gold series products, this series of products were for jewelry consumers with a growing pursuit of fashion. K gold products focused on the fashionable design, sophisticated processing, and diversified color configurations, so China's gold jewelry ushered in a new variety of colored gold. It changed the traditional image of rigid style and single color of gold jewelry in the past, and became the pioneering work of China's fashion jewelry. The fashion of gold jewelry also changed the traditional way of buying jewelry by weight and by piece in China, and to a large extent, the consumption of gold jewelry was changed from buying gold to buying culture. At that time, the pioneer of gold jewelry fashion was Italy, in order to promote the exchange between Chinese practitioners and Italian practitioners, the World Gold Council organized practitioners every year to participate in the Italian Jewelry Exhibition. Chinese practitioners had a very strong learning ability, so they quickly established a cooperation relation with Italian manufacturers to process and exchange components for Italian manufacturers and process jewelry for customers, which became the booster for the fashion promotion of China's gold jewelry. K gold jewelry has an ice-breaking significance for China's gold jewelry culture transformation. Now K gold jewelry has been an important part of China's gold jewelry system, the market share has risen from 10% to 30%. Importantly, it has prompted the fashion of gold jewelry to take a big step forward, so that China's gold jewelry has undergone a dramatic transformation.

8.1.3 A New Height of Cultural Gold

In 2002, China liberalized the gold control. Good things should be in pairs. The bull market came at the same time. The external environment for the development of China's gold jewelry market presented extremely favorable factors, and externally, the market embarked on a cultural gold road, and thus the development of China's gold jewelry market enters a new stage - A stage of climbing and surpassing international peaks. An important sign was that

Chinese Gold: From Following to Surpassing

in 2003 China's gold jewelry market ended the difficult period of declining market demand from 1997 to 2002 and entered a period of development in which market demand rebounded. Although the rebound was very slow at the beginning, the demand for gold jewelry reached 324.4 tons in 2008, exceeding the traditional gold jewelry production and demand countries - Italy and Turkey, and ranking third in the global demand for gold jewelry. The demand growth accelerated markedly after 2013, with demand rising 109.25% to 716.5 tons, surpassing India and ranking the first in the world. Until 2018, the title has been maintained for six years. The formation of a gold jewelry market with the largest scale in the world was an important achievement of gold market in China.

The emergence of the new platinum jewelry market in the country and the revitalization of the traditional gold jewelry market cannot be separated from one common element - culture. China's gold jewelry market has attached importance to capital, products, equipment and belittled culture, practitioners have finally understood in the gold jewelry market that the crisis of development begins from cultural crisis, and we have to reshape the culture first to go out of the crisis, thus China's gold jewelry market has begun a cultural transformation, tradition is integrated with fashion, the cultural attributes of gold jewelry are restored, and this effort brings a qualitative leapfrog to the quality of China's gold jewelry. The workmanship is becoming more refined, designs are becoming more fashionable, and varieties are increasing. The market is getting more and more subdivided, the products are increasingly personalized, and the diversification of products has surpassed the diversification of functions. Even a piece of jewelry with the same function has different cultural connotations, gold processing enterprises can differentiate the design and produce jewelry according to different cultural connotations suitable for different age groups, different occupations and different scenarios. Now, the diversification of gold jewelry is not only about the difference in shape and color, but also personalized culture. In particular, our country's hard gold technology can use very little gold to make very large pendants and ornaments, with only 0.1 grams of gold, which greatly improves the expressive power of gold.

China is now not only the world's largest gold jewelry market in terms of demand and production, but also an important production center for platinum jewelry, silver jewelry, and gemstone jewelry, and can already be compared with, or even surpass traditional jewelry-producing countries such as Italy, Belgium, and Japan. China's gold jewelry consumer market has gone to the forefront of the world.

8.2 Gold Demand for High–tech Products

Gold culture has a long history, but wealth and decoration have been the two main functions of gold for thousands of years. Gold is either hidden or worn, and thus the utilization is relatively single-purpose. Gold needs innovation, but little progress is made. Now there is a possibility of making up for this shortcoming of gold and it is the application of gold in the high-tech field thanks to technological progress.

Due to the characteristics of electrical conductivity and corrosion resistance, gold becomes the only choice for the manufacture of high-tech electronic products working in extreme environments, so the use of gold in high-tech electronic products has become an increasingly important application, it can also be said that the technological progress of mankind continues to expand the breadth of the use of gold. In nearly 10 years, the use of gold globally in this field has accounted for about 10% of the world's total gold consumption, or about 320 tons. Gold is mainly used in the manufacture of chips, electronic devices, computers, mobile phones and high-end instruments, experts have pointed out that: "If there was no gold surface coating, electronic, telecommunications, electronic computers would not exist". These chips, devices, instruments are used in production of aviation, aerospace, nuclear power, launch vehicles, computers and other high-tech products. Gold is very stable in general, but when it is micro-particulated, it

Chinese Gold: From Following to Surpassing

is very active to some elements, so gold catalysts, gold isotopes and gold purifying agents begin to gradually appear, these gold products are widely used in medical care and environmental protection and are regarded as essential raw materials for modern high-tech industry, so we can compare gold as rare earths in the high-tech electronic industry.

The use of gold in the high-tech field in the country is a new situation that emerged in the new century. There are three reasons for this situation: The first is the increase in the demand for supporting electronic devices with the development of high-tech industry in China; the second is that the supply of gold for industrial use can be guaranteed as the gold control is liberated before which the industrial application of gold was strictly restricted. Third, thanks to technological progress what was impossible to produce can be produced. Therefore, a new high-tech gold product processing industry has emerged in the country. Although we have made progress in the use of gold for high-tech industries, we are not the masters of core technology. The masters are foreign investors. They took advantage of China's deregulation of gold and began to establish enterprises to produce gold for the electronic industry. Now Japan's Tanaka, Germany's Heraeus, Switzerland's Metalor, and other international century-old stores have set up factories in China. Since industrial gold was strictly controlled, only scientific research units in the country produced a small amount of industrial gold products in laboratories before 2002, and large-scale production was basically blank. Therefore, foreign investors were pioneers in the production of gold products for high-tech electronics in the country, and domestic companies were followers, and lacked their own core technology, so that it was a field to be improved.

According to CPM Gold Yearbook published by the United States, the production scale of China's high-tech electronic gold products continued to grow from 35.6 tons in 2008 to 76.8 tons in 2017, an increase of 1.16 times, accounting for 23% of the world's total industrial gold for high-tech electronics at that time, second only to Japan, ranking second in the world. Compared with 2016, there was a year-on-year growth of 20.9%. The production in Japan has been on the decline in recent years, while in China the growth trend has not changed, so we have the potential to become the champion, and that is a gold market with a rapid growth in China. However, the gold needed in the high-tech electronic industry is not gold ingots in its original state, but high-tech gold components or accessories processed with high technologies, so the production of high-tech gold products should be subdivided into an independent industrial sector, which did not exist in the country before the marketization of gold in China.

8.3 Production Needs for Industrial Gold Raw Materials

If we try to understand the industrial demand for gold in a greater picture, we will find that the high-tech electronic field is only one of the fields in which gold is used, and gold is also used in many industrial fields, but the raw materials used are all processed gold products. Gold ingots are the initial state of existence of gold in the real society of mankind, while the industrial raw materials of gold are processed, in which the form and quality of gold ingots are changed. The forms of existence of industrial gold raw materials are solid and liquid. Gold raw materials in the solid state can be massive, foiled, filiform or powdery, and those in the liquid state can be slurried, pasty or watery. These gold raw materials not only change the form of gold, they also change the quality. The change of form and quality of gold expands the application of gold, makes gold a raw material for production in other industrial sectors, this is the extension of gold commodity attributes. So China's gold marketization is not only a change of trading methods, but also gives birth to new industries. Industrial gold raw materials processing industry is a new industry which has a history of only 20 years. Now, China's industrial gold raw materials have many varieties.

1. Gold salt: A gold chemical product, scientifically known as gold potassium cyanide, used for the surface coating and electronic circuit

board production, is currently an industrial gold product using the largest amount of gold, or more than 30 tons per year. Zhaoyuan of Shandong Province is already the largest production base of gold salt in China.

2. Gold wire: Contemporary processing technology can pull gold into fine gold wires thinner than hair. It is a basic materials widely used for the production of integrated circuits. What is used now is not pure gold wire, but alloy wires containing other trace metal, so there are different formulations, most are patent technologies. The annual amount of gold used for gold wires is 20 tons.

3. Gold foil: Mechanical or chemical methods can process gold into foils thinner than cicada wings, mainly used for decoration. China has a long history of gold foil production, and Nanjing is a traditional gold foil production base. The annual amount of gold used for gold foils is 2 tons and the product has been exported to more than 40 countries.

4. Gold powder: Modern processing means can process gold into ultra-fine powder, which is the raw material for production of gold slurry, gold paste, gold liquid and gold water, and these gold products are basic raw materials used in electronics, printing and other industries.

5. Gold slurry: Gold slurry is a new material developed with cutting-edge electronic technologies and machine miniaturization. It is an important material for the utilization of microelectronics technology, and the basis of thick film hybrid integrated circuits, micro components and the surface assembly technology, playing an important role in the contemporary electronic industry. China relies on imports of gold slurry and there are many gaps in production technology to be filled.

6. Colored gold: Gold will change color when other metals are added to it, and the gold with different metal contents and of different colors is called colored gold. Colored gold enriches the expressive power of gold, and is widely used in the production of gold jewelry. It changes the rigid performance of traditional gold jewelry and its combination with gold enhances the sense of fashion.

8 Innovative Gold Consumption Demands

7. Hard gold: Gold is relatively soft, which affects its applications in some fields, and hard gold is gold with improved hardness with modern technologies. Under the condition of satisfying the gold content, the hardness of hard gold is twice that of pure gold. Hard gold improves the firmness of inlay greatly and can be made into extremely small ultra-thin gold products, so hard gold has been widely used in the jewelry industry.

8. Gold target: Integrated circuits become increasingly complex and require higher electrical conductivity, thus promoting new technologies, and sputtering technology is one of them. Sputtering technology is to film the metal directly on substrate surface by using electric field on the high energy ion body under a vacuum state. Gold target is needed to cover metal substrates by sputtering technology, and it is another important application of gold in electronic industry.

9. Gold alloy: Add other metals into gold and you have gold alloys which can change gold properties and thereby expand gold applications. Gold alloys include gold-nickel alloy, gold-silver alloy, gold-aluminium alloy, gold-iron alloy, etc. Because of the introduced new elements, gold properties have changed, so it can be chosen as soft parts, elastic parts and sliding parts in electronic industry and instrument industry.

10. Gold paste: Gold paste is a paste-like gold product with conductive properties. It can be coated on a non-conductor, heated and cured to become a conductor or resistor in the circuit. There are many kinds of gold pastes due to different compositions. Gold paste contains a variety of metals and the content of other metals is generally 5%-12%.

11. Gold catalyst: Gold has inert chemical reactions, but when distributed on a specific carrier, it reacts with certain substances in an active state. Therefore, gold can be used as a catalyst and has been used in fuel cells, environmental pollution control, air purification, and waste water purification. Gold catalyst has a market size of hundreds of billions of dollars in the world.

The supply situation of industrial gold raw materials in China is severe. Chip development is current an important issue for the

Chinese Gold: From Following to Surpassing

economic development of China. Chips have surpassed petroleum to become the largest import commodity, with a foreign exchange value exceeding US$200 billion, and Western countries led by the United States have the dominance of technology, and it is possible for them to cut off the supply at any time. This situation has already happened, so the chip industry has become a strategic choice for the country's development. Experts believe that there is no big gap between the design of Chinese chips and foreign countries. The key is manufacturing. The backward performance of manufacturing is caused by equipment and materials. Only 20% of the materials can meet the demand, and most of them cannot be produced, including many industrial gold raw materials. For instance, gold pulp needs to be 100% imported. New technology has expanded a growing number of high-tech applications of gold for the demand for gold, and has also raised new topics for us. The production and processing industry of industrial gold products has far surpassed the service scope of the traditional jewelry processing industry. This is a new high-tech industry that serves the development of high-tech fields. Therefore, we must also have strong technological innovation capabilities. Now internationally renowned producers in this area, such as Metalor, Heraeus, and Tanaka have all entered China and established their own enterprises, becoming the backbone of industrial gold production of China and maintaining technological leadership. This is the status quo of this industry, which has not attracted enough attention from us. China's gold industry should have not only gold mining and gold jewelry processing industries, but also the industrial gold raw material processing industry, which is a new high-tech field with a higher height, a deeper depth and a thicker thickness.

9

A Gold Investment Market Derived from Development

Gold is a kind of metal with both commodity and financial attributes. After China lifted gold control, the commodity attribute of gold has been given full play to. China's gold consumption demand rapidly expanded, and a gold consumption market with the most processing and demand volume in the world emerged in China. Gold marketization also stimulated the financial attributes of gold, thus promoting the emergence of an active gold investment market in the country. The development of this market is mainly manifested as the expansion of the breadth, which is then manifested as the extension of the participating groups. All kinds of gold investment products in China in more than 10 years time has developed to be available for different levels of people and different hobby groups to choose from, so gold has become the most common investment choice for people.

9.1 The Lifting of Controls Activated the Liquidity of Gold

Gold is subject matter to special management because it has special financial properties and has been strictly controlled for more than half a century, which has also greatly stifled the performance of gold's financial properties. The gold consumption market is the market that needs gold to change hands for transactions, and the gold investment market is more of a market that needs gold to flow. Gold control made gold liquidity nearly nonexistent, gold liquidity was seriously shrinking, so that gold was marginalized in China's financial market. Gold investment disappeared not only in people's

Chinese Gold: From Following to Surpassing

lives, but also professional finance textbooks since relevant content was deleted. Shanghai Gold Exchange had not taken the first step in the construction of China's gold financial market until 2004, so how to establish a gold investment market? How to make the gold market part of the financial market? Our understanding is still hazy, and no one would have predicted that our gold financial market would be what it is today, capable of attracting increasing international attention.

The financial attributes of the gold market are inherent and has not changed, so the conversion from the gold market to the financial market is strictly speaking a return, that is, returning to the inherent attributes of the contemporary gold market. The forms of realization of the financial attribute of gold are different, and the financial function of the gold market linked to the dollar was to stable the value of the dollar, the central currency of the international monetary system through the adjustment to the supply and demand of gold, so the gold market pursued the stability of the gold price, generally with a fluctuation of about 1%. The subject matter traded on the market was physical gold, and the gold market was not very speculative. After the demonetization of gold, the function of the gold market to stabilize the value of the U.S. dollar was lost, and it was no longer a stable window for the price of physical gold, and the price of gold began to fluctuate frequently. From the gold price dual track system in 1968 to the general fluctuation system with unified gold prices in 1971, the participants of the gold trading market had also changed, a large number of profit-seeking investors and speculators enter the market. They were not real demanders of gold trading, but became a dominating role of market development, so the majority of products traded by gold investors were not gold but gold derivatives, and what was formed by the market was gold logistics and not currency flow. In 2008, the total trading volume completed in the global gold market was 365,700 tons, while the trading volume of physical gold was only 3,682.2 tons, accounting for only 1% of the total, but in 2017, the proportion of physical gold dropped even more to 0.8%. That was because the increased liquidity of gold was

9 A Gold Investment Market Derived from Development

the key to the development of the gold investment market, and the convenient trading of gold derivatives was more likely to increase the liquidity of the market, so the liquidity of the gold investment market is mainly achieved through gold derivatives trading. The same is true for the development of China's gold investment market, so the extension of trading subject matter of China's gold investment market from physical gold to gold derivatives is the first choice, and thus the proportion of gold derivatives trading marks the strength of the market's financial attributes.

In order to increase the liquidity of the gold market, China should promote the innovation of gold investment products, and the innovation of the gold investment subject matter has two directions, one is the miniaturization of physical gold trading subject matter, the other paper-orientation, and we have made gratifying progress in these two directions.

The miniaturization of the gold investment trading subject matter is the miniaturization of kilogram bars. The miniaturization of physical gold subject matter was the 50g small good bars launched in 2004 and 100g small good bars launched in 2006 to meet the needs of average individual investors, but this initiative had little impact, in 2017, 50g small gold bars were basically withdrawn from the market, and the trading volume of 100g small gold bars was only 9.2 tons, so the miniaturization of the trading subject matter by Shanghai Gold Exchange was basically marginalized. Commercial banks were also promoting the miniaturization of the gold investment trading subject matter.After 2004, the four major state-owned banks, namely, ICBC, ABC, BOC and CCB, launched their own brand of small gold bars, but the transaction did not show continuous growth, and the current trading volume is only about 100 tons at present, showing a trend of being marginalized. However, the efforts for miniaturization of the gold investment trading subject matter does not stop. The internet big data technology injects new power into the miniaturization of gold subject matter. Relying on the internet big data technology, now the gold investment subject matter has been miniaturized to 1 gram, even to 0.1 grams, the emergence of this

Chinese Gold: From Following to Surpassing

product innovation lowers the gold investment threshold down to a hundred yuan, so the impact of the miniaturization of China's gold trading is to realize the gamification of gold investment. Participants can increase to hundreds of millions of people, so it can be said that this is the unprecedented gold investment innovation in human history. Of course, any new technology has a gradual process of maturation, micro gold has just appeared and still needs to break in, but it is undoubtedly an epochal innovation.

The biggest contributor to the growth of gold liquidity has been the paper-based innovation of the trading subject matter, starting with Shanghai Gold Exchange, which in 2004 launched Au (T + D), a paper-based gold subject matter, a spot deferred contract that has now grown into a series of products. The trading volume of Au (T + D) series of products in 2008 was 3,234.02 tons, accounting for 72.5% of the total trading volume of Shanghai Gold Exchange, which greatly exceeded the trading volume of physical gold subject matter, marking the completion of the transformation of Shanghai Gold Exchange into a financial market. It is the first major contributor to the transformation of Shanghai Gold Exchange into a financial market. However, as more innovative gold paper-based products were launched, the proportion of Au (T + D) products declined, and by 2017, although the trading volume of this series of products had reached 23,500 tons, it only accounted for 38.03% of the total trading volume of Shanghai Gold Exchange that year, down 34.47 percentage points.

Commercial banks are another major promoter of paper-based trading subject matter of gold. Gold passbook (account) and gold accumulation plan are the two mainly traded paper-based over-the-counter products by commercial banks. There is no trouble of gold delivery and transport, and gold investment is like paper money investment. The former can be regarded as a deposit account, and the changes of account funds can be adjusted through the network; The latter can be regarded as depositing small sums of money and drawing out both the principal and interest in a time. Fixed funds are deposited monthly, the bank buys gold according to the regulations,

9 A Gold Investment Market Derived from Development

and the investor may draw or sell the gold. Au (T + D) products are for institutional investors, and while these two paper-based gold products are for individual investors, of which the gold passbook (account) accounts for more than 80% of the total trading volume.

The above paper-based gold products are spot trading products, and what is more influential on the gold investment trading market is the innovation for paper-based forward gold products. The first mover was the launch of gold futures contracts on Shanghai Futures Exchange in 2008, which drove up the total trading volume of the gold market in China by four times in the first year. The over-the-counter gold market of commercial banks is another provider of forward gold paper-based trading products, especially interbank gold trading also use forward paper-based trading products, mainly swap contracts and advanced sales contracts. The trading volume of these two paper-based products now exceeds that of gold futures contracts.

After 15 years of development, the two-way trading volume of China's gold investment market has reached 100,000 tons, the transaction varieties of physical gold subject matter is the richest in the world, and the physical gold investment volume of ranks the first in the world. All paper-based trading products of the international gold market have settled in China and localized, completed the transformation from the dominance of physical gold trading to virtual trading. The trading ratio between the two is about 50 : 1, that is, the physical gold trading volume only accounts for 2%—3% of the total trading volume, but higher than the average value of 0.8% of the international gold market, reflecting the objective demand of China's gold market based on the development of the gold industry. The development of China's gold investment market from scratch to global influence is fundamentally the embodiment of gold liquidity brought about by gold marketization.

9.2 China's Innovation in Gold Financial Products

Liquidity is the key to the development of the gold investment market, and product innovation is an important means of creating market liquidity. China's gold investment product innovation is basically promoted in two directions, one is miniaturization of the trading subject matter, reduction of trading threshold and expansion of the participant group. Now China's gold investment trading subject matter has miniaturized to 0.1 grams of gold. The other is to realize the convenience of trading with the paper-based trading subject matter. The convenience of the transaction not only reduces transaction costs, but also is an important method and means to stabilize and attract investors. At present, the main direction to realize the convenience of the transaction is the development of network technology, and in this regard we have our own advantages.

The standard gold bars stored in the treasury are generally 400-ounce gold bars, miniaturized gold bars are generally less than 1 kilogram. After the miniaturization of the gold subject matter, buying gold is as convenient as buying gold, and that was what the Western people comment. In 1980s, the most famous small gold bars were India's 100g "Tola" gold bars. When I went to Switzerland in late 1990s, I saw workers of a Swiss banker carefully packing "Tola" bars for India. Today we have miniaturized the gold subject matter to the extreme of 0.1 grams. Trading convenience, in addition to technological advancement, should also be attributed to the innovation in the trading subject matter, e.g. paper-based subject matter and digitalized subject matter, also known as tokenization and digitalization. After more than 10 years of development, China has basically introduced all the paper-based and digital products in the international gold market and achieved its own development, of course paper-based and digital products will grow strong and weak in the Chinese soil, but they will not grow simultaneously.

9.2.1 Miniaturized Investment subject matter Products

The main products of miniaturized gold investment subject matters are mainly gold coins and small gold bars. Gold coins were launched in the 1960s, earlier than small gold bars, and small gold bars were the product of the gold deregulation in 1970s, but now the demand for small gold bars has exceeded the demand for gold coins.

9 A Gold Investment Market Derived from Development

In 2017, the gold used for gold coins globally was 256.6 tons, while the gold used for small gold bars was 778.3 tons of gold, 3.03 times the amount of the former. The miniaturized gold investment subject matters of China are as follows.

Investment gold coins. Panda gold coins are issued by the central bank and distributed by the China Gold Coin Corporation, they were put on the market in 1969, started to be issued only outside the country, and only in 1984 were they officially issued to the domestic market. The Panda Investment Gold Coin, together with the Maple Leaf Gold Coin of Canada, the Eagle Gold Coin of the United States, the Kangaroo Gold Coin of Australia, and the Kruger Gold Coin of South African, are known as the world's top five gold coins. In recent years, the Panda Gold Coin has ranked forth in terms of issuance volume among the top five gold coins, only higher than the South African gold coin, and fifth or sixth in terms of global gold coin demand. The average annual gold consumption from 2008 to 2017 was 20.09 tons, and that between 1988 and 1997 was only 4.45 tons. Panda gold coins are available in 5 sizes of 28 grams, 14 grams, 7 grams, 3 grams and 1 gram. In 2018, Panda gold coins were traded on Shanghai Gold Exchange. China's gold coin market is to some extent monopolized and closed, so the market size is inferior to the small gold bar market.

Small gold bars. Small gold bars are the re-miniaturization of kilogram gold bars traded in the general market, with more specifications and weighing in grams. Little gold bars, commonly known as "little goldfish", prevailed in the 1930s and 1940s and then disappeared because of gold control, and were followed by the millennium commemorative gold bars approved by the central bank in 1999. After the lifting of gold control, Shanghai Gold Exchange launched 50g small gold bars and 100g small gold bars in 2004 and 2006 respectively. During this period, the four major state-owned banks also launched their own branded gold bars, in addition to commercial bank branded gold bars, four major gold groups - China Gold, Shandong Gold, Zijin and Zhaojin have launched their own branded gold bars. Based on the profound zodiac culture in China,

Chinese Gold: From Following to Surpassing

a kind of zodiac commemorative gold bar has emerged, which combines the cultural needs of commemorative significance with the material needs of investment. Therefore, there is a group of special small gold bar investors who buy a fixed quantity at a fixed time regardless of price. On the birthday of his two granddaughters, a friend of mine bought 200g of small gold bars as birthday gifts, totaling 2.4kg of gold for 12 consecutive years. In fact, this is his wealth gift to his granddaughters, worth of about 720,000 yuan at the current gold price. It can be said that small gold bars have become a popular subject matter of gold investment in the country, and a choice of wealth inheritance and asset allocation for ordinary people, and this choice has even become a habit.

The demand for gold bar investment in China is the demand for household wealth storage after the lifting of gold control, and then it developed to the asset allocation demand of institutions, so the demand is gradually pulled up. The demand for gold bars was only 2.2 tons in 2002, it was 60.8 tons in 2008 and 418.1 tons in 2017, an increase of 5.88 times. Gold bar investment accounted for 23.7% of the total gold consumption. The investment demand for gold bars has become an important aspect of the people's demand for gold, about 20 times the demand for gold coins. The structure of the Indian market is similar to ours, and the first choice for gold demand in Europe and the United States is gold coins, because the logistics of gold coins in Europe and the United States is more convenient than that of gold bars, which is one of the reasons why gold coins are preferred instead of gold bars.

WeGold. It is an online trading product jointly launched by ICBC and Tencent. It is extremely miniaturized to 0.1 grams and we can buy and sell it after we set up a special account online. Because of the extremely low barriers, China's 800 million Wechat users can easily trade gold online and become potential customers in the gold market. Customers can conduct virtual transactions or extract gold online. WeGold is supported by physical transactions of gold, so we classify it as the miniaturization of gold rather than the virtualization of gold trading, which seems to be similar to the operation of

9 A Gold Investment Market Derived from Development

London Gold. I think gold is only a name for the WeGold product launched by Tencent. In fact, it is necessary to expand the use of internet technology, because there is a huge amount of transaction information to be processed, and the processing of a huge amount of information can only be completed by network technology. Although the network technology we have ranks among the best in the world, this is, after all, the innovation of gold trading in China on the basis of the application of new technology, so it puts forward new requirements for supervision. The security of a trading platform with the participation of hundreds of millions of people must be handled with care, improved and run-in, so although the platform has been officially launched, it has not been run on a large scale and is still in the stage of trial operation.

Gold ETF. If we say the innovation of "WeGold" originated in China, gold ETF was an authentic import. After the demonetization of gold, the demand for gold has been increasingly driven by the consumption of gold jewelry, so the World Gold Council has long taken the expansion of the gold jewelry market as the focus of its work. However, the World Gold Council began to recognize the importance of gold investment demand to drive gold demand in the late 1990s, and therefore selected a new chief executive officer from among people with a financial background, Kimberton, an American who retired from the post of CEO of the largest civilian servant fund in the United States, and therefore how to achieve a breakthrough in gold investment in the existing financial system became Kimberton's responsibility. It has already been pointed out that the development of gold investment is mainly to increase the liquidity of gold which requires virtualization innovation of gold trading subject matter. Based on the background of the World Gold Council's gold producer marketing, this innovation must be linked with the corresponding physical gold, and that is the reason for the design of gold ETF.

The design idea of gold ETF is to divide 1 ounce of gold into 10 parts and securitize them, and then circulate and trade them in the securities market, with the corresponding gold stored in a third party to ensure the authenticity of the gold. The third party generally stores the gold in an international bank with good security. Investors who own gold ETF can buy and sell gold ETF in the securities market for profit and loss settlement, and if they withdraw, they can take away the gold ETF they own corresponding to the gold. The transaction fees of the investors are allocated proportionally by the issuer of the ETF, the securities company and the gold storage bank. Because the World Gold Council is the world's largest issuer of gold ETF, the fee income from the gold ETF accounts for two-thirds of its funding, drastically reducing members' dues.

The gold ETF was originally scheduled to be launched in the United States, but Australia went ahead of the United States and became the first country to launch gold ETF. The response to the launch of gold ETF was enthusiastic. Many countries including Britain, France, Italy, the United States, Germany, Singapore, Sweden, Turkey, the Netherlands, India, have Switzerland a number of gold ETFs, and the amount of gold owned exceeded 2,000 tons at the highest, but it declined for three consecutive years after 2013. In 2016, it rebounded and grew, and it declined again in 2017. In 2013, China successively launched three gold ETFs were, Guotai Fund, Hua An Fund and E Fund, raising 410 million, 1.208 billion and 500 million yuan respectively. The size of China's gold ETFs is not large, and much marketing work is needed to be done a deeper understanding of this innovative work with many advantages.

9.2.2 Paper–based Products of Investment subject matter

Paper-based subject matter in gold trading is also based on the convenience of the transaction, and the difference from the miniaturization of subject matter is that there is not standardization requirement for physical trading subject matter. Paper-based gold is to hold gold certificate vouchers, certificates of deposit, gold IOUs, gold passbooks and gold accumulation. Some paper gold may be used to exchange for physical gold, and some may not. At present, China's paper gold only includes gold accounts and gold accumulation launched by commercial banks.

Account gold. This is a kind of paper gold investment product for

9 A Gold Investment Market Derived from Development

the general public.After setting up a capital account, investors can buy and sell gold from the over-the-counter gold dealing platforms of commercial banks according to the quotation by commercial banks. Gold accounts can generate profit and loss, but physical gold cannot be withdrawn. This is the currently the largest proprietary gold business of commercial banks at present, but the volume of trading has fluctuated relatively widely since launch, falling from 2019.2 tons to 988.7 tons from 2013 to 2014, a decline of 51.04%, rebounding to 2130.8 tons in 2017, the highest historical record for this business, accounting for 26.39% of the bank's total proprietary business that year.

Gold accumulation. We can understand the gold accumulation as depositing small sums of money and draw out both the principal and interest in a time. The investor deposits fixed funds at a specific time, the bank buys gold in batches, the funds deposited in the gold accumulation account reduce, and the gold purchased increases accordingly. When mature, the accumulated gold can be withdrawn, or sold according to market prices. China's gold accumulation was launched by the Industrial and Commercial Bank of China (ICBC) in 2009, the trading volume in the first year of launch was only 0.54 tons, while in 2014 it reached 594.24 tons, the highest trading record since launch, but in 2017 it fell to 201.85 tons. Gold accumulation was also an import, born in Japan, it has quickly become a popular form of gold investment.

9.2.3 Physical Credit Collateralized Products

These products are investment subject matters that generate liquidity in gold without transferring ownership of gold, and the reason why liquidity can still be generated without transferring ownership of gold is that some people only need to obtain the right to use gold temporarily and do not need to have permanent ownership of gold.

Gold lease. Financial institutions transfer the right to use gold to gold production enterprises and gold using enterprises according to a certain lease interest. The reason why gold production enterprises need to rent gold is to expand the plant or acquire working capital for production, and then the produced gold is returned back to the lessor. The reason why gold processing enterprises need to rent gold is to access to low-cost production raw materials, they sell the products they have produced, buy gold with the payment for products and return to the gold lender. The gold lease interest rate is generally lower than the funds interest rate, so gold lease is one of the paths to reduce the cost of capital, and also an effective means of avoiding price risks, therefore, there are an increasing number of enterprises joining the ranks of gold leasing, bringing an explosive growth to China's gold leasing market. In 2005, the annual gold lease scale was only 2.21 tons, and 2017 it reached 2994.65 tons, an increase of 1,354 times.

Gold lending. This is the act of financial institutions regulating gold surplus and deficiency among themselves. As China's gold market is expanding in scale, the gold lending behavior between financial institutions is becoming more frequent, in 2007 the lending volume was only 1.2 tons, and the incoming 10 years witnessed a continuous growth in the lending volume. In 2017, the gold lending volume has exceeded 1,000 tons, or 1,216.6 tons, but down 2.09% year-on-year.

Gold collateral. This is an act of exchanging gold for funds, i.e., the temporary loss of ownership of gold in exchange for the right to use the funds before redemption of gold, mostly as a response to emergencies when there is a shortage of funds, so it is far less likely to occur than gold leasing and gold lending. The general size is only a few tonnes, with merely 0.83 tonnes in 2017, down 75.64% year-on-year.

9.2.4 Virtualization Products of Investment Subject Matters

Gold virtualization products is gold derivatives. Relative to physical gold, this kind of gold trading subject matter is not for the completion of the delivery of gold and realize the possession of physical gold, but in order to achieve profit, or transfer or avoid the uncertainty risk of the gold price. The subject matter virtualization

9 A Gold Investment Market Derived from Development

products of gold investment are mainly the following:

Spot deferred delivery contract. In 2004, Shanghai Gold Exchange needed to increase liquidity in spot gold market due to its transition to a financial market, and launched the first spot deferred delivery contract - (Au + D), followed by four gold deferred contracts - Au (T+5), Au (T+1), Au (T+2) and Mini (T + D), which developed a spot deferred delivery product series. The launch of gold spot deferred products enables Shanghai Gold Exchange Market a function of avoiding price risks and the market has a greater liquidity. By using spot deferred contracts, investors can delay delivery at risk, thereby avoiding adverse situations. Therefore, deferred fee is to be paid, in case of oversupply, the seller pays deferred fee to the buyer, vice versa, continuous deferring is accepted and the deferred fee rate is 0.02%. This actually balances the supply and demand relationship at spot market by means of deferred fee instead of transferring spot market risks to forward markets, so it has Chinese characteristics.

Spot deferred contracts have played an important role in the transformation of Shanghai Gold Exchange, as the proportion of spot deferred contracts trading reached 72.5% in 2008, becoming the dominant subject matter traded on Shanghai Gold Exchange, marking the completion of the transformation of Shanghai Gold Exchange into a financial market. The volume of deferred products traded in that year was 3,234.02 tons, and in 2017 it has reached 23,500 tons, an increase of 6.27 times, and the product has been the main force in the development of Shanghai Gold Exchange.

Gold swap contracts. Gold swap contracts, as the name suggests, are a tool to adjust the time of performance, those contracts, same with spot deferred contracts, have the same function of postponing the real market risk, the difference is that the swap contracts are contracts traded in the over-the-counter market. So the swap contracts are non-standardized contracts, and personalized contracts agreed between the two sides of the transaction, and have a greater flexibility, and the biggest problem is that the transaction information is controlled by both sides and lacks of social openness.

Chinese Gold: From Following to Surpassing

The lessons of the international gold market tell us that the lack of openness of information will lead to fraud, therefore the openness and transparency of trading information is the goal of the reform of the international gold market. Our response is to introduce swaps from over-the-counter to Shanghai Gold Exchange's floor inquiry and trading platform for settlement and filing, and to place the whole swaps trading process in a transparent market environment.

Gold swap contracts were first launched on the market by ICBC in 2011, and have a history of only a few years, the trading volume in the first year was only 5.6 tons, 3 years later it grew to 100 tons. It maintained at 100 tons for 2 years, and reached the 1,000-ton level in 2017, or specifically 1,119.3 tons, an increase of 86.14% year-on-year. This was the highest value of this product in the 7 years of its launch and accounted for 13.86% of the total volume traded over the counter at commercial banks that year.

Gold futures contracts. They are the first standard forward contracts launched on China's gold market and an important driver of the size of China's gold investment market. Gold futures contracts were launched in 2008 on Shanghai Futures Exchange, and in the same year, the gold futures contract market had been the largest gold market in China since then before it was surpassed by Shanghai Gold Exchange until 2017, but gold futures contracts are still the largest gold trading subject matter in China. The trading volume reached its highest since launch in 2016, with the two-way trading volume reaching 69,500 tons, while in 2017 it fell to 39,000 tons, and then to 32,000 tons in 2018. Futures contracts have a history of a hundred years, and gold futures developed in the 1970s. The gold futures contract market is an extremely liquid market, and now the trading volume of merely New York Mercantile Exchange in 2017 reached 23.46 tons, while the same year the one-way trading volume of Shanghai Futures Exchange was only 34,800 tons, only 14.83% of that of New York Mercantile Exchange, so China's gold futures market still has a long way to go.

Gold option contracts. Gold option contracts were born in the 1980s. Option contracts are about the right of selling or buying a

9 A Gold Investment Market Derived from Development

certain amount of gold at a certain price, the right can be exercised or abstained, in case of abstention, the loss is just the option fee, thus the maximum profit opportunities may be maintained by locking one's own losses. There is a close correlation between option contracts and futures contracts, and it can be said that options are a safeguard against the risks of futures trading, thus after the gold futures contracts were launched in 2008, the launch of option contracts became inevitable, but it was not until 2015 that option contracts were tested on Shanghai Gold Exchange inquiry and trading platform. The trading volume was 14.46 tons that year, 15.79 tons in 2016, a 72.61-fold increase to 1,162.23 tons in 2017. This explosive growth reflected the market's strong demand for gold options as a product. In 2018, Shanghai Gold Exchange also launched the Renminbi gold options volatility curve for the first time to provide guidelines for options trading. The launch of gold forward options on Shanghai Futures Exchange was also reportedly on the agenda.

Advanced sales contracts of gold. There are the following inconveniences for investors to use gold futures contracts to lock in the uncertainty risk of future gold prices. First, To maintain the contract according to changes in gold prices, one has adjust the margin at any time, or forced liquidation will occur, so there must be sufficient capital flow for assurance; second, the gold futures contract market is rapidly changing, the operation requires a strong professionalism, and the professional quality requirements of practitioners are very high; third, standardized contracts lack of flexibility, and do not adapt to the changing requirements. To a large extent, forward contracts that may overcome above-mentioned shortcomings are advanced sales contract of gold, which complete physical transactions of gold of certain purity, specifications and quantity according to agreed time, price, and delivery mode in the form of a contract established between the two parties. This is an over-the-counter market trading of forward contracts, flexible and can realize the individuality of the contract. Once signed, the contract cannot be adjusted and this ensures low cost and convenient management. So standardized gold futures contracts are more suitable for investors and speculators, and advanced gold sales contracts are more suitable for gold producers and processors. Due to the existence of the biggest gold industry in China, so we have a great demand for advanced sales contracts of gold, and it has already ranked first in the proprietary trading volume of China's commercial banks.

It was Bank of China and Industrial and Commercial Bank of China which took the initiative to carry out the advanced sales business of gold. In the beginning, the trading was dollar-denominated, and only after that there were Renminbi-denominated forward contracts. In 2008, the trading volume was only 178.78 tons, after that basically the growth momentum was maintained, in 2015, the trading volume exceeded a thousand tons and reached 1488.82 tons, the highest record after the product was launched. After two years, the trading volume fell back but still maintain the level of a thousand tons, and it was 1,294.27 tonnes in 2017. The trading volume of advanced sales contracts was higher than that of swaps, or 1,119.3 tons, and options, or 1,162.23 tons, ranking first among proprietary gold derivatives of commercial banks.

9.3 From Product innovation to Platform Innovation

The key to the development of the gold investment market is to increase the liquidity of gold, innovation in gold trading subject matter is the driving force of gold liquidity, and each such innovation can expand the function of the market and bring new market participants, and therefore new liquidity to the market. But China's financial market is separately managed, the basis of which is product-based management, the management is under different authorities according to difference in product attributes, so the separate management system is the prerequisite for the innovation of gold products. In 2007, Shanghai Gold Exchange planned to launch gold futures contracts, a product regulated by the CSRC, hence

9 A Gold Investment Market Derived from Development

there was a regulatory problem. Gold, foreign exchange, currency, securities, futures, commodities and many other financial products are interchangeable, so how would gold achieve cross-border interoperability through innovation in the separate management system of China? To this end, Shanghai Gold Exchange has moved from product innovation to platform innovation, which means striving to build a trading platform that can be used jointly by gold financial subject matters supervised by different authorities, so as to realize cross-border gold flows without changing the system of separate product supervision, thereby raising the liquidity of China's gold market to a new level. Shanghai Gold Exchange inquiry and trading platform has made a useful exploration in this regard, but the choice of this path may not be intentional, but rather the result of China's separate management "system".

9.3.1 Background of the Birth of the Gold Inquiry and Trading Platform

On December 3, 2012, Shanghai Gold Exchange and Shanghai Foreign Exchange Bourse jointly established an inter-bank inquiry and trading platform based on the need to promote platform innovation, which began with the cultivation of China's gold market maker system. 6 ministries and commissions, including the central bank, issued Opinions on Promoting the Development of the Gold Market in 2010, requiring Shanghai Gold Exchange to introduce the market maker system into the over-the-counter market. The issue of market makers was raised as an issue for the development of China's gold market, indicating that the market maker system is an important system for the gold market, a guarantee for the liquidity of the over-the-counter gold market and an important promoter of the forward contract and the gold paper contract market, so the development of China's gold market also needed market makers. As a result of more than half a century of isolation from the gold market, after the market liberalization, we did not have qualified gold market makers, which was a shortcoming of the development of China's gold market, so the cultivation of market makers and establishment of market maker system became a development problem of China's gold market.

Market makers had to face the pressure of two-way risks of long position and short position, so they were special members of the market born after market and assuming special responsibilities. We established a market maker system and cultivate market makers. If we took the road of free competition, the road of the survival of the fittest, there would be a waste of social resources and a lot of uncertainty, so we chose to let market makers to play a role in a rule-based environment and control risks in the growth of market makers, so we need to create a "special" market environment for the development of market makers, which was the top design of "invisible hands", which introduced the market maker system into the market. That was the background of Shanghai Gold Exchange and Shanghai Foreign Exchange Bourse Exchange jointly creating Shanghai Gold Exchange Gold Inquiry and Trading Platform.

On the inquiry and trading platform of Shanghai Gold Exchange, the recognized market makers quote prices, buyers and sellers trade freely, complete the settlement process and are put on file. Therefore, China's market maker trading mechanism and the international traditional market maker mechanism are both free trading with over-the-counter and floor two-way quotations, and the difference is that the settlement and filing are completed in the floor market. Shanghai Gold Exchange inquiry and trading platform actually provides a "special" market environment for the development of market makers in China's gold market, or in other words, establishes a special gold trading zone, thus China's gold market has also developed a proper noun: Market makers on the gold inquiry market (Floor market makers).

9.3.2 The Development of Gold Inquiry Market Maker System

From 2012 to 2018, this gold market platform with Chinese

9 A Gold Investment Market Derived from Development

characteristics had been in operation for 6 years and has extended outward from inter-bank inquiry trading to inquiry trading between banks and enterprises and international board inquiry trading. The research team on the development of Shanghai Gold Exchange inquiry market has divided the development history of market makers in China's gold market into 3 stages.

■ Start-up Stage of The Development of Market Makers (Before July 2014)

This stage was mainly to initiate inter-bank forward and swap trading and provide a basis for market maker trading, which was a product preparation for the inquiry platform, while the institutional preparation was the piloting of the gold forward price curve quotation syndicate mechanism in July 2013, which constructed the prototype of the market maker quotation trading mechanism. In November of the same year, the Interbank Market Exchange Association issued the Basic Terminology of Over-the-Counter Gold Derivatives Trading in China, defining the concept of market makers in the gold quotation market, a concept that was innovative in the Chinese sense.

■ Initial Stage of The Development of Market Makers (July 2014– December 2015)

This stage was mainly to promote the following aspects of reform: First, the central bank issued the Notice of Relevant Matters on the Establishment of the Market Maker System for Trials of Interbank Gold Inquiry Transactions, which laid the policy foundation for inquiry market maker trials; second, 21 commercial banks that attempted to be market makers were identified, and a specific quantitative assessment index system was simultaneously developed, providing a standard for the selection of official market makers; third, new trading products were launched in addition to forwards and swap subject matters. Shanghai gold inquiry and lending contracts were launched in July 2014, the international board inquiry varieties were rolled out in January 2015, and the inquiry physical gold options were released in February 2015; fourth, the market's participation groups were expanded, the first brokerage firm entered the market in 2014, and two major currency brokers entered the market in 2015. An increasing number of cross-border traders entered and expanded the service base of the inquiry trading platform.

■ **Official Launch Stage of Market Makers (January 2016 – Present)**

In January 2016, Shanghai Gold Exchange officially launched the inter-bank market maker system, identifying the first batch of 10 market makers and six attempted market makers, consisting of state-owned banks, banks of gold export-import, joint-stock banks and foreign banks. The establishment of the market maker system greatly promoted the scale of China's inquiry trading. 55 institutions participated in the trading that year, with a cumulative transaction of 17,700 tons, an year-on-year increase of 72.83%, an increase of 1116.09% over the 1,455.49 tons that Shanghai Gold Exchange's inquiry trading market makers were ready to launch in 2013.

9.3.3 Significance of the Gold Inquiry and Trading Platform

In 2017, the number of institutions involved in trading increased to 61, of which 47 were domestic and foreign banks and securities companies, while the rest 14 were non-financial institutions. Thus, the significance of the construction of Shanghai Gold Exchange inquiry and trading platform has transcended "inter-bank", and the reason for this transcendence was that the inquiry and trading platform provided a specific development space for market makers, and the difficulty of risk control in this specific development space was much lower than the difficulty of controlling the global risk, so more reforms and trials could be carried out and thus banks' own gold derivatives trading could be expanded on this trading platform. In 2011, before the establishment of the inquiry trading platform, the trading volume of commercial banks' self-owned forward derivatives was only 139.17 tons, while after the establishment of Shanghai gold

9 A Gold Investment Market Derived from Development

inquiry trading platform, the trading volume reached 45,600 tons in 2018, an increase of 326.7 times. Therefore, the establishment of the inquiry trading platform has advanced the reform and promoted the development of the banks' self-operated gold derivatives market, which is one of the significance of the establishment of the inquiry platform.

The gold inquiry trading platform was jointly set up by Shanghai Gold Exchange and Shanghai Foreign Exchange Bourse, inquiry market makers can quote on main board of Shanghai Gold Exchange or on Shanghai Foreign Exchange Bourse platform, so which not only inadvertently realizes the connectivity between the gold market and foreign exchange market, but also makes gold a choice of institutional asset allocation. The gold asset allocation is a new trend today, and the establishment of the gold inquiry trading platform allows this trend to be realized in China. Tullett Prebon SITICO (China) Ltd. and Shanghai CFETS-NEX International Money Broking performed well in the inquiry market. In 2016, these two currency companies completed 0.556 million tons of gold transactions on the inquiry platform , in 2017 the trading volume increased by 108.63% to 11.6 million tons, respectively, 31.44% and 50.66% of the total trading volume of the inquiry market of the two years, and 11.42% and 21.36% of the total trading volume of Shanghai Gold Exchange. The performance of these two currency brokers showed the huge demand for institutional allocation of gold wealth, and the establishment of the gold inquiry market facilitated the cross-border flow of gold, which was a necessary condition for the landing of gold asset allocation and another important significance of the inquiry market.

The establishment of the gold inquiry trading platform promoted the development of China's gold forward trading and provided more application scenarios for the application of "Shanghai Gold". "Shanghai Gold" was priced under a transparent mechanism, this process formed the Renminbi pricing, which is another independent price for international transactions in addition to the traditional dollar pricing in London, thus the birth of "Shanghai Gold" was internationally revolutionary. However, "Shanghai Gold" only provided a pricing standard for gold trading, and the use of this price was of greater strategic significance, as it was necessary for the internationalization of Renminbi. The activation of the international board inquiry trading opened up a market space for the use of "Shanghai Gold". If the derivatives of gold option quotation were linked to "Shanghai Gold", and the offshore Renminbi used "Shanghai Gold" pricing as the cash settlement price of gold futures, then "Shanghai Gold" could also be widely used in over-the-counter funds, wealth management products and ETFs. Expanding the application scenarios of "Shanghai Gold" was another important significance of Shanghai Gold Exchange's inquiry and trading platform.

Another important significance of the gold inquiry market was that the development of the inquiry market changed the trading structure of Shanghai Gold Exchange - from dominance by spot gold trading to dominance by forward gold trading. The trading volume of forward inquiry exceeded the trading volume of spot bidding, marking the transformation of a marginalized market of the financial market to a basic market, which was an important change for Shanghai Gold Exchange. The development of the gold inquiry market also drove the overall improvement of the social function of China's gold market system.

9.3.4 Trajectory of the Development of the Gold Inquiry Market

The trading platform of Shanghai Gold Exchange was launched on December 3, 2012, with a trading volume of 14.31 tons in that month, an annual volume of 171.72 tons in 2013, an annual volume of 957.6 tons in 2013, and an average annual growth rate of 115.12% in the following four years. The three years witness three order of magnitudes. The trading volume reached 22,900 tons in 2017 and 45,600 tons in 2018, an increase of 99.13%. Its proportion in the total trading volume of Shanghai Gold Exchange also increased year

9 A Gold Investment Market Derived from Development

by year, from 8.25% in 2013 to 42.13% in 2017 and 67.56% in 2018, an increase of 25.43 percent points and surpassing the traditional competitive price trading volume for the first time. Shanghai Gold Exchange, which started with spot competitive price trading, has always been the dominant trading method, but in 2018 it was surpassed by the forward inquiry trading mode, which essentially indicated another qualitative change in the trading structure of Shanghai Gold Exchange. In 2008, spot deferred contract trading replaced physical gold competitive price trading as the dominant trading, which meant that Shanghai Gold Exchange was changing from a gold commodity market to a gold financial market, so what did the replacement of spot competitive price trading with forward inquiry gold trading as the dominant market mean? This meant that the transfer of the marginalization of gold in the financial market to the basic position, indicating that there were more and more financial products that were linked to gold, or used gold in price settlement price, or existed in currency, foreign exchange, funds, or asset markets, which was an upgrade of the financial attributes of Shanghai Gold Exchange, so the gold market became an important part of the financial market, and it was no longer a theoretical determination, but an objective fact.

As evidence of this, Shanghai Gold Exchange Annual Report 2017 disclosed that 22,900 tons were traded on the inquiry platform that year, while 14,700 tons of the trading volume, or 64.19%, were completed on Shanghai Foreign Exchange Trading Centre platform, and only 0.82 million tons, or 35.81%, were completed on the platform of the main board of Shanghai Gold Exchange and international board platform, which meant that nearly 2/3 of the gold inquiry transaction that year was not completed on the gold trading platform, but on the foreign exchange trading platform. Didn't it prove that gold had been part of the foreign exchange market trading, and the existence of the foreign exchange market? The innovation of a product can bring about the expansion of the size of a market, and the innovation of a trading platform can bring about a qualitative change in the market.

10

A Gold Market with Diversified Means of Transaction

The way of trading is a part of the market structure, different market structure has different ways of trading, today's gold market mainly has two dominant ways of trading: the United States is a field gold futures market, thus the market trading way is bidding trading way; Britain is an over-the-counter gold trading market, so the market trading way is market maker quotation trading way. And for a country, if the gold market is a specialized single market structure, the country not only the market trading target is a single, and the trading method is also a single. If it is a multi-market structure, the country's gold market trading method is multifaceted. Our country is a pluralistic gold market structure, and therefore our country's gold market trading method is pluralistic. The diversification of gold trading methods is an important symbol of the development of China's gold market, and is one of the Chinese characteristics of China's gold market.

There are 5 types of gold trading methods in China: Competitive price trading, quotation trading, inquiry trading, priced trading and lease mortgage. The trading volumes completed by these 5 trading methods are not the same, and in 2017 the ratio of the volumes of the various trading methods were: Competitive price trading accounted for 68.24% of the total trading volume of that year, quotation trading accounted for 22.57%, quotation trading accounted for 5.02%, lease mortgage accounted for 2.96%, and priced trading accounted for 1.28%. Although competitive price trading accounted for more than 2/3 of the total trading volume, quotation trading increased rapidly, and in 2018, the volume of quotation trading increased by 99.13%

over 2017, from 22,900 tons to 45,600 tons, already become the number one trading method in Shanghai Gold Exchange, accounting for 67.56% of the total trading volume the Shanghai Gold Exchange.

10.1 Competitive Price Trading of Floor Market

Competitive price trading is the trading method of the over-the-counter market and is the main trading method of the two over-the-counter markets, Shanghai Gold Exchange and Shanghai Futures Exchange. The main board of Shanghai Gold Exchange and the gold futures trading of Shanghai Futures Exchange both use the competitive price trading method. The competitive price trading is to rank the quotations in order, and to match the buyers and sellers through the electronic system. Initially, the quotations were loudly declared by traders who shouted out the buying prices or selling prices, other traders also shouted out accordingly and achieved the transaction, and then a contract was established for final confirmation. The exchange in the past was very noisy, but now it has become very quiet, because the development of computer technology makes the quotation from shouting out to remote digital input, through computer matching, the transaction can be completed in an instant with the computer system. The process of floor competitive price trading is transparent, fair and fast, making it the prevailing way of trading in the contemporary international gold market. In China, the gold trading volume completed through competitive price trading in 2017 was 69,200 tons, accounting for 68.24% of the country's total in that year as the kind of trading with the largest trading volume. Among them, the gold trading volume of Shanghai Gold Exchange completed through competitive price trading was 30,200 tons, 29.78% of the country's total gold trading volume in that year; the gold trading volume of Shanghai Futures Exchange through competitive price trading was 39,000 tons, 38.46% of the country's total trading volume. While Shanghai Futures Exchange adopts a single competitive price matching trading method, Shanghai Gold Exchange has introduced a diversified

10 A Gold Market with Diversified Means of Transaction

trading method. The diversification of trading methods has created a huge lifting force for Shanghai Gold Exchange and is the main way to expand the scale of Shanghai Gold Exchange. Shanghai Gold Exchange is a gold market with multiple trading methods, in addition to competitive price trading, it also has inquiry and priced trading, which constitute one of the elements of Shanghai Gold Exchange with Chinese characteristics. Although competitive trading remained the trading method with the biggest share in 2017, its share decreased by 28.26 percentage points compared to 2008, and the new trading methods are beginning to squeeze the market share of competitive price trading methods.

10.2 Over-the-Counter Market Quotation Trading

Quotation trading is the trading method of the over-the-counter market, the quotation trading method was about free quotation, identification of buyers or sellers, which was very inefficient. Then some special market participants who quoted the selling prices and buying prices at the same time as sellers and buyers, they were called market makers, thus market makers have become liquidity providers of the over-the-counter market and market trading organizers, and they are also the main bearers of market risks. Under normal circumstances, market makers are both buyers and sellers and can hedge their risks, but when the market is unilateral, market makers, who are responsible for assuming market liquidity, must quote prices in both directions and become the biggest bearers of market risks, so not all market participants are qualified as market makers and have sufficient financial strength, and after years of market trials and tribulations, those who have proven to be outstanding may become market makers. Therefore, market makers in the international gold market are generally large international banks, and thus the over-the-counter gold market has become a market dominated by commercial banks.

Our gold market was a latecomer, and in the early stages there were no qualified market makers who were experienced and tested

Chinese Gold: From Following to Surpassing

by the market. Due to the absence of this important condition, China took a very cautious approach to the development of the market-making market, i.e. a controlled development. As a result, Shanghai Gold Exchange handover individual customers in comprehensive members to financial institutions, internet gold enterprises are rectified for compliance. While the country actively supports the growth of genuine market makers, China stays highly vigilant of the proliferation of fake market makers. Therefore, although the over-the-counter gold trading market of commercial banks in China's gold market system is the smallest market, of which the innovation performance is not satisfactory, this cautious attitude the general defect of the gold market in the country, namely the deadlock of either too strict regulation or too loosen regulation. We have actively promote the reform of the market maker system, and developed the inquiry trading mode, that is an innovation, and also a part of the cautious policy.

The over-the-counter quotation trading of market makers is completed on the over-the-counter business platform of commercial banks. Generally speaking, the quotation trading increased from 356.55 tons in 2008 to 5,080 tons in 2017, an increase of 13.24 times. However, the average annual proportion of over-the-counter quotation trading in the four years from 2013 to 2017 was only 4.66% of the total trading volume. It is a marginal trading mode related to the reform of the market maker system in the country. We did not made great efforts to cultivate over-the-counter market makers, but established Shanghai Gold Exchange inquiry and trading platform to actively cultivate floor market makers. A large number of quotation transactions are completed by market makers on the floor, which will naturally affect the trading volume of over-the-counter market makers. In addition, the lack of innovation in the over-the-counter gold market of commercial banks is also a reason.

China's commercial banks mainly participate in floor gold trading on Shanghai Gold Exchange and Shanghai Futures Exchange, while their own market maker quotation trading is mainly completed on the inquiry platform of Shanghai Gold Exchange, so over-the-counter quotation trading by market makers of commercial banks account for less than 5% of the domestic trading volume, while the overseas gold trading of China's commercial banks is mainly completed in London over-the-counter market maker market. This is because six Chinese commercial banks are already market makers in London market, but they are rarely involved in floor gold futures and options trading in New York. In 2017, the overseas gold trading volume of Chinese commercial banks was 12,600 tons, and the gold trading volume of over-the-counter market maker quotation market was 12,500 tons (Excluding futures and options trading volume), accounting for 99.21% of the overseas gold trading volume of commercial banks. Commercial banks' overseas transactions are basically done in the over-the-counter market, that is, the London Bullion Market.

10.3 Innovative Inquiry Trading

Inquiry trading is an innovation of China's gold market, which was originally introduced into the over-the-counter market in order to promote the establishment of the over-the-counter market maker system in China's gold market, and turn it into a market maker of the gold inquiry market of China or a market maker of the floor market. Therefore, this floor market maker is different from the original over-the-counter market maker, because this market is no longer the other market. The transaction in this market is still quoted by the over-the-counter market maker, but a process of inquiry is introduced to the quotation, which is intended to make the quotation more transparent, the formation of the quotation more fair, and the transaction is settled on the floor and put on record on Shanghai Gold Exchange. This is different from the traditional over-the-counter market maker, it is an improved market maker, so it is called inquiry market maker. Inquiry trading is another new way of trading after competitive price trading and quotation trading, and this new trading method is genuinely created in China. The market maker system of the London Bullion market has been there for a century, but it collapsed due to the

Chinese Gold: From Following to Surpassing

gold price manipulation fraud of Barclays Bank in 2013, and the international over-the-counter market maker system was forced to be reformed. In 2010, six ministries and commissions including the People's Bank of China released Several Opinions on Promoting the Development of the Gold Market, which initiated the reform of the over-the-counter gold market maker system in China, that was, requiring Shanghai Gold Exchange to introduce the market maker system. Therefore, the inquiry products were launched in 2011, the inter-bank gold inquiry trading market was launched in 2012, and the inquiry market maker system in China was gradually formed. The over-the-counter market in London was also reformed in 2015, which was a passive reform after something went wrong, while we took the initiative to reform. as a result, the market maker system did not become a disaster in China, but became a driving force for development. Inquiry trading has become the fastest growing form of trading on Shanghai Gold Exchange. The transparency of trading information is an important issue in today's gold market reform. Although the market maker system reform in China has not yet made the trading information of market makers public to the whole society, the openness in the market has taken a step forward, and the action has been made traceable, which can have a great restraining force on the evilness of human nature and increase the security of market transactions.

The greater significance of the launch of the inquiry trading platform is to set up a new wholesale trading platform for institutional gold investors, different in terms of functions and quality from the original competitive price platform. Therefore, this new platform has the possibility to promote new reform experiments, and the market trading participants quickly go beyond "inter-bank". In addition to small banks, foreign banks and securities institutions, there are also non-bank institutions. However, more and more non-bank institutions are beginning to use the gold inquiry market, which shows the richness and extension of the service function of Shanghai Gold Exchange, so the gold forward derivatives trading of commercial banks is increasingly transferred

10 A Gold Market with Diversified Means of Transaction

to the inquiry trading platform. the significance of building such a gold inquiry trading platform has gone beyond the significance of "gold" and has a pulling impact on the whole financial market of the country.

The inquiry market was jointly set up by Shanghai Gold Exchange and Shanghai Foreign Exchange Bourse, which enabled Shanghai foreign exchange trading platform to inadvertently connect the gold market, the monetary market and the foreign exchange market. That was a functional breakthrough for the development of China's gold market, and gold assets became a part of monetary asset allocation. This breakthrough strengthened the financial nature of Shanghai Gold Exchange and immediately created two major customers in the gold inquiry market: Tullett Prebon SITICO (China) Ltd. and Shanghai CFETS-NEX International Money Broking. Their trading volume was 5,600 tons in 2016 and more than doubled to 11,600 tons in 2017, accounting for 31.44% and 50.66% of the total inquiry trading volume of the two years respectively. That was something cannot be done in the competitive price main board market. With the establishment of the inquiry and trading platform of Shanghai Gold Exchange, the important products in the over-the-counter gold market could be sold in advance, swaps and option contracts could be implemented, so that the trading of gold spot and forward contracts in China developed rapidly. There was another big increase in gold forward trading in the over-the-counter bank market in 2017, with a gold forward trading volume of 1294.27 tons, a trading volume of swaps of 1119.3 tons and a trading volume of options of 24.15 tons, up 5.91%, 87.64% and 52.92% respectively.

The interbank inquiry trading market was born in December 2012, and the annual inquiry trading volume in 2013 was 0.096 tons, while in 2018 it reached 45,600 tons, surpassing competitive price trading and becoming the largest trading method on Shanghai Gold Exchange. The volume and proportion of gold inquiry trading between 2012 and 2018 are shown in Figure 10-1.

Chinese Gold: From Following to Surpassing

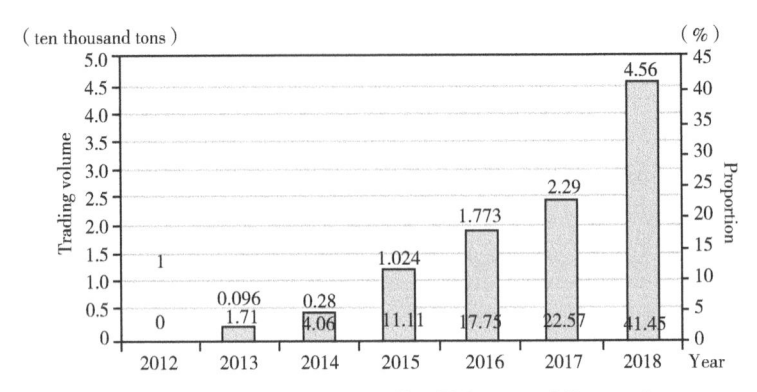

Figure 10-1 Gold Inquiry Trading Volume and Proportion from 2012 to 2018

10.4 Priced Transaction out of the Chamber of Secrets

Shanghai Gold Exchange launched priced trading in 2016. Due to the formation of the benchmark price of "Shanghai Gold" and the construction of "Shanghai gold" trading platform, a new scenario of Renminbi pricing and trading was formed in Shanghai Gold Exchange, and a new market different from the main board that changed with the changing prices of U.S. dollar was established. Therefore, the launch of "Shanghai Gold" broke the dominant pattern of dollar pricing in the international gold market, and provided another choice for gold investors. For the international gold market, that was the emergence of a new trading pattern. For China's gold market, that was not only a specific application of Renminbi internationalization, but also an effort to improve the voice of China's gold market.

In 2017, the participants in the "Shanghai Gold" pricing market had 10 bidders and 8 quasi-bidders, then the number grew to 30, and the members participating in the pricing transaction were domestic commercial banks, gold-using enterprises and overseas members, so it had a wide range of representativeness. In the

10　A Gold Market with Diversified Means of Transaction

"Shanghai fixed" pricing transaction, 18 market makers first quoted the initial reference price, and after many rounds of negotiations, the "Shanghai Gold" benchmark price was finally presented, and then the transaction was carried out according to the benchmark price. In 2017, "Shanghai Gold" conducted a total of 488 sessions, 2,433 rounds of pricing, with an average of 4.99 rounds of adjustment each time. This pricing process was similar to the pricing process of the five major gold merchants in London founded in 1909, but the biggest difference was that the five gold merchants priced in a secret chamber, and the information was opaque, while the pricing processing of "Shanghai Gold" was made public and published in time, transparent and fair. That was a great change in gold pricing in China after it had experienced planned fixed pricing-planned floating price-floating price that changed with the US dollar-dominated gold price. That also reflected the voice and influence of China's gold market in formation of international gold prices. Although it took a process to improve this voice and influence, we had taken the first step. Priced trading had been launched for only three years by 2018, so the trading volume was small and accounted for less than 2% of the total trading volume. Priced trading volume rose from 569.19 tons in 2016 to 1,262.74 tons in 2017, an increase of 121.85%, before another increase of 16.79% to 1,474.71 tons in 2018.

The launch of the "Shanghai Gold" pricing trading platform of Shanghai Gold Exchange enhanced the brand effect of "Shanghai Gold", expanded the scope of use of the benchmark price of "Shanghai Gold", and became a benchmark settlement price for the development of forward products. Therefore, it had a wide application prospect in the fields of over-the-counter financial management, funds and gold ETFs, so the benchmark price of "Shanghai gold" has gone beyond the gold market and produced a wide range of premium effect in the financial market. The "Shanghai Gold" benchmark price is also used abroad, and Dubai Gold has been authorized by Shanghai Gold Exchange to use the "Shanghai Gold" benchmark price as the settlement price in the development of offshore Renminbi-denominated gold futures contracts.

Chinese Gold: From Following to Surpassing

The diversification of the trading mode of China's gold market is the product of the diversification of the form of China's gold market, and the diversification of the form of the gold market is the result of the pursuit of the extension of service function of the gold market. The extension of service function is one of the main reasons for the scale expansion of China's gold market, so over the past 17 years, with the expansion of the scale of China's gold market, it has begun to establish an increasingly close relationship with the various factor markets of the financial market, transformed the gold market from an isolated marginal financial market to a basic market. The so-called basic financial market is a market that can provide settlement standards, transfer risks and maintain the stability of the financial market. With the increasing integration with the financial factor market, China's gold market is moving towards the financial basic market step by step.

11

A Gold Market under Progressive Internationalization

Gold has a characteristic of global liquidity, the gold market is a global 24-hour continuous trading across time zones, so the gold market has the gene of internationalization. To survive and develop, the gold market must promote internationalization, this is the only choice of the development of the gold market, and the pursuit of internationalization necessitate the selection of the path of opening. China's gold market also needs to open up and take the road of internationalization, but the internationalization of China's gold market should have its own characteristics, it is not immediately internationalized but gradually internationalized.

11.1 Rectification of Name for a Gradual Internationalization Road

Gold market must be internationalized, and the road of opening up must be taken for internationalization. London Gold Bullion, New York Gold Market, and other backbone markets in the international gold market system must be internationalized to take heavy responsibilities, and regional markets must take internationalization as their own development path and achieve development in an open environment, because gold market is a global continuous trading market system for which synchronization of transactions is very important and any market non-synchronization may damage the market itself by offering arbitrage opportunities. In 1990s, gold was controlled in 1990s, and gold smuggling rose due to arbitrage opportunities with international gold prices, and Hong Kong and

Chinese Gold: From Following to Surpassing

Macao received smuggled gold from mainland China. In order to prevent gold smuggling, China had to strengthen management, increased management costs, it was still difficult to fundamentally eliminate gold smuggles. Therefore, it was not that we chose not to internationalize, we could not internationalize, because we did not know whether our gold market had enough attraction to attract international investors to the market. There were different roads to choose from for opening up and internationalization, and we chose a road of gradual opening up.

Since 1978, China has embarked on the road to reform and opening up, which has been fruitful, beneficial and left no reason for us shut down again. The doors opened to the world would not be shut down again. This was our commitment and determination to demonstrate to the world. However, there were still some doubts about our opening up, not always internationally, sometimes there were doubts in China, mainly on different choices in opening up the market. We were practitioners of neo-classical economics based on imperfect understanding of markets, so the opening up took steps gradually under the intervention of the visible hand. However, economic liberals opposed the "visible hand" and they wanted to settle the matter at one go, because they believed markets could rectify themselves and achieve balance, and naturally challenged gradual step-by-step openness. Actually, our reform and opening-up practice has shown that although full opening up at one attempt seems quick, it may cause new conflicts that are tough to handle, while gradual opening may yield twice the result with half the effort. Internationalization with gradual opening up is not only theoretically demonstrated, but also proved by practice, so it is a correct choice to develop gold market gradually and realize internationalization.

11.2 Gradual Internationalization of China Gold Market

The internationalization of the gold market in China is an practice case of gradual opening up. Before 2002, the People's Bank of

11 A Gold Market under Progressive Internationalization

China was a direct operator of gold products, but after 2002, it has been a regulator of China's gold market, so the People's Bank of China did not change its role because of the abolition of the gold system of unified collection and distribution, and only the object and content of management changed, previously products and now market. The intervention of the visible hand in gold market has always existed because of the existence of this regulator, the opening up is not a radical and one-stop action, but gradual. This is because the People's Bank of China is not only the regulator of the gold market, but also the bearer of risks in opening up. Therefore, openness is a political choice for the People's Bank of China, and also a realistic choice. Opening up must be necessary, but it will bring uncertainty risks. So the door can only be gradually opened with enhanced risk management abilities of the People's Bank of China against risks in opening up, which is essential reason for the gradual internationalization of the gold market in China. Market opening up is provided with a top design. Therefore, two presidents made it clear on 2002 and 2004 respectively on the direction of internationalization of gold market in China, but no specific progress was given. Actually, the policy orientation of the People's Bank of China is to take natural steps forward according to actual situation of gold market development.

The impact of gradual opening up is that China's gold market has a relatively mildly competitive market environment, this environment provides protection to the newly born and still weak gold market, which is conducive to its growth. When China's gold market has a certain scale and then enhances the opening up, it has the ability to dialogue with international investors on an equal footing. Precisely because of this, the internationalization of China's gold market is not to open up and invite teachers, but to cater to commercial partners, when China's gold market chooses to promote openness and internationalization, it has the initiative and the decision-making power to determine when and how to open up.

In June 2007, five years after the operation of the gold market in China, the People's Bank of China approved Shanghai Gold Exchange to introduce foreign bank members to carry out gold

Chinese Gold: From Following to Surpassing

business. In February 2008, Standard Chartered Bank became the first foreign bank member of Shanghai Gold Exchange, which was the first step towards opening up gold market in China. Up to then, Shanghai Gold Exchange had become the largest spot trading market in the world. The trading volume reached 1,828 tons in 2007, with an increase of 144.19% in 2008, reaching 4,463.77 tons. That was why the gold market in China was so confident in opening up and advancement internationalization. After that, the number of foreign bank members increased to 8, but foreign bank members have been equal participants in the market rather than dominant players.

Shanghai Gold Exchange took another step forward and launched the international board of Shanghai Gold Exchange on September 18, 2014 in Shanghai Free Trade Zone, allowing overseas members to participate in gold trading on the main board of Shanghai Gold Exchange using offshore Renminbi (Closed management of funds and logistics were practiced to maintain the independence of the international board). When Shanghai Gold Exchange took a step of internationalization of practical significance, its trading scale had reached a 10,000-ton magnitude, reaching 11,600 tons in 2013. Shanghai Gold Exchange became an eye-catching star, an important gold market in Asia, showing huge growth potentials and having a greater attraction to foreign investors, Therefore, the international board has attracted 15 international members, 34 domestic members engaged in transactions soon after it was launched. By 2018, the international board of Shanghai Gold Exchange had had 69 international members, 71 international customers represented by international customers, completing 4,776.98 tons of gold trading volume, which was 8.8% of the trading volume of Shanghai Gold Exchange, or 54,300 tons. Due to the launch of the international board, Shanghai Gold Exchange set up a treasury in Shanghai Free Trade Zone, Gold began to be imported via Shanghai Customs and this accounted for 35.83% of imports in 2017.In 2018, the number of international board members increased to 151.

Shanghai Gold Exchange launched "Shanghai Gold" on April 2016, providing gold trading standard for international

11 A Gold Market under Progressive Internationalization

gold investors. "Shanghai Gold" was formed in the over-the-counter market. To avoid frauds of London "London Gold" for nontransparent operations, the pricing process of "Shanghai Gold" insisted on fairness, openness and transparency, and recorded all processes. 18 quotation members offered the initial quotation, after multiple rounds of quotation (Averagely 4.99 rounds in 2017), the transaction benchmark price was produced and issued timely. There were 26 institutions participating in the priced trading of "Shanghai Gold", completing a trading volume of 569.19 tons. Participating institutions included commercial banks, brokerage firms, smelters and gold-using enterprises. The number of enterprises participating in transactions rose to 30 in 2017, the trading volume reached 1262.74 tons, and in 2018 it was 1474.7 tons, maintaining a growth momentum, but only accounting for 2.18% in the total trading volume of 67,500 tons of Shanghai Gold Exchange, so "Shanghai Gold" was not the main force of Shanghai Stock Exchange.

The trading volume of "Shanghai Gold" was still at a thousand-ton level in the first three years after the launch, and it did not create an impressive pulling force for the expansion of scale of Shanghai Gold Exchange. However, for the development of Shanghai Gold Exchange, even the gold market in China, the launch of "Shanghai Gold" had an epoch-making significance.

Firstly, the internationalized application of "Shanghai Gold" pricing indicated that our country has developed from opening up of market to opening up of rules, while the internationalization of rules was the symbol of transformation of the Chinese gold from a follower to a leader. "Shanghai Gold" was important not only because it was a new trading product, but also because it provided a settlement standard between domestic and foreign financial derivatives and financial products linked to gold, thereby integrating gold into the financial market.

"Shanghai Gold"'s first overseas application project was that the offshore Renminbi gold futures launched by Dubai Gold and Commodity Exchange was settled on "Shanghai Gold" as standard prices. Another important significance was to create market

Chinese Gold: From Following to Surpassing

scenarios for Renminbi international application and provide an important supporting force for Renminbi internationalization. Dollar was pegged to gold to form dollar exchange standard, and GBP was pegged to gold to form gold standard and gradually became an international currency from a domestic currency. Historical experience can be used for reference. Establishing and forming gold supporting force in various forms is an important national strategy, and the release of "Shanghai Gold" provided a handle for the formation of gold support of Renminbi.

11.3 A Near-term Vision for the Internationalization of China's Gold Market

In 2008, China's gold market developed overseas bank members and opened up the main board market of Shanghai Gold Exchange; in 2014, the international board was created and the offshore Renminbi gold market was opened up; in 2016, the "Shanghai Gold" priced transaction was launched and international gold institutions started to participate in the Renminbi gold pricing process, which was the history of internationalization of China's gold market, and today it has developed to a new stage.

In 2017, Shanghai Gold Exchange focused on opening up to the outside world to interact with the Belt and Road Initiative and promote cooperation between markets along the route. To this end, Shanghai Gold Exchange held cooperation discussions with countries along the route and signed a memorandum of cooperation with Budapest Stock Exchange. In particular, China and Southeast Asia are similar in culture, civilianization and geography, so the opening up to Southeast Asian countries will be the focus of the internationalization of China's gold market. Southeast Asian countries are at different stages of economic development, and countries such as Myanmar, Laos, Cambodia, Thailand, Malaysia and Indonesia have similar gold consumption culture with China, and we should focus on the opening up of logistics of gold jewelry market to pull both markets. Exchange and cooperation in the

11 A Gold Market under Progressive Internationalization

gold trading market should be carried out with countries with more developed financial markets such as Singapore. The focus of the opening up should be "Shanghai Gold" trading and Shanghai priced derivatives innovation, and a closer link to the needs of the internationalization of Renminbi.

The broader vision for the internationalization of China's gold market is the formation of an central market in Asia which is the region with the largest number of gold markets. It was world's largest gold-producing continent between 2012 to 2016 and the second largest in 2017. In past 10 years, Asia has been the world's number one in both gold jewelry consumption and industrial consumer goods of gold, and thus Asia is well positioned to replace Europe as the global gold logistics center. In addition, Asia is the most active area of the contemporary economy and has a huge potential gold investment demand. Japan, India, Singapore, Turkey and other gold markets occupy a place in the international gold market system, but the Asian gold market lacks a central force. The development of Shanghai gold trading market has increased the weight of the Asian gold market in the world, if Asia becomes a whole, it will have a pivotal position in the global gold market system, and China's gold market should take this as its responsibility and make unremitting efforts.

Although Asian gold markets are quite a lot in number, they are small in scale and not good in quality. There is not a central market, making it difficult to form a coordinated interactive operation mechanism. In 1980s, Japan was the central gold trading market in Asia, from which China learned in the initial development of its gold market. However, instead of making progress, the gold market in Japan backslid, with a current trading volume of less than 10,000 tons, on the contrary, China's gold market, as a latecomer, has development rapidly with a two-way trading volume of more than 100,00 tons. The dual competitive structure of the international gold market has been replaced by a situation of three major gold markets in London, New York and Shanghai. The market position of the gold market in China as the central gold market in Asia has

Chinese Gold: From Following to Surpassing

been established. So the future internationalization of China's gold market is to gradually establish the mechanism and system of interoperability and interaction with Asian gold markets and form an important place for Renminbi gold trading. Shanghai Gold Exchange and Dubai Gold and Commodity Exchange have jointly promoted the launch of forward derivatives of Renminbi "Shanghai Gold", which is the first step in the design of derivatives with "Shanghai Gold" as the standard price, and this effort will be further deepened and expanded in the future, which will be a new task and a new level of internationalization of the gold market in China.

The internationalization of the Renminbi needs to form a gold support force, any credit paper currency needs to provide value support for physical commodities, the linkage with gold is a historical tradition, so recently in the face of the uncertainty of the world economy, central banks are jumping on the bandwagon to increase their gold reserves. The People's Bank of China also joined the ranks in 2009, increasing gold reserves is a choice to increase the currency gold support, but more importantly, to improve the control ability and influence of the gold market, so the establishment of a global gold logistics center market is another important goal of the internationalization of China's gold market, which is undoubtedly extremely important for the achievement of the goal of the internationalization of Renminbi.

Now China is already the world's largest producer, the largest consumer, the largest importer and the largest wealth accumulator of gold, and therefore it basically has the "hard conditions" to replace Switzerland as a global gold logistics center, but what is lacking is the "soft conditions". First, the management policy for two-way flow of gold import and export is not formed, and now the import and export of gold cannot flow freely; Second, there is a lack of top-level design, a global gold logistics center must realize the free flow of gold, it needs management and is not to be left unattended because the free flow of gold may also cause money laundering, smuggling and other illegal acts, so the construction of the global gold logistics center market needs top-level design, until now only a concept has been presented, and the specific top line design has not yet been developed.

12

Prospect: Thoughts on Future Development

The development of China's gold market in just 17 years has been a gratifying achievement, especially China's gold market has a special DNA, and takes a development road with Chinese characteristics. This road of development has drawn attention from international gold professionals as the development of international traditional mainstream gold markets encounter challenges, they hope that China's gold market becomes the pioneer and future leader of the international gold market transferring from the west to the east, and there are expectations and blessings for the future of the gold market of China. But the future goals and the path to achieve them are not yet clearly directed, and the relevant top-level design has not yet begun, which in turn seems to indicate that there are still many uncertainties in the future development of China's gold market, so our discussion on the future development of the gold market is necessary. I think that for the future development of China's gold market, first of all, we need to clarify the national strategic positioning of the development of the gold market, that is, what is the national purpose of the development of the gold market. The national strategy for the development of the gold market is not fixed, and necessary adjustments need to be made according to the actual situation, and the national strategy for the development of China's gold market today is to establish the international gold support of Renminbi.

12.1 Market Development Is a Need to Fulfil National Strategies

The strategy is a big picture, and the national strategy is a big picture for the nation as a whole. We cannot say that all economic activities should be linked to the national strategy, but for the gold market, we must recognize that the development of the gold market is to complete the needs of the national development strategy. This is because gold has its special financial properties, the gold market is not a general commodity market, but a tool for the "visible hand" to control the economy, this is the reason why the development of the gold market is linked to the national development strategy, and it is also the special nature of the gold market. The special nature of the gold market —— the special nature of its development path, so it is inevitable that China's gold market is a product of the design by the "visible hand".

Between 1949 and 2001, China did not have a gold market, which was the need of gold control by the country, and gold control was to serve the overall situation of the country at that time. The establishment of Shanghai Gold Exchange in 2002 was the need for the country to complete the reform of the gold market, which was also the strategic situation of the country. The development of the gold market was a requirement of this strategic situation, and since 2004 when the strategic goal was completed, the national development strategy of the gold market has been to improve and enrich the service function of the financial market to make up for the long-term deficiencies of China's financial market and to increase China's financial capacity, and this strategic goal has been or is being accomplished. Every stage of the development of the gold market embodies the will of the state, but the "visible hand" is not the runner of the gold market, which is strictly defined, but it is the decision maker of the direction of the development of the gold market, it decides what to do or not to do in the gold market, this is a fact, so the future development of China's gold market must also be a development with a top-level design.

12 Prospect: Thoughts on Future Development

Reality is the best teacher. In 2007, the subprime mortgage crisis in the United States triggered the financial crisis of 2008, culminating in a persistent global economic crisis with such serious repercussions that, more than 10 years later, it is still considered a once-in-a-century event. This crisis has affected the world and exposed the truth about the operation of the international financial system: Under the banner of free market economy, selfish desires in the name of financial innovation are uncontrollably proliferating, virtual transactions in the financial market are emerging and dominating, leading to price manipulation and market risks that are infinitely magnified, which finally make the crisis erupt and free market theorists are questioned. The crisis was caused by free marketers, who then turned on each other and looked to the "visible hand" for help. The outbreak of the crisis revealed the truth of the matter, which told us the necessity of the "visible hand" to take charge of the economic development, thus the development of the gold market in China with a top-level design began to be increasingly recognized. But the development is a continuous process, the future development of the gold market also needs a new top-level design, and this top-level design is derived from the needs of the national strategy. So what the national strategy is for the future development of China's gold market becomes the premise for our discussion on the future development of China's gold market.

Suggestions for the future development of China's gold market have two different perspectives: one is not to consider the national strategy of the gold market development changes, that is, in the present national economic strategy for the future development of the gold market to put forward suggestions for improvement and perfection; one is to gold market development of the national strategy has changed or will change as the basis for new thinking on the future development of the gold market, suggesting to cultivate the new functions of China's gold market to adapt to the changes in the national strategy.

The change in national strategy stems from changes in the international development environment, which is now so uncertain that it can be said to be changing to a dangerous degree, not to mention on an annual basis, but even on a monthly or even daily basis. While any assessment of our future development is uncertain, thinking in terms of the worst and biggest changes is necessary to take control of the future, so we need to be prepared for and face changes in national strategies, even if we are not happy about it.

12.2 Voice from Authoritative Research Institutions

The Financial Research Institute of the Development Research Center of the State Council, an intelligent institution directly under the State Council with high authority, completed a research project titled Report on Suggestions for the Future Development Direction of China's Gold Market in July 2018. The project put forward the following recommendations for the improvement and perfection of China's gold market based on the existing foundation.

12.2.1 Establishment of a New Approach to Regulation

The report considers that the essence of this recommendation is to form a legal basis for the intervention of the "visible hand" in the gold market, and to determine the path and boundary of the intervention of the "visible hand" in the development of the gold market. The report gives a positive assessment of the practical activities of the People's Bank of China, and stated "the People's Bank of China has the ability to lead the entire industry and put long-term strategic issues at the core of development...". It has specific recommendations for the People's Bank of China to move forward with its future endeavors: Development and promulgation of new market regulation regulations.

China's gold management regulations are *The Gold and Silver Management Regulations promulgated* in 1980s, since China has liberalized gold control, the regulations have actually lapsed even through they are not abolished. In 2010, six ministries and commissions including the People's Bank of China jointly

12 Prospect: Thoughts on Future Development

issued *The Opinions on Promoting the Development of the Gold Market*, the opinions are instructive, but are not binding enough. Now China's gold market has developed into a diversified market system, and become the leader of Asian gold market leader, with a trading volume steadily ranked the third in the world, so the market development needs normative regulations. In 2008, before the issuance of *The Opinions on Promoting the Development of the Gold Market*, the Legislative Affairs Office of the State Council started the drafting of the gold market regulations. I, as a consulting experts for the regulations, know of the situation. We were very divergent, because the conditions were not mature and finally the regulations were not drafted. This also shows that although there is an objective need for the gold market management regulations, there are a lot of problems to be solved for the formulation and adoption, because we are still not clear and even have no idea about the law of development of the gold market, and this is the difficulty we encounter.

The research report of the Financial Research Institute of the Development Research Center of the State Council puts forward recommendations on the gold market management regulations, suggests that the regulations to be titled "Gold Market Regulation Rules", and proposes that the formulation of regulations should fully learn from the lessons and experiences of the incorrect international response to financial crisis in the previous ten years, for this purpose, the Institute proposes that the formulation of regulations should follow the three following principles:

1. Principle of fairness. The report states that it is important to ensure that participants in market transactions of different identities are treated fairly and that market practices and standards of conduct are applied in a clear, consistent and transparent manner.

2. Principle of orderliness. The report states that strong trading facilities are needed to create effective and orderly market competition and to support price formation and trading.

3. Principle of regulation. The report states that the market and the conduct of market participants must be overseen by a credible

regulator, and recommends the establishment of a dedicated gold market regulator to ensure that the regulation and supervision of this regulator is unified and not fragmented. In addition, the introduction of a gold leasing information sharing platform and an over-the-counter master agreement should be prioritized.

12.2.2 Formation of Two-way Cross-border Flow of Funds and Gold

The realization of the two-way cross-border flow of funds and gold is the need for the international development of China's gold market, the realization of the two-way cross-border flow of funds and gold can be piloted first, and then gradually expanded.

1. Pilot the free import and export of gold and the free conversion under the Renminbi capital project in a specific customs territory within Shanghai Pudong Free Trade Zone.

2. Increase the certainty for foreign investors to participate in capital controls and quotas to attract more foreign investors to participate in gold trading.

3. Promoting the implementation of the Belt and Road Initiative, encourage countries along the Belt and Road to ship gold to China for trading, and encourage more investors from countries along the Belt and Road to participate in hedging transactions through the China's gold market.

12.2.3 The Development of Higher Market Standards

High standards in the market will not only improve the quality of market participants and market operations, but will also radiate the influence of the gold market brand of China internationally. The report recommends that the following three standards should be given priority to:

1. Develop standards applicable to trading on all online gold investment platforms and gold supply platforms, regulate trading practices in this sector and meet the needs of digital investors.

2. Standardize and legalize the social and environmental

12 Prospect: Thoughts on Future Development

responsibility of China's gold enterprises, which would take the international reputation of the gold industry in China to a new level.

3. The operation and regulation of the market need transparent and complete data as the basis, and the occurrence of some fraud incidents also shows that there are problems in this area, so the future development of China's gold market must have a high-level data transparency and complete high standards.

12.2.4 Market Access for Institutional Investors

Although China's gold market is developing rapidly, the investor structure is still relatively small and scattered. The market is lack of institutional investors, so there are many short-term investors and few long-term investors. The problem is the poor stability of the market, insufficient depth of the service, and the role of gold in the protection of China's wealth is not given full play to. Regarding the role of gold in protecting China's wealth, the report makes the following recommendations for the future development of the gold market.

1. Allow pension funds and insurance companies to enter the market. Allowing pension funds and insurance companies to invest in gold can increase the safety of futures and insurance portfolios, which is already a common international practice.

2. Enhancement of the education of institutional investors on the importance of gold in asset portfolios is essential for institutional investors to change their mindset and accept gold as a fundamental asset.

3. Customize investment products for institutional investors. China's gold products have been tailor-made for the retail market, institutional investors have very different requirements for cost structure and liquidity, their needs for tailor-made products are also different, the specific suggestion is to consider the establishment of joint ventures for market product design and marketing.

12.2.5 Infrastructure Construction of Gold Market

The current state of China's gold infrastructure has been

satisfactorily evaluated, but there is still room for improvement, and the report's main recommendations are as follows:

1. Establish a market setup that can support a monitored two-way cross-border flow of funds and gold. Based on the freedom to import gold, limited export freedom can be achieved by the issuance of export quotas before the gradual development into the freedom to import and export gold.

2. Shanghai Gold Exchange and Shanghai Futures Exchange should cooperate in the research and design of products that can meet the needs of large institutional investors, and in this process should listen extensively to the opinions and suggestions of domestic asset management companies and banks that provide investment services to futures.

3. Shanghai Gold Exchange and Shanghai Futures Exchange should establish closer and friendly relations with potential clients, and provide advice and services on risk management for a longer period of time, so that clients from abroad who directly provide products to China's gold market can manage their risk exposures.

12.3 Observations and Reflections from a Different Perspective

In 1991, without any preparation, I became involved with the study of gold market issues, from then on I have became an observer, researcher and promoter of China's gold market. In the blink of an eye it has been 28 years, and I have changed from a middle-aged man into an old man, but never like today I feel the strong urgency of the gold market change. Changes often happened in the previous 28 years, but most changes had a clear goal and the direction of the change was also relatively clear, but only this change is both profound and highly uncertain. Therefore, in my opinion, the future development and change of China's gold market is extremely profound, and there is great uncertainty, because the development prospects of China's gold market are linked to the changing international political and economic situations.

12 Prospect: Thoughts on Future Development

My observation of the development prospects of China's gold market has the following four basic points:

First, China's gold market has a top-level design and the realization of the national strategy is the direction and goal of gold market development; second, the national economic development strategy has been or is being adjusted; third, the adjustment and change in China's development strategy will certainly affect the future development of China's gold market, so the strategic objectives of China's gold market must also be changed or adjusted; Fourth, the change of the environment is fundamental, we should think profoundly and take further measures for the future development of China's gold market. Why do we say that the changing environment in which the gold market is developing today is fundamental?

12.3.1 Change has Happened, and It's Fundamental

Change is the result of comparison, and when we say that this is a world that has changed radically, we are comparing it from the dimension of a century. Billions of people live on the same planet, as social beings, so there must be tremendous relationships, and the management of interpersonal relations is a major issue of survival. There are two options for the management of interpersonal relations: Violence in hatred, or coexistence through peace. The first half of the twentieth century was a period of human suffering and social turmoil, with two world wars, and between them the world was plunged into the period of a great depression of the 1930s. Humankind was dragged into a "war" without the sound of guns, with tens of millions of people going bankruptcy and millions struggling for subsistence. Mankind, faced with the enormous loss of wealth and the painful ordeal in the first half of the 20th century, began to rethink its behaviors. In the second half of the 20th century, after comparing the pros and cons, mankind abandoned violence and confrontation and chose peace and coexistence. That was why in the second half of the 20th century, although the two camps confronted each other, a "cold war" state was maintained, and there was no general imbalance, and the United Nations, a political organization to balance the disputes between nations, and the WTO, which promoted global economic integration, emerged, and economic development became the main theme of humanity. However, in the tide of global economic development, there was a competition between the planned economy and the market economy, and the two economic forms represented the political confrontation led by the Soviet Union and the United States at that time respectively. In the early 1990s, the socialist camp, represented by the Soviet Union, collapsed, the planned economy was abandoned, and the market economy became the dominant global economic model. China's reform and opening up started in 1978, the 14th Party Congress in 1992 decided to establish a socialist market economic system, and began to change from a planned economy to a market economy. China joined the WTO in 2002, and boarded the train of economic integration. In this process, China and the United States became partners, and thus our economy and the U.S. economy began to be closely linked and inseparable. Reform and opening up presented China a period of sustained economic development, and in 2010, our economy surpassed Japan's to become the second largest economy after the United States and China began to take the central place on the world stage. We entered the first decade of the 21st century with glorious hopes for the revitalization of the Chinese nation, believing that the lofty goal of a century was not far away. But the changes have been more rapid than we thought, and we find that the second decade of the twenty-first century is so different from the first: for the world, the global economic crisis caused by the outbreak of the subprime mortgage crisis in the United States in 2007 has caused humankind to rethink the economic system established after the war and the path of development it has chosen.

12.3.2 Currency Competition is a Grade National Strategy

Changes in the competitive relationship between China and

12 Prospect: Thoughts on Future Development

the United States are inevitable, and competition has become an important development strategy for our country. This may not be our choice, but it is a reality. Striving to win the competition has naturally become our unanimous goal, from top to bottom, because it concerns the prosperity and well-being of every individual, every family and the family of Chinese nation. Competition is epistemologically a matter of confidence in the choice of the socialist market economy, and politically a matter of struggle against hegemony and the pursuit of equality. For this reason, we must adjust our original development strategy, the core of which is to make us stronger for competition, and the building of a financial breakwater should be a priority.

Why should building a strong financial breakwater be a priority? This is because today's human wealth has been monetized, whether it is exchanged to meet the needs of the human reality, or stored to meet the needs of the future of mankind, money is the main means and tools of use, so who has the right to money has the right to the distribution and use of the wealth of human society. The dollar hegemony is an important part of the international power of the United States - the dollar is the main means of payment and settlement in international trade and the main international reserve currency, accounting for more than 60% of the total global demand, so the United States can manipulate the dollar settlement system and dollar supply system to make the social economy suffer or collapse without starting a war, so the dollar hegemony is a powerful weapon for the United States to win in competition or wars. The monetary and financial game is therefore the main field of international competition today. We should understand how the United States achieves and consolidates dollar hegemony by we know ourselves as well as our enemies.

The performance of the dollar hegemony is first of all the status of the international central currency, the status is achieved with the pegging between the dollar and gold for the formation of the dollar gold exchange system to maintain the stability of the value of the dollar and defeating the GBP in the Bretton Woods international

Chinese Gold: From Following to Surpassing

monetary conference in 1944. The gold reserves of 22,000 tons of was the confidence of the United States to maintain the stability of the value of the dollar as the central currency. But in the 1970s, the gold was depleted, so the United States changed over to new ways, pegged the dollar with staple commodities, especially petroleum, and maintained the status of the central currency of the dollar through the usefulness of the dollar. The value of the dollar stability was no longer the focus of the United States, and the dollar embarked on a road of sustained devaluation. The super currency of the dollar has become a means of "sheep shearing" on a global basis for the United States. This is the hegemony of the dollar, but also the weakness of the dollar. From a competitive point of view, to build a strong Renminbi breakwater is to build a strong support for the value of Renminbi, and only with a stable value can Renminbi become an international currency.

The competitiveness of Renminbi is the stability of its value, and the greatest reflection and gain brought to mankind by the subprime mortgage crisis in the United States in 2007 and the global economic crisis that erupted as a result of its impact is that integrity is not a stable asset, so it cannot bring stable value support to paper money, and it must be pegged to physical commodities to obtain value support. The U.S. dollar was pegged to physical gold and replaced the GBP as the international central currency, after it was de-pegged with physical gold, it was pegged to staple commodities and gold, so as to ensure the usefulness of the U.S. dollar to obtain its value support, and that is the long-term hidden mystery of the U.S. dollar.

The value stability of Renminbi has always been based on the country's economy as a reference system, although China has been a politically independent entity in the world stage, it has been a non-dominant force, economically, and the specific performance is that Renminbi has been a marginal currency for a long time. In the Asian financial crisis in 1991, the Chinese government said it would never benefit itself at others' expense, Renminbi would not devalue, and would peg to the dollar. From the perspective of today, it was great wisdom and doing the right thing at the right time. To peg Renminbi

12 Prospect: Thoughts on Future Development

with the dollar, the strong currency, was a very common practice. Especially after China became the world's largest dollar reserve, maintaining nearly 4 trillion U.S. dollars at the peak and currently more than 3 trillion dollars, the value of Renminbi obtained the value support of the strong international currency, and the international reputation of Renminbi rose rapidly. So now Renminbi has gone international and become one of SDR's basket of currencies in the international monetary system, accounting for 5%; Renminbi has also become the settlement and reserve currency for international trade, with a share of about 3%, surpassing the yen.

12.3.3 A New Thinking: Pegging Renminbi with Gold

It is a tradition for paper currencies to be pegged with gold for value support. For more than 200 years, mainstream paper currencies in the world have been pegged with gold, except for in 1971, when the dollar declared to de-peg with gold as it could not handle the gold run, and practiced the so-called gold demonetization. Even then, global central banks still maintained gold reserves of 29,000 tons, which has until now increased to 34,000 tons, and this indicates that paper currencies are still to some extent pegged to gold and not de-pegged from gold.

Strengthening the connection between Renminbi and gold was our long-term policy, before the 1990s, China has been increasing gold reserves as an important strategic initiative, but after that period, because of the dollar income increased, gold was gradually marginalized in the national reserves and even considered useless, but in 2007, the United States subprime mortgage crisis unveiled the mysteries of dollar mystery, the idea that gold was useless was suppressed, so in such a situation, proposing that Renminbi should be linked with gold will get more people's response, but how to peg Renminbi to gold is still an unsolved problem.

The method to peg gold and currencies is changing, in the early period of gold standard, gold was a currency because gold was a means of payment. After that, as a result of the convenience of using banknotes, it increasingly became a circulation means of payment.

Chinese Gold: From Following to Surpassing

At that time, there was a correspondence between banknotes and gold, so paper money was the proof of gold. Later, there was no longer a correspondence but a kind of proportion. Gold was the basis of the paper money issue, a country established gold reserves to peg the issuing scale of paper money to that of gold reserve. And then, in the gold exchange standard period, the national reserves began to diversify, in addition to gold, there were foreign exchange banknotes, so then the issue of banknotes was only partly pegged to gold, and now gold is not pegged to the issue of banknotes. Gold reserves just provides a kind of insurance for banknotes as the substitute of the payment function. In general, in a system of dollar hegemony, the link between currencies and gold is increasingly distant, and the enhanced link between gold and Renminbi goes against this trend of alienation.

Now although gold was demonetized and the dollar has been de-pegged from gold, in fact the dollar still maintains a close relationship with gold, but this relationship is no longer tied to the amount of gold but to the price of gold. The dollar is used as the standard for gold pricing, the purpose of which is to increase the usefulness of the dollar. If people are able to use the dollar to the maximum extent possible, the value of the dollar will be reflected, the usefulness of the dollar becomes the supporting force for the value of the dollar, and thus supporting the trading value of dollar. This is a way to reflect and increase the stability and authority of the value of the dollar by trading liquidity of gold. So how does the United States create liquidity of gold?

The U.S. started by making the gold market functionally alien and developing gold derivatives trading, and now less than 1% of the trading volume in the gold market is traded with gold, while more than 99% is traded with dollar-based paper currencies, because the gold market has become a long/short manipulation market dominated by speculators with no actual gold trading needs. Because the trading in the gold market has nothing to do with the balance of supply and demand, it can create liquidity of gold as it wishes.

The gold price is manipulated like this: Before the close of the

12 Prospect: Thoughts on Future Development

New York Futures Exchange, a large number of short orders are thrown out so that the long position investors continue to take orders, declining gold prices eventually make those long position investors to stop loss and leave the market. Then the manipulated low price of gold is spread out to disappoint investors, more fund firms will follow and sell more gold, the gold price continues to fall and reach the bottom, then they will reenter and harvest the "wool". This manipulation process does not require much capital because the futures market allows for leveraged trading, with a leverage ratio of 1: 20. That is to say, with 1 dollar you can generate a market liquidity of 20 dollars, so market manipulation is not easy to detect and market manipulation is not an isolated case.

Now our mainstream thinking is to increase the trading volume of gold priced by Renminbi and thus increase the support of gold to the value of Renminbi. When we understand the structure of the contemporary gold market, we know that the dollar and the gold price is pegged to increase trading volume, only the demand for dollars is expanded, and the dollar is still depreciating. This is the driven by expanding the hegemony of the dollar, not by stabilizing the value of the dollar. When the dollar was competing against the GBP, it needed to pursue its stability, now it choose to expand the trading volume of the gold market to increase the use of the dollar. Different methods are used for different purposes. In different stages of development of the currencies of China and the United States, there should be different thinking and different methods of response.

China's Renminbi is pegged to gold in order to obtain a stable support for the value of the Renminbi, so this support needs to be built on the basis of physical gold. In order to execute the national strategy, it is necessary to make adjustments to the future development of China's gold market, therefore I hereby put forward the proposal to establish a gold bank, that is, to form a Renminbi gold support on the basis of the liquidity of the stock of gold. The gold bank is a new concept arising from judging the changing environment, and it will be discussed later as a separate chapter.

13

Gold Market: The Third Segmentation

China's gold market was established in 2002, the first market segmentation began in 2004, and was basically completed in 2008, realizing the transformation from a gold commodity market to a gold financial market. A commercial bank over-the-counter gold trading market was established, and it was a gold retail market for the public. In 2007, the gold market began the second segmentation that was basically completed in 2010, realizing the segmentation from the spot gold market from the forward gold market, marked by the launch of Shanghai Futures Exchange's gold futures contracts in January 2008. It was primarily a market in which investors and speculators participated. Based on the national strategy, to form the gold support of Renminbi, and to put this strategy into practice, I believe that we should promote the third segmentation of China's gold market, that is, establish a national gold bank to achieve the segmentation of the stocked gold and incremental gold.

13.1 Stocked Gold vs. Incremental Gold

Gold stock and incremental gold are two forms of existence in trading process of the gold market. Because gold has excellent physical and chemical properties, so it is not easy to be oxidized or corroded, and can exist independently for a long time, this is the eternal nature of gold. In 2018, more than 97% of the more than 200,000 tons of gold produced in human history was still in the world, but gold as a commodity gold is mobile in the market is. Gold will continue to enter the market, and flow out of the market after

Chinese Gold: From Following to Surpassing

transactions. One kind of gold trading needs to complete the transfer of ownership of gold, the other does not, so there are two kinds of trading methods on the gold market, namely selling and buying, borrowing and lending. The reason why there are two methods of trading, because most of the gold will not disappear because of "consumption", but is made into commodities as processing raw materials, recirculated and traded on the gold products market, or stored up as human wealth. So for a country, at a certain point, there is gold traded in the market and gold stored up, so the gold owned by the country can be divided into incremental gold and stocked gold. Incremental gold refers the gold flowing in the market and needing to be delivered, and stocked gold refers to that ceases flowing and is in the stage of storage. As human wealth, stocked gold will re-enter the market for trading in case of special needs, not to complete the transfer of ownership, but to gain some benefits through the suspended transfer of the right to use, so gold produces liquidity on the market not through delivery, but loans. So there are two kinds of gold market. One is the incremental gold market, which needs to complete ownership transfer for delivery, and the other is the stocked gold market, which does not require the transfer of ownership, but achieves the transfer of the right to use with loans. The incremental gold market and the stocked gold market have differences in trading purposes and functions, and there are also differences in management, the incremental market is mainly about capital flow management, while the stocked gold market is mainly about gold logistics management.

The incremental gold market and the stocked gold market have different functions, so the two have the reason to stratify, but now the gold market is integrated, gold loan is just an variety of the incremental gold market, and to satisfy the needs of forming a Renminbi gold support, an independent market should be established. This is because today's gold market is gold derivatives trading dominant market, the trading volume of physical gold accounts for less than 1% of the total. So the loan trading with physical gold as the subject matter is subordinative and marginal

13 Gold Market: The Third Segmentation

trading, which makes it unnecessary to develop into an independent market. In addition, most of international gold trading markets are financial capital markets, and there are no demand for physical gold, with just the flow of gold, and no accumulation of gold, so basically there is no or very little stocked gold, and accordingly there is no condition to form an independent stocked gold market. There was no necessity and possibility for the segmentation of the stocked gold market and the incremental gold market in China at the beginning.

Now there are two reasons for the formation of an independent incremental gold market based on the segmentation between the stocked gold market and incremental gold market in China: The first is that China is the world's largest gold demander, and it has the world's largest gold products manufacturers who has the actual need for gold loans; the second is that China is the world's largest gold importer and consumer. Officially and civilianly, there is increasing gold wealth, as well as the demand and capabilities for gold loans after 17 years of opening up of the gold market. In the face of the current profound changes in the international political and economic landscape, China places financial stability in a prominent and urgent position, the core of financial stability is the stability of Renminbi, for which China must form the gold support for Renminbi, so the task of segmentation between the stocked gold market and the incremental gold market is put on the agenda of reform.

13.2 Pegged to Gold: Self-redemption of Paper Currency

Based on the convenience of use, human currency has gradually become paper-based in modern times, but there has always been the problem of unstable value, which constantly threatens the paper currency and there have been many paper currency crises. In fact, during the Song Dynasty, China was the inventor and the earliest user of paper currency. after the Jin Dynasty and the Yuan Dynasty, in the Ming Dynasty, although the founding emperor Zhu Yuanzhang strictly forbade the use of metallic currency and introduced paper

Chinese Gold: From Following to Surpassing

currency, in 1435, Emperor Ying restored the copper currency, and then the silver currency in the next year, and China's silver standard system had existed since then until the beginning of the 21st century. The failure of paper currency originated from the vicious devaluation, the people's wealth was looted, eventually paper currency was abandoned, and the stability of paper currency became the biggest threat to its existence. So how to stabilize the value of paper money? That is to be pegged to gold. In 1944, the Bretton Woods International Conference determined that $35 could be exchanged for an ounce of gold, so the gold content of one dollar was 0.810 grams, it was this policy that ensured the stable value of the dollar, national currencies were then pegged to the dollar at a fixed exchange rate, so that each banknote had a legal gold content, for example, one mark's gold content was 0.222 grams, 1 yen's gold content was 2.469 milligrams, and once the gold content of one Soviet Union ruble was 0.222 grams. Pegging to gold made paper currency a kind of gold certificate. Paper currency was pegged to gold to obtain the value support, it also constitutes an integrity commitment and behavioral restraint of paper currency issuers, and gold became the core element of currency stability in the gold exchange period. Because the United States had up to 22,000 tons of huge gold reserves, it had the confidence to compete against the GBP and gain advantages, thus replacing the GBP as the international central currency. Pegged with gold, paper currencies jumped over the trap of vicious devaluation to achieve the stability of the international monetary system, and the world had entered a period of sustained economic development.

In 1971, because of the inability to cope with the emergence of gold squeeze, the United States cut off the link between the dollar and gold after the loss of large number of gold reserves, and human society entered the era of credit money. The credit money system without the support by gold only lasted less than fifty years. In 2007, the subprime mortgage crisis erupted in the United States, and led to the global economic crisis that has caused influences until today. After the outbreak of the crisis, the United States took advantage of

13 Gold Market: The Third Segmentation

the right to issue dollars and over-issued dollars. The United States printed an additional 3.7 trillion dollars between 2008 and 2014, while only 800 billion dollars were printed in the two hundred years before 2008. The over-issuance of dollars has led to a significant devaluation of dollar reserves and holdings of dollar assets of other countries, and the United States has transferred the dollar crisis to the world, exposing the vulnerability of the dollar as well as the injustice of the dollar-centric international monetary system, thus leading to calls for reform, which is now underway on multiple levels, though not radical. Even within the United States, some members of congress have proposed a return to the gold standard, and three state governments have already resolved to go on the gold standard.

The stability of the value of Renminbi was linked to its own gold and foreign exchange reserves, but due to China's very small gold and foreign exchange reserves, the support was very small, so Renminbi had long been regarded as a weak currency in the international arena, and it was in a marginal position in international trade and a weak position in the international financial competition. Today, after the reform and opening up, with the world's largest foreign exchange reserves of more than 3 trillion U.S. dollars as the the value support of Renminbi, the currency has gradually become stronger, and now has become one the SDR's basket of currencies of the International Monetary Fund, occupying a market share of 3% in international trade as an international reserve currency.

There are 2 purposes to be achieved by the construction of the Renminbi gold support task. The first is to meet the needs of Renminbi internationalization. With the development of China's economic internationalization, the internationalization of Renminbi has become a realistic and urgent strategic task. The U.S. dollar is the main settlement currency of contemporary international trade, the United States is the controller of the international trade settlement system, the development of international trade in China expands the payment scale accordingly, the risk of reliance on this system increases, once it is blocked, there will be huge losses. Russia

Chinese Gold: From Following to Surpassing

and Iran were subjected to U.S. financial sanctions, they could not settle with the United States dominated international settlement system, their foreign trade encountered great difficulties, so we must expand the use of Renminbi in foreign trade and achieve the internationalization of Renminbi. Only when the value of Renminbi is strong, other countries are willing to choose Renminbi as the settlement means and reserve currency of foreign trade, and a strong gold support must be established to keep Renminbi strong. The second is to change the dominance of the dollar in China's foreign exchange reserves. Now the country's foreign exchange reserves has exceeded 3 trillion U.S. dollars, and 80% is U.S. dollar assets. It is dangerous in the current international political and economic situation that is full of uncertainty, so we must promote the diversification of foreign exchange reserves. Increasing gold reserves is one of the measures of foreign exchange reserves diversification, because gold is the absolute wealth of mankind, so increasing gold reserves can reduce the risk of devaluation of reserves.

13.3 What Is the Gold Support for Renminbi?

Generally speaking, Renminbi gold support to about setting up a "gold treasury" with a large enough scale and linked with the issuance of Renminbi. While building a international gold trading center, we have to become a gold logistics center, so that we can become the place where global gold assets are gathered, for which we have to vigorously expand the scale of stocked gold in the country. China's stock of gold includes government stock and civilian stock, so the formation of the gold support for Renminbi requires us to establish a linkage conversion mechanism for two kinds of stocked gold, to use regulations to determine the connection between Renminbi and gold, which is the legalization of Renminbi gold support. The Renminbi gold support requires the liquidity of stocked gold that flows but is not to be lost, that is, to achieve controlled liquidity of gold, so there is a problem for innovation in

13 Gold Market: The Third Segmentation

the management mode.

What is able to provide support for the value of paper currency is stocked gold, not incremental gold, so the establishment of Renminbi gold support is mainly about doing a good job about stocked gold. The question is we have focused on incremental gold since the birth of the gold market in China, we have expand the market scale with the trading liquidity. Actually, this liquidity is mainly to increase the use of money, not to improve the support of currency value. But now because the strategy of building the gold support for Renminbi support is put forward, the incremental gold market is stratified from the stocked gold market, and that is the third segmentation in 17 years since the gold market in China came into being, this means that China's gold market is ushering in another new development stage, because a stocked gold market with new functions will be established.

The liquidity of the incremental gold market is a liquidity based on the transfer of ownership of gold, while the liquidity of the stocked gold market is a liquidity based on the transfer of the right to use gold. The incremental gold market is traded by delivery, while the stocked gold market is traded by loans. As gold derivatives dominate today's gold market trading, the incremental gold market is mainly about capital flow, so capitals are mainly regulated, and the stocked gold market is mainly about logistics, so gold is mainly regulated. The two markets are different in functions and management, so they need to be stratified. However, the two markets can be integrated as the trading scale of stocked gold is not big and the liquidity is not strong.

A noticeable gold loan market has emerged in China, but it is largely based on borrowing gold from abroad. For China, it is still incremental gold trading, not stocked gold trading. The liquidity of our domestic stocked gold is still problematic, and the gold loan market that already exists is not yet the same as the gold loan market needed to establish the Renminbi gold support. As a result of Renminbi gold support strategy, the stocked gold market has become an important development target, which has become an important opportunity to promote the segmentation from the incremental gold market and the stocked gold market, and has multiple implications.

The significance of the development of the stocked gold market is firstly to push the Renminbi support to a new stage, to accelerate the accumulation of China's gold wealth, and to further promote the development of the international pattern of "flow of gold from the east to the east"; secondly, as the virtualized trading of the international gold market is confronted with bottlenecks and difficulties, the third segmentation of China's gold market is to focus on activating stocked gold, and to place the development of China's gold market on the basis of physical gold, which provides another kind of thinking and choice for the future development of the international gold market. China is the world's largest gold demander and the largest gold products manufacturer, so there is a huge demand for gold loans. China is the world's largest gold importer and gold consumer, after 10 years of development, it has achieved a considerable scale of gold wealth accumulation, so there is an increasing demand for gold loans in addition to the gold loan capabilities. So the development of the stocked gold market can drive the liquidity of the gold wealth of the general public, bring low-cost financing to the gold processing industry, and provide support for the development of the gold industry.

13.4 Size of Official Reserves for Gold Support

Establishing international support for Renminbi is a national strategy, so the question of how to determine the size of the country's gold reserves is brought forward. The task of establishing a Renminbi gold support is first proposed, so is the pegging of Renminbi to gold, we have no ready-made answers to copy, so we can only seek answers from what we have learned.

First, the best object to learn from is the United States, because the dollar has a rich history of being pegged to gold and can provide us with a direction to think about.

Before 1944, the United States also put gold in strict control, so

13 Gold Market: The Third Segmentation

all stocked gold in the United States were held by the state. After the outbreak of World War II, most countries abolished the gold standard, but the United States still adhered to the gold settlement mechanism in international trade, so during World War II, the United States became the world's main gold recipient and deposition. After Word War II, the gold reserves of the United States gold reached a total of 2.2 million tons, 75% of the global official gold reserves, accounting for 49.4% of the global gold stock of 4.45 tons, or nearly a half. The United States, with huge gold reserves, held high the banner of gold standard and challenged the GBP, promised that U.S. dollars might be exchanged for gold at a fixed rate, and finally defeated the GBP in the Bretton Woods International Conference in 1944 and became the international central currency, thus establishing the dollar centered international monetary system. Then the 22,000 tons of gold was the scale of support for USD gold in the period of dollar and gold exchange monetary system in which the dollar was pegged to gold.

In 1971, the dollar was de-pegged from gold, and the process of demonetization of gold begin, the United States' gold reserves should be theoretically reduced to zero, but in fact the United States, to support the value of the dollar, buy a gold insurance and keep 8,134 tons of national gold reserves, accounted for 75% in foreign exchange reserves, or the sum of the rest 2-4 countries, ranking first in gold reserves and the proportion in foreign exchange. China has increased its reserves several times after 2009, reaching a peak value of 1,885.5 tons in April 2019. Although the United States continues to devalue gold in public opinions, it has always maintained the dollar's gold reserve support advantage. In addition to this, the United States has used its financial advantage to mortgage the gold reserves of its trading partners, which amounts to more than 7,000 tons of gold, to itself in the name of facilitating settlement, and the said gold reserves is controlled by the U.S. government. The sum of the mortgaged gold and the national reserves of gold of the United States is more than 15,000 tons, that is to say the United States can now directly control more than 15,000 tons of gold, or 45.45% of

Chinese Gold: From Following to Surpassing

the official global gold reserves. That is, the United States provides 0.8 million tons to 15,000 tons of gold support for the stability of the value of the dollar under the condition of gold demonetization. This is still a low configuration with the dollar hegemony to maintain currency stability.

Second, the scale of China's Renminbi gold support can also be observed from the perspective of the proportion of the world's gold reserves in global foreign exchange reserves.

In order to support the value of their own paper currencies, countries have established a system to peg to strong international currencies and set up foreign exchange reserves, including gold reserves, which can be regarded as the gold support established by those countries in order to achieve stability in the value of their paper currencies. The specific situation of each country is different, the scale of gold reserves is different, and the proportion in foreign exchange reserves is also different. The global average level of gold reserves in 1979 and 1980 had reached 62%, when the proportion of gold reserves far exceeded foreign exchange, but then it continued to decline and fell to less than 10% in 2013. From 2013 to 2017, the average of the proportion was 9.45%. Based on this percentage, the scale of China's foreign exchange reserves by April 2019 was 3.04 trillion U.S. dollars. According to the average proportion of countries around the world, China's gold reserves should be 287.3 billion U.S. dollars, and based on the current price of the gold dollar, it should be about about 8,960 tons. If China has reached the gold reserves, it will surpass the gold reserves of the United States, or 8,134 tons and rank first in the world. From the perspective of the proportion of gold reserves in countries around the world, China's scale of gold support for Renminbi should be about 9,000 tons.

The above analysis for China's official gold reserve scale provides a direction of thinking on the scale of gold support for Renminbi. Under the condition of gold demonetization, the scale of a gold insurance maintained for Renminbi should be 9,000 tons to 150,000 tons, 4.77 times to 7.96 times the current scale of China's gold reserves of 1885.5 tons. If Renminbi and gold form a closer exchange

13 Gold Market: The Third Segmentation

relationship, it is necessary to have a larger gold reserves, but in the current situation, in order to build a solid financial breakwater, it is still necessary to maintain a gold insurance for Renminbi, so China's national gold reserves still have a lot of room for growth.

Third, it needs to be pointed out that, gold ownership is not equal to gold control, and gold control is more important, so in the current situation, Germany and more than 10 countries have shipped their gold in the United States back to their own countries and set off a campaign titled "sending gold home", while the United States requests its trade partners to store and mortgage some of their gold reserves in the United States in the name of facilitating the settlement, which is indicative of the importance of the gold control. This is only one aspect of the issue; control of the gold market is a higher form of gold control, and in this respect the US is also worth learning from. During the gold exchange period, the international gold market was a window to stabilize the dollar-centric international monetary system, while after the demonetization of gold, the gold market was a tool to increase the usefulness of the dollar. The control of gold market is obtained through the market system regulations, the former is achieved through the gold supply manipulation, the latter is achieved through the gold dollar pricing, in short, the international gold market, regardless of all the changes, always serves the development strategy of the United States. So China must pay attention to the market system innovation, which is an important soft power of gold control. From the requirements of establishing China's Renminbi gold support, China's gold reserves still have a lot of room for growth. There is an even greater gap in market system innovation, a gap not only in the reality of the results, but also in our cognition.

13.5 How Big Is the Potential of Civilian Gold Deposits?

The civilian gold storage is an important part of the gold support for Renminbi, and a part of the stocked market with the highest

Chinese Gold: From Following to Surpassing

requirement for liquidity. During the Asian financial crisis in 1999, an economic crisis broke out in South Korea, the government mobilized people to donate gold to solve the international trade imbalance. South Korea fully mobilized the power of stocked civilian gold, and took the country out of the predicament, and it was a typical contemporary case of salvation of the country with gold. China's stocked gold from history was not much. In the early years since the People's Republic of China was founded, the gold maintained by the general public was only about 156 tons, and then it has grown with the development of China's gold market, and in the 21st century, Chinese people entered a period of rapid growth of gold wealth.

In 1979, the country issued the Panda Coin, and the domestic issuance was not practiced until 1984 to satisfy the domestic market. In 1982, the country resumed the supply of gold jewelry, the public began to possess gold in the form of jewelry. In 2004, the country opened the gold bar market to the public, who could officially own gold wealth. From 1949 to 2002, China produced a total of 2,372 tons of gold, in 2002, China's gold reserves were 600.23 tons, about 1,700 tons of mineral gold was used, so what was the gold used for?

During the period of gold control in the country, the civilian use of gold was strictly controlled, and the data of gold allocated for civilian use was kept secret. The quota for jewelry production every year was only a few tons, which was far from being able to meet the needs of the jewelry industry and led to the spread of gold smuggling. But about 400 tons, or 15% or 20% of total gold production, were still available for rationing, and some were used for international payments and flowed abroad. In addition, gold was sold on consignment in Shenzhen from 1999 to 2002, with an estimated 150 tons, so before 2002, civilian deposits totaled more than 700 tons (Historical deposits + domestic gold rationing + consignment sales of foreign gold). As a result, more than 90% of China's civilian gold deposits is formed after the opening up of the gold market in 2002.

After 2002, China's gold has realized the transformation from

13 Gold Market: The Third Segmentation

official storage to civilian deposits, the national gold reserve has only increased slightly, and the supply of gold market has mainly become civilian gold deposits. From 2003 to 2018, China produced a total of 5,457.8 tons of gold. During this period, the central bank's gold reserves increased from 600.23 tons to 1,885.5 tons, an increase of 1,285.27 tons, accounting for 23.55% of the total gold production, and the rest 76.45% were civilian deposits.

After the opening up of the gold market, the huge demand for gold was released. Since 2007, China has changed from an exporter of gold to an importer, and in 2013, it overtook India to become the largest importer of gold in the world. After 2013, China imported more than one thousand tons of gold for five consecutive years. From 2007 to 2018, China imported a total of 8,587 tons of gold. Import has become the largest source of gold supply for the country. While importing gold, China also exports gold at the same time. Before the opening up of the gold market in 2002, gold exports were mainly about processing of supplied materials, while after the opening up of the gold market in 2002, gold re-exports has appeared, most of which were normal exports of gold products (Mainly gold jewelry) exports, and some were exports for arbitrage. According to the data of the China Gold Yearbook, the average annual export volume of gold was 311.22 tons from 2003 to 2018. This data only gives us a direction of thinking. The export volume at the initial stage of market opening up was lower than this average. Therefore, we estimate that 3,000 tons to 4,000 tons of gold was re-exported from 2002 to 2018, and the stocked civilian gold formed by gold imports was about 5,000 tons.

The stocked civilian gold from gold produced in China is about 4,878 tons, and that from imported gold is about 5,000 tons, totally 9,878 tons. From 1949 to 2018, the level of civilian gold deposits in China has reached 10,000 tons, which is the evaluation of the current situation of the stocked civilian gold in the country, of which about 93% was accumulated in the 17 years after the opening up of the gold market.

In the future, the further growth of the scale of civilian gold in

Chinese Gold: From Following to Surpassing

China is a high probability event, because after nearly 10 years of sharp decline in the stock market and the depreciation of the US dollar, people have gained a better understanding of gold. More and more people begin to regard gold as the first choice of asset allocation. The average annual demand for gold in China from 2003 to 2018 was 2,002.45 tons. After deducting 311.22 tons of exported gold and 263.77 tons of recycled gold, China's average annual stock of gold increased by 1,427.46 tons, of which only a small amount of gold was used as national gold reserves, and most of the gold would become civilian gold deposits, that was to say, China's civilian stock of gold had the potential to increase by more than a thousand tons a year. In the next 10 years, there will be another 10,000 tons of civilian stock of gold. Coupled with the established civilian stock of gold, China's private deposits will have a potential of exceeding more than 20,000 tons in the next 10 years, which is equivalent to 5.6 trillion of capital precipitation at the current gold price. So we have to consider how to use its liquidity, how to manage this liquidity, because this is an important part of the gold support for Renminbi.

The stocked gold is a kind of precipitation of social wealth, it is based on the requirement of the appreciation of the stock gold and needs liquidity. The liquidity management of the stock gold is based on the requirement of maintaining the gold support for Renminbi which is "flowing without loss", that is, it flows within and not out of the country. To this end, human beings generally used the method of gold control in history, but this made the stocked gold lose its liquidity, so how to flow without losing gold becomes a challenging problem. This is also the reason why I propose to develop the gold loan market and realize segmentation from the incremental gold market and the stocked gold market, and the measure to materialize the proposal is to establish a gold bank.

13.6 Gold Bank: Operator of Stocked Gold

The concept of the gold bank has been put forward for many years, and it is not a new concept. Some commercial banks have

13 Gold Market: The Third Segmentation

announced the birth of the gold bank, and some internet enterprises have put forward the concept of internet gold, and on this basis, they have established online gold banks. But none of these has made any substantial progress. The former lacks clear business positioning and the latter lacks credit. The central bank has a clear policy guidance for the development of internet gold enterprises, that is, it is only the auxiliary rather than the main body of the gold business of commercial banks in the future. For commercial banks, the segmentation of stocked gold market and incremental gold market brings an opportunity for the clear positioning of the gold bank.

As a new form of commercial banks, the gold bank should have its own special functions and positioning, which is the vitality of the gold bank. The functions and positioning of the gold bank is gradually clear due to the third segmentation of China's gold market: Renminbi needs to be supported by the stocked gold, and the accumulation and growth of the stocked gold has create increasing liquidity requirements, and the construction of the value support for Renminbi requires this liquidity that "flows without loss", that is, the stocked gold flows in and not out of the country, which is a new issue of China's gold market management. Solving this problem requires practice, and practice requires practitioners to establish a special trading platform for the flow of stocked gold, which is the gold bank, so our functional positioning for the gold bank is the operator of stocked gold.

What is the operator of stocked gold? It is the manager and operator of the liqudity of stocked gold liquidity. In order to achieve the "flowing without loss", the gold bank does not operate on the basis of the transfer of ownership. Different from the current incremental gold trading platform, it uses physical gold as the subject matter of trading, therefore different from the current financial institutions with currency as the subject matter; gold bank also has bill transactions, but all correspond to physical gold, different from current commercial banks that use paper currency as capital. The gold bank with professional characteristics should create a market environment in which gold "flows without loss",

Chinese Gold: From Following to Surpassing

the formation of this environment allows the realization of things that could not be done previously on the platform, and can promote the general innovation and transformation of the financial market in China.

Capitalization of gold. Using stocked gold as the founding capital of the gold bank is actually building a storage for stocked gold to absorb stocked gold, and gold entering the storage may generate liquidity through loans. The transfer of ownership will be strictly in accordance with the regulations, and the supervision of society is accepted, so that the liquidity of the stocked gold can be controlled in order to achieve the purpose of "flowing without loss". This is in effect the capitalization of the stocked gold under the gold bank, which has positive implications for promoting pure paper currency reform.

Issuance of gold certificates. For the convenience of transactions, the gold bank can issue gold certificates that strictly correspond to physical gold, because there is a correspondence to physical gold, gold certificates have the authentic value and authority, they can be pledged, used as physical asset certificates, and applied in asset evaluation and transfer. This is actually to say that gold has the function of quasi-currency and replaces the functions of credit money in a specific range, which also has a positive significance for the improvement of financial stability.

The creation of an anchor of gold stability. To create an anchor of gold stability and inject the stability of gold into the credit paper currency system is an ideological trend of gold re-monetization after the outbreak of the subprime mortgage crisis in the United States in 2007, the gold bank itself is the product of this trend, every step of its development should reflect the requirements of gold re-monetization, so China's gold bank can become a special pilot zone and a cradleland of gold re-monetization in China.

To this end, the gold bank can initiate the establishment of a gold monetary fund, collect stocked gold from society for Renminbi transformation, that is, the central bank approves and issues the line of credit according to the quantity of stocked gold submitted

13 Gold Market: The Third Segmentation

to the treasury by the gold bank. The loan amount increases and decreases with changes in the amount of gold in the treasury, once the realization of linkage between gold and Renminbi is achieved, it is equivalent to the fact that the issuance of a certain number of Renminbi is based on gold, then isn't it an anchor of gold stability? In addition, this is an effective way to enhance the control of the central bank over gold.

Gold lending. Gold as a financial asset has two ways of trading in the financial market, one is to deliver, one is to lend. Based on the requirement of "flowing without loss" for the gold support, gold lending is the dominant transaction mode for the gold bank. Although China has more than a thousand tons of gold lending scale, what needs to be done is gold incremental trading rather than stock trading, so the process of gold lending of the gold bank gold should be redesigned. Now money laundering and arbitrage occur in gold lending because a gold lending loop is not formed, while it is very easy for the gold bank with physical gold as the capital to form a closed loop of operation for gold lending. Lending gold is lending their own capital (gold), and recovering gold is recovering capital, so a loop is formed accordingly. Therefore, China's gold lending will see a big step forward, the significance of which is that it can promote the growth of China's gold stock and further build up the gold support for Renminbi.

Afterword

I've been associated with the gold market in China since I started working on gold economics. At the end of 1991, I was transferred to the Development Research Center of the National Gold Bureau from the China Materiel Newspaper, and was assigned to work in the Economic Research Office. At that time, although the working system of gold control prevailed, after several years hesitation and observation, the market-oriented goals have become increasingly clear for China's economic reform, and marketization reform of gold has definitely become a direction of thought. In 1992, I led the completion of the first project report as the leader of a research group, maybe the first research report about China's gold marketization. From then on, I have become attached to China's gold marketization reform, and become an observer and participant in the whole process of the development of the gold market. In 2013, 11 years after the comp letion of the first research report, I published a book titled Cocoon Breaking: Deciphering the Course of China's Gold Marketization", which recorded the course of China's gold market from scratch. In the years after the publication of this book, China's gold industry and market entered a period of rapid development and transition, ushered in a "golden age" in history of gold in China. The development of the gold industry and market created the gold glory that attracted global attention and comments. The true face of Lushan is lost to my sight, for it is right in this mountain that I reside. When I heard the comment by international professionals that "China's gold market is already a leader in the future development of the international gold market", I was more perturbed than I was inspired, because I was confused about this

Afterword

comment. So I am starting again to explore what made it possible for our gold market to transform form a follower to a leader, which for me may be somewhat of a catch-up.

When I embarked on the road to learning, I was not bound by any preconceived ideas, and started out in a state of complete uncertainty, but when I focused on the "system" as the answer, I was very perturbed because the international community was full of curiosity and criticism about the path of development with Chinese characteristics. When I was writing this book, there were fierce trade frictions between China and the United States, and the constant smearing of our "system" by some people in the United States weighed heavily on my conclusions, so I also needed to find another answer, namely, is the path of development with Chinese characteristics an alternative, or does it have universal values that mankind is pursuing together? So my observation starts from a relatively small area of the development of China's gold market before an extension to the thinking on the road of human development, because the small issue of the gold industry and market development is also part of the big issue of economic development of the mankind. When I look at the road of China from the perspective of human development, I find that human development itself is a process of trial and error, a process of discovering and correcting mistakes. After the Great Depression of the 1930s, mankind discovered that the "invisible hand" had its own insurmountable defects, so they placed hope in the "visible hand" and revised the free market theory. The theoretical foundation of the necessity of the "visible hand" was neoclassical economics, which led to the practice of extensive involvement by the "visible hand" in human economic development. For example, from the perspective of the evolution of human economics, the path of China's economic development is a practice of neoclassical economics, so the experience and lessons learned in the process of practice have "universal values", thus confirming my cognition of China's "system", or my confidence in the "system", and that is a boost in self-awareness during the writing of the book.

Chinese Gold: From Following to Surpassing

The book I now present to readers is a small summary of my understanding of the stages of China's path, the Chinese gold industry and market are still developing, and this development process is still a process of trial and error, which is also part of innovation. The development of China's gold industry and market has gone from nothing to something, from small to large, and then to being entrusted with a great responsibility. Leading the way forward is a historical fortune and at the same time a historical responsibility. Is China ready for this? Maybe we have not come up with a well-thought-out plan, but there's a future for sure, so we must stride forward!

References

China Gold Association. China Gold Yearbook (2000-2018)[M]. China Gold Association, Beijing.

China Gold Association. Global Gold Yearbook (2016-2018)[M]. China Gold Association, Beijing.

China Gold Association. CPM Gold Yearbook (2014-2018)[M]. China Gold Association, Beijing.

Shanghai Gold Exchange. China Gold Market Report (2008-2018) [M]. Shanghai: Gold Exchange.

Shanghai Gold Exchange. Financial Statistics of China (1952-1991) [M]. Beijing: China Financial Publishing House.

Gold Market Analysis Team. Report on the Development of China's Gold Market [M]. Beijing: China Finance Press.

Ping An Bank. Report on the Development of Gold Business in China's Commercial Banks (2017-2018) [M]. Beijing: Social Sciences Academic Press.

Wang Zhongqiu, Wang Xiaoyu. China in 1750-1950 [M]. Beijing: New World Press.

This book is the result of a co-publication agreement between China Financial and Economic Publishing House (China) and Paths International Ltd (UK).

Title: Chinese Gold: From Following to Surpassing
Author: Liu Shan'en
ISBN: 978-1-84464-686-9
Ebook ISBN: 978-1-84464-687-6

Copyright © 2022 by Paths International Ltd (UK) and by China Financial and Economic Publishing House (China).

All rights reserved. No part of this publication may be reproduced, translated, stored in a retrieval system, or transmitted in any form or by any means, electronic, mechanical, photocopying or otherwise, without the prior permission of the publisher.

The copyright to this title is owned by China Financial and Economic Publishing House (China). This book is made available internationally through an exclusive arrangement with Paths International Ltd of the United Kingdom and is only permitted for sale outside China.

Paths International Ltd

Published in the United Kingdom
www.pathsinternational.com